Culture Rules

School culture is unarguably central to a school's success or failure. While there is no single "correct" school culture, there are lessons to be learned. *Culture Rules* examines the factors that create an environment where students want to learn, and adults want to teach.

Culture Rules explores staff culture, student culture, team building, establishing and maintaining norms inside and outside the classroom, and lessons learned from top-performing schools. By sharing her personal journey in school leadership, Jo Facer:

- explores the different factors that can affect a school's culture;

- considers hot topics such as teacher workload, discipline, marking, CPD and shows how these can influence a school's culture and success; and

- includes real case studies to show how schools have developed a strong culture and the impact on performance.

Full of practical, sustainable ideas for schools to implement in the short and long term, this is essential reading for all school leaders in primary and secondary schools looking to build a great school culture in their organisations.

Jo Facer is the principal of Ark John Keats Academy in London, and the author of *Simplicity Rules*, published by Routledge in 2019.

Culture Rules

Creating Schools Where Children Want to Learn and Adults Want to Work

Jo Facer

Routledge
Taylor & Francis Group

LONDON AND NEW YORK

First published 2022
by Routledge
2 Park Square, Milton Park, Abingdon, Oxon OX14 4RN

and by Routledge
605 Third Avenue, New York, NY 10158

Routledge is an imprint of the Taylor & Francis Group, an informa business

British Library Cataloguing-in-Publication Data
A catalogue record for this book is available from the British Library

Library of Congress Cataloging-in-Publication Data
A catalog record for this book has been requested

ISBN: 978-0-367-56254-0 (hbk)
ISBN: 978-0-367-56257-1 (pbk)
ISBN: 978-1-003-09707-5 (ebk)

DOI: 10.4324/9781003097075

Typeset in Melior
by Apex CoVantage, LLC

For Dr Byrne. One day, I will be as good a teacher as you, Sir.

Contents

Acknowledgements

In the course of writing this book, my thoughts have been shaped by senior leaders in education and other sectors, and I am extremely grateful to them. Many of the ideas presented as my own originated with these people. My thanks in particular go to Lizzie Bowling, Tilly Browne, Sarah Cullen, Stuart Lock, Carly Moran, Pran Patel, Natasha Porter, Barry Smith, David Thomas, Jenny Thompson and Ed Vainker.

Many people say that headship is a lonely profession, but that has not been my experience at all. I am indebted to all my colleagues at Ark Schools, and in particular Becky Curtis, Jerry Collins, Sarah Donachy, Fiona Chapman, Peter Haylock, Oli Knight, Matt Burnage, Paul Bhatia, Max Haimendorf, Aishling Ryan, Katie Marshall, Nat Nabarro, Sean Mullarkey, Fran Freeman, Aaron Collingwood-Williams, Amy Baird and Mide Ola-Said for their support, guidance and advice. I have learned more from you than I can express.

Finally, to the teachers, leaders, support staff and children at Ark John Keats: you give me joy and hope every single day. It is an absolute honour to work with all of you.

Introduction

I decided to write a book about school culture because over the course of a year spent building the foundations of a brand new free school I became convinced that culture is the single most important facet of any school.

With a start-up school, this is more rapidly apparent. Before being appointed to open a new Ark school in west London (Ark Soane Academy), I had worked in a series of established schools, and for a series of established headteachers. I had slotted into a culture they had created and embedded years earlier, and that was still going strong. The problems we were solving were to do with curriculum or teaching; occasionally strengthening behaviour systems or improving student ethos, but I had never experienced 'fixing' a culture problem.

In a new-start school, you exist in a void. For a year, it felt surreal to be called a 'principal' when I led precisely zero staff, had exactly zero children, and had absolutely no school building.

In a new-start school, all you have is the idea of a school.

I spent the first months of my headship racing towards the October admissions deadline. I went from primary school to primary school in west London, held event after event in local Church halls and in the grounds of other local schools, and talked about the idea of a school.

In a world where ideas are all you have, culture seems the clearest thing you can hold onto.

As the year went on, I was lucky enough to visit some of the top-performing schools in our network, Ark Schools, as well as schools in other networks and some stand-alone schools. I visited a lot of new-start schools, and found cultures which permeated everything they did. I found a strong correlation between successful schools and a great school culture.

Whatever aspect of schools we discuss, my executive principal Becky Curtis always asks: 'what does great look like?' We have to be able to answer this question before we start trying to improve our schools. I did not want to build a school in a vacuum, so I wanted to ensure I was clear about this.

When I think about the best schools I have worked in or visited, I think about:

- Children straining to put their hands higher when asked a question in class.

- Classrooms so focused you don't realise people are in them when you walk down the corridor.

- Assemblies that genuinely inspire, where children lean forward to listen, or laugh or smile.

- Dining halls that are full of calm animation.

- Children who are grateful to the adults who teach them.

- Children chatting merrily and without prompting to complete strangers visiting them about how great their school is.

- Staff members who gush about how much they love their school at the slightest provocation.

- Every child filing into silent lines when they are asked to, and smiling as they walk to lessons.

- Leaders who are fixated on improving their school when they talk to external visitors, but are equally fixated on telling their staff what an amazing job they are doing.

Ultimately, great schools are full of happy children, happy adults, and lots of learning. From May 2019, when I was appointed the principal of Ark Soane, I became obsessed with culture: how could we found a school that would go on to rival these incredible places of learning?

Then, in March 2020, everything changed. Just as I recruited the final member of our founding staff team, all the schools in the country – almost all the schools in the *world* – closed. Our future was placed in peril. We went into emergency mode, sourcing alternative sites and alternative ways to open in September. We put case after case to the Department for Education, and watched not one but three contingency sites be taken out of our grasp.

By May 2020, our fate was sealed. The school we had so focused on founding was to be deferred until at least September 2021, as the Department for Education rightly chose to prioritise supporting existing schools to remain open through a time of incredible challenge.

The phone calls I made on 4 May 2020 remain the hardest conversations I have had – not just in my career, but in my life. Without exception, though, every member of the founding team responded with kindness and grace. Before I made the calls, I asked Becky Curtis, who had long been a trusted colleague, for advice. 'What would a great response be?' she asked me. I had already called the one other member of Soane staff in post – my executive assistant – to tell her the devastating news. The first thing she had said was: 'Are you OK?' I told this to my colleague Becky and she replied: 'Well, I mean – be realistic.'

Yet every single member of founding staff who I delivered the message of disappointment and uncertainty to did indeed ask if I was OK. Their care and lack of self-interest at that crushing moment only secured my knowledge that we had hired an extraordinary founding team.

One of the huge benefits of being part of a large network was that we could find alternative placements for every teacher who wanted to stay with us for the year (some chose to stay in their current schools), and in the process of re-homing teachers, I found a new home as well.

In September 2020, instead of opening the doors of a shiny new start-up of 180 children and 11 teachers, I found myself at the helm of Ark John Keats in Enfield – an all-through, 3–18 school with over 1700 children and over 200 members of staff.

When I came to read the first draft of this book over, I was struck that the first chapter I wrote (and the one you will read next) opens with a quote overheard at Ark John Keats. At the time I wrote it, I was referring a school I greatly admired. I am now privileged to lead that very school.

I share this story to provide the context of my personal journey in school leadership. I have been extremely lucky to have worked in five schools in London and Kent, before setting up Ark Soane for a year, during which time I also worked three days a week in two other schools. During the eleven years of my career, I have been lucky to visit more than twenty schools up and down the country, and in other countries as well. I hope that this book will begin to uncover what we mean by a great school culture, and how we get there.

Part I
The adults

According to Eva Moscowitz, the founder of one of the most successful chains of Charter Schools in America, 'Education is for kids, but about the adults.'[1] For Moscowitz, adults are the change-makers. A school succeeds or fails because of what adults do, not children. So this book starts with the adults, because children do not set school culture, adults do.

In a nutshell, what we need to do to create an environment where a scholarly culture can flourish is two things: recruit the right people, and then make sure they don't leave. This is a simple idea which is difficult to do.

In Jim Collins's *Good to Great* he famously talks about getting the 'right people on the bus'.[2] It is widely accepted that to succeed as a school, you need the right people in the building. And what do we mean by the 'right' people? While every school in the country wants teachers to be qualified and kind, different schools have different values and priorities. Knowing what you stand for is a prerequisite for attracting and securing the right people who are not only qualified and kind, but who will work with you to further your mission for your community. And great people can only flourish in the right kinds of environments: I have spent my career working in schools which serve disadvantaged communities, but I'm not sure I'd adjust well to schools in rural areas – the challenges facing them are nothing I have ever contemplated – or to schools serving more affluent communities. Similarly, I've seen colleagues struggling in one school (and even, horrifyingly, told they 'can't teach' in some institutions), only to go on to have enormous career success in a very different kind of school.

So recruitment matters, and we open this first part of the book with that.

Once you have your A team, the worst thing that can happen is they leave. Great people in the right subjects to serve your curriculum plan who are aligned to your vision are not the easiest to find. Moreover, high staff turnover is largely accepted to be a terrible thing for children. So much of learning relies on children being receptive to learn, and if they are spending time working out who this new teacher is, what their expectations are and if they mean them, and the particular ways they open up their subject to children, they are not using that brain-space to learn new material.

DOI: 10.4324/9781003097075-1

1

So, how can we create schools where people don't want to leave? Although much is made of well-being initiatives and perks of certain multi-academy trusts with well-lined pockets (one local school to me boasts an indoor swimming pool that staff can use out of hours), what actually matters most is a sense of team. Ensuring your people buy into what the school is doing and feel their voice is heard in shaping the direction of travel is infinitely more useful to children in the long run and more effective in retaining them.

Of course, it is not all about vision and mission (and I have some colleagues who might scoff at the 'airy vision', but I'm going to argue for its importance, so do bear with me). Teachers are professionals like any other, and unlike the kinds of jobs I did to pay my way through university, they will not be happy doing the identical same thing ten hours a day for the forty-five-plus years of their career. A teacher is not, after all, a waitress. While waitressing, to my knowledge, has not appeared to change very much at all from when I did it twenty years ago, education does adapt. Education changes with different governments, different exam syllabuses, and, most crucially in my view, new research. We have a responsibility to develop the people we employ, and I'll explore some ways we might do that.

Finally, while toxic internet memes might suggest that teachers are 'candles' who 'consume themselves to light the way for others', it is widely accepted now that teachers are in fact entitled to a life beyond their career. When I trained to teach, the Charter Schools of America and free schools of the UK were in their infancy and largely staffed by unencumbered twenty-something-year-olds; time (and, for some, additional responsibilities of family) has shown that a human cannot, in fact, sacrifice their entire life for their work for very long. We have a duty as school leaders to consider the workloads of our teachers and do something about it when that burden becomes excessive.

My hope in these chapters, and in this book, is not to indoctrinate the reader in a 'right' kind of school culture, but to rather share experience and research that any leader or teacher can make use of to build the culture they desire.

Notes

1 Eva Moscowitz, *The Education of Eva Moskowitz: A Memoir* (Harper, 2017).
2 Jim Collins, *Good to Great: Why Some Companies Make the Leap ... and Others Don't* (Random House, 2001).

How can we recruit the right teachers?

Recruitment is at the heart of what we do in schools. I once worked for a headteacher who insisted on meeting every individual who interviewed to work at their school. At the time, I was surprised they would invest so much time in this process. Once in the post myself, I thought this to be a stroke of genius. Indeed, if you're going to invest a huge chunk of your time anywhere as a head it ought to be choosing the right people to staff your school!

Advertising for teachers: writing the ad

When you are appointed the principal of a new-start school, you have the enormous privilege of getting to hire every single member of staff from scratch. It is a blessing: if you hire every single person, you shape the direction of your school. The pressure to get it right is enormous. Every single person we hired for Ark Soane would be hired by me, and if any did not work out, I was the person who had made the mistake. Our ads needed to be worded perfectly.

Unfortunately, I did not recognise this until very late in the recruitment process.

My initial wake-up call came when interviewing a candidate. Describing applying to another school, he said: 'they had the best worded advertisement I've ever read'. My pride was hurt, but my curiosity was piqued.

'What was so good about it?' I asked.

'Oh, everything. They say what they stand for. Strong behaviour, a sensible approach to workload, their idea that the teacher is the expert. It's just great, and it's all backed up when you visit.'

I looked up the Magna Academy shortly after. Here is what I found:

Do you want to be part of a team where you will help make a lasting impact on our students, many of whom are disadvantaged, and rapidly accelerate their progress?

Do you want to work in a school where you are free to teach, with impeccable student behaviour and unhindered by bureaucracy?

DOI: 10.4324/9781003097075-2

Despite being a 'secondary modern' in a selective grammar school borough, our mind-set is that we are a 'grammar school for all'. We are unapologetically ambitious for every child, no matter what their background, prior attainment or needs. Our mission is to prepare every student to be able to go to university or high-powered alternative. We believe in the traditional values of hard work and kindness. Our Academy is a vibrant and exciting place to work and was graded as outstanding in all areas by Ofsted in June 2015 and December 2018. In 2018, Magna achieved a Progress 8 score of 1.15, placing us 24th nationally (top 1%).

We believe that we are starting to do something for our pupils that is really special. However, we know that our results, whilst ground-breaking, are not yet enough to achieve the vision that we have for our academy: for all pupils to 'climb their personal mountain to university or aspirational alternative.' Addressing this, is the exciting next stage of our journey.

We value our staff highly, and treat workload very seriously. Our systems ensure you can really focus on your core purpose – teaching, in a sustainable way, unhindered by bureaucracy or poor behaviour.

What we offer:

- Great students who behave impeccably – you can make a massive difference to them

- Tight, robust 'no-excuses' behaviour systems

- Highly visible/supportive senior leaders who have your back

- Same-day centralised detentions, including homework detentions (you do not need to organise/run/chase them at all), helping to underpin impeccable behaviour, so you are free to teach

- A feedback policy focused on whole class feedback – we do not have onerous/impossible marking policies

- A centralised homework system at KS3 – you do not need to check/mark KS3 homework

- No formal graded lesson observations – just ongoing 'no-stakes' feedback, helping you to continuously develop – we believe that trusting our staff with autonomy helps to develop a strong staff culture

- Collaborative planning with centralised, shared units of work and resources

- CPD starts as soon as you are appointed

- Excellent ongoing CPD, career development and promotion opportunities

- A professional progression model to enable great teachers to remain in the classroom via our Lead Practitioner (LP) and Specialist Leaders of Education (SLE) routes

- State of the art facilities and a very pleasant location in beautiful Dorset

What we are looking for:

The successful candidate will be:

- an excellent teacher of Maths who will play an important role in helping to move Maths into its next stage of development.

- someone who does whatever it takes to ensure the life chances of all our students are maximised. They will blend extreme personal humility with intense professional will.

- totally aligned to our values and mission. If you are the type of person who fits with our culture, you will love working here.

It is an excellent opportunity for an NQT or ambitious practitioner wishing to further develop their career. As a Teaching School you would also have the opportunity to become a Specialist Leader of Education.

We actively welcome visits and would be delighted to show you around our Academy to fully appreciate our excellent learning environment.

Richard Tutt, headteacher at Magna Academy at the time this ad was out, now an executive principal for United Learning's Bournemouth and Poole Cluster, and with whose kind permission this advert is reproduced, told me:

I realised over time that staff alignment to the vision and systems of a school is of critical importance (especially so when the school is doing something very different). And this needs to start with making the advert as explicit and honest as possible about what the school is about, otherwise it wastes everyone's time. Demonstrating alignment at the interview is then critical. The interview process also included a thirty-minute presentation from me and a written exercise which tested alignment.

When writing job adverts, I learned, always include what is special about your school. Who are you serving, and what is your aim? What are your non-negotiables?

Shout your values loudly

When we struggled to recruit an art teacher, I realised that our advert was not explicit enough about what we believed in. Noting that those who came for interview were employing group work and 'busy work', we got explicit, adding that 'our founding art teacher will believe in direct instruction and cultural capital: that all children can be artists, if taught well, and that all children deserve to know about the greatest artists who have lived'. For this position, the distinctive alignment we were looking for was two-fold: a belief in direct instruction, and a belief in teaching art as a vehicle for cultural capital.

Another great example of an advert that fronts its values is this from Bedford Free School's search for a head of maths from February 2020:

> At BFS our values drive everything that we do and as a result our teachers enjoy impeccable behaviour in lessons and hardworking, highly motivated students. Open for just 7 years, Bedford Free School is a genuinely comprehensive school that provides a knowledge-based education for students of all backgrounds. We teach an unashamedly academic curriculum consisting of the best that has been thought and said, and as you would expect, maths is at the heart of this.[1]

The advert goes on to talk about leadership capacity, the department and the development on offer – all after this explicit paragraph on school culture.

Writing a job advertisement

What is it about your school's culture and ethos that you'd like to front in your advert? Think carefully about your beliefs about education. Do you passionately believe in working with the most disadvantaged young people? This might be something you'd look for in prospective teachers. What is your pedagogy position – group and project work, or traditional and didactic? Again – be upfront about this. I had assumed my school was so obviously in the latter category that I did not need to say this, but this was not the case – as evidenced by not one but many interview lessons I watched centred on group work. What about your approach to extra-curricular: do you pare it down so teachers just teach, or does every teacher get to run a club that interests them? How about your ways of working – is all planning done centrally, saving workload? Or is planning devolved to teachers, ensuring absolute autonomy in lesson creation? Either extreme can be big draws for different professionals.

Of course, in a recruitment crisis it is understandable why schools are increasingly emphasising what they offer to staff, and not just the kind of person they are looking for. Teachers are increasingly looking for places which will nurture their development, as well as offer opportunities to progress, and it is, frankly, a buyer's market.

Think about what makes your school a great place to work, and put it front and centre in the advert. Do you use a sensible marking policy, meaning teachers can do most of their marking in lessons? Perhaps you have no written reporting to parents, or no late evening events? Maybe you offer the option to work from home on inset days? The list of workload incentives is potentially endless – think about what your school does well, and sell it. Similarly, we know that many schools manage behaviour centrally, with the aim of making lessons disruption free for teachers and minimising administration. This undoubtedly makes these schools attractive places to work.

You won't be able to list everything that makes your school special in one advert. The best candidates will do their research, so it would be good if they can find out more if they are keen, perhaps from an online prospectus or school website. The best approach might be to limit yourself to five things that are great, or 'different' about your school – not unique, but different perhaps to 'how things are done' elsewhere. Find multiple trusted members of staff from all places in the school hierarchy and ask them to do the same. What comes out over and over again? That will probably be the key to what makes your school great. In fact, a great exercise to build staff morale is to get people to reflect on why they love working at your school, so ask people this in staff surveys, and share the responses.

Spread the word

Hopefully a time will come when schools don't collectively have to spend hundreds of thousands each year advertising their jobs in the education press, but the reality remains that if you want great swathes of the teaching profession to see your job adverts, you really do need to advertise them in it, though the government does appear to be (slowly, very slowly) creating its own centralised vacancy portal.[2]

To advertise in the TES is not enough, however. There is an enormous teacher community on Twitter, and a growing one on LinkedIn – in fact, if we looked at where Ark Soane's founding teacher applications came from, most were from TES, followed by Twitter, followed by LinkedIn (which surprised me greatly, as I very rarely posted anything on LinkedIn – though we were very lucky to have a HR team who owned that piece more comprehensively for us).

One headteacher I met a number of years ago said that we should not be relying on an interview day alone to recruit someone – it must be more of a relationship over time. As a senior leader and headteacher, it is crucial to spend time investing in your network – you never know when someone will know someone wanting to relocate who happens to be perfect for your school.

Of course, we must beware of recreating the 'old boys' network' through such methods. It has been long reported that female teachers as well as those from ethnic minority backgrounds are underrepresented in leadership positions in schools.[3] If we tend to hire those who resemble ourselves, our schools will never be as good as they can be; will never serve the diverse needs of any school population. My job as a leader is to beware of people who look and sound like me, and to actively seek out those from other backgrounds with different perspectives.

Pran Patel, a former senior leader and teacher trainer, told me:

> *Why Diversity Matters*[4] states that gender-diverse companies are 15% more likely to outperform financially, and ethnically-diverse companies are 35% when comparing the top quartile to the bottom for diversity. In 2018 *Delivering Through Diversity*[5] stated: 'The statistically significant correlation between

a more diverse leadership team and financial outperformance demonstrated three years ago continues to hold true on an updated, enlarged, and global data set.' Diversity is not only the right thing to do morally but leads to gaining the best expertise and talent. There are real advantages in looking at the retention rates and HR records of staff who possess protected characteristics, the longer a member staff stays in your organisation, the better it is for everyone. Day to day, leaders should embrace dissident and diverse thinking within their teams; aiming to build innovate collaborative cultures to provide support and also to recognise the value of dissonance inside and outside the organisation.[6] A group of like-minded individuals are likely to fall prey to the groupthink cognitive bias, and this may lead to more of the same, as leadership is almost solely about change; this is a systemic dead end.

The crucial thing is to be aware of our own bias. Though we cannot escape the limits of our subjective perspective, if we are aware of this we will inevitably get closer to preventing it. Indeed, awareness of our own bias can in many ways provide a foil to our own shortcomings. In her fascinating book *Invisible Women: Exposing Data Bias in a World Designed for Men*, Caroline Criado Perez warns:

> Studies have shown that a belief in your own personal objectivity, or a belief that you are not sexist, makes you less objective and more likely to behave in a sexist way. Men (women were not found to exhibit this bias) who believe that they are objective in hiring decisions are more likely to hire a male applicant than an identically described female applicant.[7]

What I learned from seventeen interviews in two days

When we first opened applications for Ark Soane Academy, I assumed we would have a lot of interest. As a new school, in a well-known academy trust, it was a very attractive proposition for people seeking to move into their first leadership position. I was not prepared for quite how many applications we actually received, however. We had 65 applications, and after I had read the first five it became apparent that these were all incredibly high-quality applicants.

Our original plan had been to shortlist four candidates and run an interview day in a host school. As we had no school or children of our own, we were reliant on colleagues in other schools loaning a few classes they could spare for the day, and as we would be leaning on people thirteen further times at least to fill our other positions, we couldn't shortlist more candidates. At the same time, we didn't know how to cut so substantially down from so many quality applicants.

We decided, therefore, to run short initial interviews in our central offices. We scheduled thirty minutes per interview, back to back, over two days. We invited seventeen of the best applicants, assuming some would cancel. No one cancelled. Myself and my then executive head, Peter, interviewed seventeen candidates over a day and a half.

Conducting so many interviews over a short time was a challenge in several ways. Simply staying focused and attentive by interview 17 at 5 p.m. on a Friday was difficult. Ultimately, the job was impossible, but we learned a lot through the process.

As the interviews were short, we had to be prepared. For each applicant, I had written questions and uncertainties I had on their applications. I was interested to see to what extent their views aligned with mine, so I had a few broad questions about education that were open to start with. We were then incredibly direct: there was just no point in leaving something unsaid which might rule in or rule out a candidate.

It was clear from even limited probing who had done their research, and who had just looked for a senior leadership team (SLT) role in a school – any school. It was easy to separate out those who had read the website, read some of the (many, many) blogs I had written on education, and taken the time to illustrate their suitability and fit to our vision. We sent out pre-reading in advance, and anyone who had not read it was easy to rule out – the very minimum of preparation for an interview is to read what the school sends you.

Ultimately, though, it was clear by the end of two days that we probably could have saved a lot of people a lot of time and energy by conducting these interviews by phone instead of in person. Phone interviews can feel staged and uncomfortable, but as an initial 'sift' of a large and strong field that can save people time and putting in a request for absence from their school, and still give you good information on whether they might be the right fit for your school.

The hardest part of conducting so many interviews was when candidates requested feedback. Given the strength of the field, coupled with how short the interviews were, it was just very difficult to give useful feedback – ultimately, when you see so many people in such a short period of time, you are essentially using comparative judgement: is this person better or worse than that person?

It would be impossible to avoid the question of bias in interviews today. Thankfully, we have become a lot more aware of the possibility of bringing bias to bear on our appointments, and awareness of a bias is a good way to start. At Ark, we always ensure more than one person is involved in shortlisting – something that proved wildly helpful in every instance, as other people always see things you do not.

According to David Didau's excellent blog, we should be swayed by a candidate's strong educational background (a good degree, good A levels and good GCSE results are all strongly correlated with great new hires), but worry less about their personal statement, which only tells you 'whether someone … was able to guess right as to what you wanted to hear'.[8] At the same time, the statistics will only reveal what is *usually* the case, and some of the best educators I have ever worked with have had woeful academic records for a variety of reasons.

In *The Art of Thinking Clearly,* Dobell writes eloquently of mankind's inevitable biases, saying: 'if we could learn to recognise and evade the biggest errors in thinking, we might experience a leap in prosperity'.[9] Of the many biases Dobelli explores in this text, a number should ring loud alarm bells for leaders, in particular 'groupthink' and the 'in-group out-group bias'. Dobelli refers to group-think as 'the calamity of conformity', and particularly cautions against 'the illusion of unanimity' in which 'if others are of the same opinion, any dissenting view must be wrong'.[10] It is very tempting when someone spouts your own ideas to assume this is the person for you. While doing your research and being aligned is to be applauded at interview, we must check our biases at the point a candidate speaks our website back to us and probe more deeply. In the 'in-group out-group bias' Dobelli refers to the idea of groups as historically helpful for humanity's survival, but as now being more likely to drive 'prejudice and aversion': 'identifying with a group has been a survival strategy for hundreds of thousands of years. Not any longer; identifying with a group distorts your view of the facts.'[11]

Ultimately, we can only be aware of our biases and ask others to help to overcome them. A generally good rule when interviewing someone is to ask:

- Do I like them because they remind me of me? (If the answer is yes: beware)

- Do I dislike them because they are different from me? (As above)

- What different skills or perspectives can I learn from this person? (Always seek to enrich the perspectives of your team, once your non-negotiables on culture and ethos have been set down)

Running interviews

What fascinated me was that in those twenty-minute SLT interviews, two candidates stood out particularly. When we brought them back as part of a larger pool of candidates, and I interviewed them again – this time with a *different* second interviewer to get a different perspective, they felt exactly the same. Watching those candidates teach – in fact, watching all of the SLT candidates teach – I was completely unsurprised by how wonderful they were at teaching. Their teaching had almost no impact on my choices, because the field was so strong in every way.

Yet I've also interviewed candidates who were a mess of anxiety in the interview, who couldn't give a coherent answer, who couldn't talk about themselves at all… Who then delivered an absolutely stunning lesson.

What is more rare in teaching is someone interviewing well and then not teaching effectively, and I think that is because someone who 'presents' well, and confidently, in the high-pressure situation of an interview is very likely to do well in teaching, the thing they do every single day; whereas it does not always follow that those who teach well have the same skillset required at interview. It is simply so much easier to be at ease in a classroom full of young people than it is in a room with one or two people whose sole purpose is to judge you.

The interview

Preparing for interviewing candidates is important but need not be time consuming. If you have a well-organised application system, whereby you can clearly see candidates' experience and reasons for wanting to join you, annotate what stands out and what raises questions. What is their current school like? Have they left a position mid-year? Does a line in their personal statement raise questions on alignment, or lack of? It is worth adding or tailoring interview questions depending on the candidate.

For example, we used a bank of similar questions for teaching candidates, and would decide which were most relevant to that candidate. The opening question was always the same – a warm up – what made you apply for this post, and why are you a good fit?

Following this, depending on what question marks we have, we might ask:

- How do you plan a lesson?

- How do you ensure children remember what they've learned for the long term?

- How high are your high expectations when it comes to behaviour?

- If you have a class from year 7 to year 11, what would you expect in terms of their progress and attainment?

- What enrichment are you passionate about offering?

It is not always clear from their taught lesson – particularly when they are teaching a lesson you yourselves have planned – how candidates plan learning. Here, we look for their thinking around planning – are they focusing on content and how to get children to understand it? Or are they distracted by activities and buzzwords? If they have let some behaviour slide in their lesson observation, we might probe around expectations – are they able to raise these with coaching feedback, or is there a philosophical objection to strict discipline? Are their expectations of what children can achieve high enough? Sometimes this is clear through other questions, but we think it is worth asking explicitly, particularly as possibly my only non-negotiable is: must believe all children can achieve all things. Finally, we should always be looking for a culture fit – some people want to just teach their lessons, and that is absolutely fine in many, many schools. In many Ark Schools, we're looking for people who are happy to spend all of that extra 'soft time' with the children in corridors and on the playground at break and lunchtime.

With all interviews, though, we liked to stay responsive – some of the most illuminating answers came from a series of unplanned questions where we probed something specific to the candidate, or picked up on an aspect of their answer that we could not have foreseen. I think it is most important in interviews to stay responsive, in the moment, and be willing to go in a different direction to find out what you want to find out before committing to hire someone.

Leadership questions

For candidates for middle or senior leadership positions, we ask additional questions focusing on whether they are aligned in our leadership style. We try and keep our questions as open as possible and let candidates talk. Questions we might ask would be:

- How do you conduct line management?

- How do you deal with a colleague who is underperforming?

- How do you retain someone who is excellent?

- How do you motivate people to work hard?

- How would you give feedback to a Vice Principal/Principal?

One question Jerry Collins, Ark's director of secondary education, likes to ask is: how would you go about setting up and running enrichment/coaching/teacher development? His interview mantra is 'How you do anything is how you do everything', and Jerry feels that you can tell a lot about someone by how they think through a very specific aspect of school life (particularly one they might not have had direct management experience of before) and execute it. The other question that Jerry likes to ask, which I have shamelessly stolen ever since, is 'who or what has most shaped your educational philosophy?' If you're interested in alignment, this one is almost always effective in telling you if the candidate speaks your language.

Openness and honesty should always be prized. One candidate, after flailing on a particularly challenging high-level safeguarding question, looked my colleague in the eye and said: 'I actually don't know. That's definitely an aspect of my practice I need to work on. I'm committed to undertaking additional training, and I have some colleagues who could get me up to speed on this before September.' His humility, willingness to learn and, above all, honesty, was welcome: he was subsequently offered the job and became a hugely successful Assistant Principal in the network.

Teaching at interview

I have to see candidates teach at interview. I try to make it the first thing they do, and I flag at the start of the day how crucial it is that they teach well. I've sent people home after their lessons plenty of times, because I knew it just would not work, and I think that is on balance, the right thing to do: we have only so many hours in the day, and any time we are interviewing is time we can't be doing our jobs – making our schools run well, and giving children a great educational experience. To sacrifice that to bring in more great people is one thing, but to sacrifice that to be polite to someone you would never put in front of children at your school doesn't seem right to me.

Plenty of people would argue that, having turned up to a job interview, you have the 'right' to the full day, including the professional development an interview gives you. I have a lot of sympathy for this view, and having never been sent home from an interview have little concept of how gutting it must be for people who have prepared a lot only to be cut short. But the reality is that we cannot do everything, and that the hurt feelings of adults should not be our main concern. Of course, treat people with compassion and respect – tell them your expectations clearly, and ensure they know that there is a cut at a particular point in the day.

Set up the teaching

In terms of their teaching, set them up for success. David Didau writes: 'The worst way to use a sample lesson in an interview is to send candidates a loose brief and expect them to guess what type of teaching you like. This not only creates undue stress and hours of pointless work, it also results in a performance which is unlikely to tell you much you couldn't have found out in other ways. My advice is to send candidates a lesson plan you would like them to teach. Not only does this cut down on their preparation, they're no longer having to guess about what you want to see. The benefit for the employer is that you get to see whether the candidate can adapt to fit your expectations. I think it's helps to debrief the lesson at some point, but the emphasis on this should not be to offer feedback – any such feedback in a highly artificial setting will serve no practical purpose – instead it should focus on what the candidate might have done differently and how they think the lesson might be improved.'[12]

Certainly, this was the conclusion we came to at previous schools I have worked in. When contacting candidates with the details of their interview, we would include the lesson the children would normally have, and ask them to prepare to teach it. For schools which work from a shared curriculum, this is surely the only sensible way to work. (For schools in the process of creating their curriculum, it is understandable that you might like to see how well a teacher plans – though whether you can tell this from an artificial stand-alone lesson where they don't know any of the children is another argument.)

When starting a new school, however, we conducted our interviews at any host school that had capacity. (In the weeks we were interviewing, I would have to scrupulously check and re-check my calendar lest I found myself in Acton when the actual host school that day was in Barnet.) Though all the schools we used were part of our academy trust, which largely does share resources, it still proved too challenging to share the lessons for a number of reasons: coordinating with the host school's head of department would prove an unreasonable burden on people whose good will we were relying on, or (for languages) the schools did not offer the languages the candidates could teach, or (for maths) we were re-purposing a history class, and so the mix of children could not simply plough on with the maths curriculum without causing issues when they returned to their 'home' maths lessons.

While teaching is, as I've said, the most important aspect of the interview process, it is also the hardest to get right at interview. The ideal, as many educators would probably agree, would be to visit every candidate in their own school and watch them, live and unannounced, teach their own children. Only then could you really judge what a teacher can do over time. Sadly, the time investment required to do this would mean we could see far fewer candidates.

For a fully up-and-running school with a shared curriculum, I would strongly favour allowing Heads of Department to send the lesson to prospective candidates. Candidates would then teach the lessons of the HoDs, who are in the room to observe, which means no cover. If you organise for candidates to teach only part of the lesson, the usual class teacher might be there to swoop in and finish the lesson. This has the added benefit that if candidates do not successfully cover the material, the teacher is in the room and can note what they need to catch the children up on next lesson. Ultimately, this enables us to cover the curriculum and not have to 'waste' any of the children's time in learning something inappropriate or distracting, and we believe this gives them a better overall experience of school.

Lesson reflection

We always ask candidates to reflect on the lesson they have taught, primarily to see if they've noticed what we've noticed. The perfect lesson is, of course, not expected, and if candidates know this it is a good step towards making that coaching relationship work for the long term. Asking candidates what they would change if they could teach the lesson again is very revealing on whether they are able to identify the same elements you would on making their lesson better – it helps to see whether you are aligned on what makes a great lesson.

Another aspect of the lesson observation is the candidate's willingness to take feedback. I've been surprised by how many people make excuses or refuse to own, when given feedback, that an aspect of their lesson could have been better. For a school like ours, where we have an open-door policy and lesson drop-ins are the norm, it is vital everyone is open to feedback and eager to improve.

Following feedback, if a candidate has huge potential but has delivered a poor lesson, I have actually asked them to teach another class the same lesson again. I stole this idea from King Solomon Academy, who have done this for a great many years as a matter of course. Everyone teaches a bad lesson sometimes, and no one teaches their best lesson to a class they have never before met. But if you give someone feedback and they execute it, it tells you a lot about their potential and willingness to learn.

On-boarding new staff

Too often, we do not think carefully enough about what happens between the offer of a job being made and the 1st September the following year. Early in my career, I was lucky enough to be guided through what could possibly be the exemplar for how to on-board new members of staff.

For my first appointment as a head of department, I was hugely inexperienced, and a big part of accepting the role had been the assistant head's promise to do quite a lot of hand-holding (he didn't call it that – he was professional to the nth degree). After my appointment, he waited a couple of weeks before asking if I'd like to come by after school one day. My current school was quite far away, and so despite racing out of the gate with the students (something I had never before experienced) I made it at about 5 p.m. He introduced me to the two members of the team who were still in the English office, and then led me to a classroom, where he presented me with a large flip folder.

Inside the folder he had copied the overviews of each year group, along with the Autumn 1 schemes of work. He had copied the GCSE syllabus the school used and the mark scheme. He then had a document explaining what year 10 had already done, and so what would be needed with year 11.

I remember the school closing up during that first meeting at 6 p.m., and the assistant head taking me for a drink around the corner, before launching into the 'softer stuff' – what the team was like, general advice for my first middle leadership position, how I would manage people that year.

For each of the follow-up meetings, the preparation was equally clear, and although nothing can prepare you for your first leadership position (and my goodness – what I did not get wrong that year might almost fill a postcard), I felt far more prepared than I have been in subsequent jobs, despite the step up being considerable.

When moving schools at a later point in my career, I experienced a more concerted attempt to on board a whole team. Although my line manager there also arranged numerous meetings on site after school, and a one-day visit, the school also arranged a day for all new staff in the summer. Present on that day were key members of the leadership team, and the sessions were well run to give an excellent understanding of what it would be like on 1 September. After the day, we were treated to a lunch where we could all get to know each other more, and others attended, including teachers currently at the school who did not hold responsibility, so it was a lovely mix of individuals.

Inspired by this kind of on-boarding process, we designed a similar day at one school I subsequently worked at, but this time in the summer term. We coordinated with all new starters to come on the same day, taking into account the days our Teach Firsters would be on site to ensure everyone was there (some training routes mandate specific days in school). This worked well for department heads, who then could take all of their new starters at once rather than having to spend additional one to one time on different days. It also enabled us to run some centralised sessions, for example on teaching and learning, the behaviour policy, and how to be a form tutor effectively in our school.

At new-start Ark school which may not have a school to host new starters, leaders plan a 'residential' – two days, over a Friday and a Saturday, in the July before opening. Almost all schools will grant teachers a day in their new school, and this provides an excellent opportunity to get a founding team together for the first time.

One of my greatest regrets of the Ark Soane deferral was not being able to deliver the founding residential we had planned. Speaking to Becky Curtis focused my thinking that these sessions must tack clearly towards culture. She made me realise that, in a team where everyone is new, there is no trust in the room, and that our first step as a team had to be focused on building that trust: without a strong team, nothing will be brilliant.

With this in mind, we scripted the first day around a series of what we felt were the most pressing questions:

1 Who are we? (Welcome and introductions)

2 Where are we going? (Our mission)

3 How will we work together? (Staff culture)

4 How will we get where we want to go? (Our priorities)

5 What do we believe? (Our values)

Only after these introductory sessions would we move to the most pressing logistical questions:

6 What and how will we teach? (Curriculum and planning)

7 How will we create this school? (Ethos and culture)

It was our thinking that these questions would help us dig deep into what was most important to get right, as well as uniting everyone around a shared purpose, shared values, and shared ways of working that would stand us in good stead to face the inevitable challenges of the coming year.

Our induction day

We prioritised culture absolutely in our new staff induction day. Having hired a team of excellent practitioners, we felt that nothing was more important than an introduction to the ethos and culture of our school, particularly as this was a new-start school that we would, in many ways, create together.

One way of building trust in a team is to encourage vulnerability. In *The Advantage*, Patrick Lencioni writes:

> The kind of trust that is necessary to build a great team is what I call *vulnerability-based trust*. This is what happens when members get to a point where they are completely comfortable being transparent ... with one another, where they say and genuinely mean things like 'I screwed up', 'I need your help', 'your idea is better than mine', 'I wish I could learn to do that as well as you do', and even 'I'm sorry.'[13]

It is important for the leader to model that vulnerability, and always go first to set the groundwork and ensure a safe space for all team members. We had planned to start with a series of questions that, I hope, don't feel too invasive, but that also start to unlock personal motivations and values:

1 What made you choose to be a teacher?

2 What was your experience of school?

3 What do you want our children's experience of school to be?

4 What made you want to work for Ark Soane Academy?

The next aspect we would move onto, again inspired by Becky Curtis's sage advice, was to provide clarity around roles and responsibilities: Becky pointed out that people feel anxious when they don't know who to go to about different queries, and when lines of command are blurred. In any school, you must begin with introductions, and also by explaining clearly what people 'owned.' A strong organisation relies on everyone knowing where to go for what.

We would next move onto our mission. I was a big mission sceptic, and had many difficult moments over this (my first mission was so generic as to be meaningless, and this very feedback was embarrassingly given to me at my first trust-level meeting). After spending a long time honing what we were doing, it was important to have something meaningful around which to point our efforts. Beginning by thinking carefully about *why* we want this for the children we serve, and what some barriers might be, begins to make people think strategically as a team around our larger purpose as a staff body and connects teachers to their deeper purpose.

Another stage-setting piece I had planned to run in the residential and which I ran early on with my new leadership team at Ark John Keats was our ways of working, introducing ideas I will go into much more detail in this book in Chapter 2. Ways of working, for me, encompasses the way we will interact, the expectations of how we will behave in our roles, and the ways we will ensure our time is spent most effectively to have maximum impact on the running of our school.

Finally, we planned to move on to cover the basics of how we would create the culture of our school – again, the subject of Chapter 2. Frontloading the culture in this way was hugely important to me at this early stage – having visited a great many schools (which I explore in the final part of this book), it seemed clear to me that our culture would determine our school's success.

Keeping communications open

As soon as you appoint a new teacher, ask heads of department to make one contact each half term from the time of their appointment until the time they begin. They will inevitably have questions and information for their appointee, so it's worth batching this into a considered email to make people feel in the loop.

In the intensity of the school day, it is easy to forget about new hires until they join in September, but keeping communication open is critical to ensuring a smooth start. At Ark John Keats, we kept our September inset programme light, but built in a five-minute 'huddle' with new teachers each day where they could request specific help, guidance or support in any areas they required, and built in additional inset sessions that they had requested.

After recruiting your dream team, you probably want to ensure they stay with you for the long term – which is what the next chapter explores.

Take-aways

■ Make sure your values sing through your job advertisements.

■ Be on the lookout for different perspectives through the hiring process.

■ With a large strong field, use short pre-interviews.

■ Question your biases.

■ Be aware of what you do and don't learn from candidates teaching at interview.

■ Keep communications flowing with new hires before they are in post.

Notes

1 Retrieved from www.bedfordfreeschool.co.uk/vacancies/head-of-maths-september-2020 (accessed 21 February 2020).

2 At the time of writing, the DfE's job portal was in its embryonic stages, but it is hoped that in time this free route will replace the expensive publications schools have had to rely on (retrieved from www.gov.uk/find-teaching-job, accessed 2 March 2020).

3 Retrieved from https://schoolsweek.co.uk/revealed-the-lack-of-diversity-in-education-leadership-roles (accessed 2 March 2020).

4 Retrieved from www.mckinsey.com/~/media/McKinsey/Business%20Functions/Organization/Our%20Insights/Why%20diversity%20matters/Why%20diversity%20matters.ashx (accessed 27 July 2021).

5 Retrieved from www.mckinsey.com/~/media/McKinsey/Business%20Functions/Organization/Our%20Insights/Delivering%20through%20diversity/Delivering-through-diversity_full-report.ashx (accessed 27 July 2021).

6 Michael Fullan, *Change Focus: The Sequel* (Falmer Press, 1999).

7 Caroline Criado Perez, *Invisible Women: Exposing Data Bias in a World Designed for Men* (Vintage, 2020), p. 94.

8 Retrieved from https://learningspy.co.uk/leadership/designing-effective-school-interviews-part-1 (accessed 26 February 2020).

9 Rolf Dobelli, *The Art of Thinking Clearly* (Sceptre, 2013), p. 4.

10 Ibid., p. 79.

11 Ibid., p. 243.

12 Retrieved from https://learningspy.co.uk/leadership/designing-effective-school-interviews-part-1 (accessed 27 February 2020).

13 Patrick Lencioni, *The Advantage* (Jossey-Bass, 2012), p. 27.

2 How can we make a school where teachers stay for the long term?

When I started teaching in 2010, it was a fairly desirable profession. The UK was still deep in the throes of a financial crisis, and some of my friends who had landed graduate contracts with top consultancy firms and banks had already found themselves redundant. Teaching, all of a sudden, seemed attractive: solid, stable, with a decent salary and a good pension. Four years later, when I was in my first year as a head of department and in the position to recruit my first English teachers, we had so many CVs we had to set a ludicrously high bar for shortlisting: we only shortlisted people with Master's degrees.

Looking back, this feels something like the glory days of teaching. Although we had strong fields for Ark Soane, a new-start school with all the 'pull' of founding a school from scratch, I was already very familiar with the difficulty of hiring new teachers: at one school I worked at, we had to reduce the hours in the science curriculum two years in a row as we simply could not hire enough teachers to teach it. This has become the more usual state of affairs in most schools.

There are several reasons for this, some to do with a stronger economy, and others within the control of schools. While we can't change the job market, we can do much to ensure the people we recruit stay with us for the long term. I will argue that much of this work relies on creating and sustaining a positive school culture. For teachers this means a few things: that we enjoy the day-to-day of coming to work, that we don't feel overloaded by work, and that we feel we are improving at what we do.

Behaviour matters

The first of these, the enjoyment of work, relies, in my view, on a strong system of behaviour management. I wrote about this in my previous book, *Simplicity Rules*. There is no shortage of news articles reporting dramatic assaults on teachers by pupils, and it should go without saying that no teacher should be expected to suffer physical abuse in the workplace.[1]

 DOI: 10.4324/9781003097075-3

But even in schools unblighted by serious attacks, the behaviour of students can become a barrier to teachers staying. For most teachers, low-level disruption and student rudeness are the things that make their jobs tough day to day. It is up to school leaders to create systems that ensure teachers can teach, and that learning is not disrupted – it is up to teachers to use these systems in their classrooms. We will look at creating a culture of polite, respectful and hard-working young people in depth in the second part of this book.

Fulfilment

To feel fulfilment in work is about much more than avoiding harm, however. In *Drive*, Daniel H. Pink identifies three things adults need to feel fulfilled in their work: mastery, autonomy and purpose.[2] These three aspects are a useful lens through which to examine teachers' work.

Purpose is perhaps the easiest of these three. It is clear that the overwhelming majority of teachers are in the profession because they find great purpose in improving the lives of the young people in their care. Teaching is ultimately a career imbued with purpose: every day, professionals come to work and help young people to reach their potential. What could be more purposeful?

But there are still ways schools can subtly undermine teachers' sense of purpose. When a teacher has a great relationship with a class, for example, and they are given to another teacher the following year – or, worse, part-way through a year – this can make teachers lose their sense of purpose. I heard of a school once taking every class away from a teacher while they 'improved their practice' and giving them endless administration tasks to do, seemingly in an effort to make them resign. Finding purpose in that kind of workplace strikes me as almost impossible.

Similarly, though, schools can unwittingly strip teachers of their sense of purpose by poorly thought-through performance management systems. Judging teachers on the results of their exam classes, without deep consideration of the particular challenges those classes may have (or consideration of the point in their school career the teacher took on that class – after all, who actually owns the results of a child who has been in school for eleven years, and is it right to assign all that responsibility to their teacher to the final year of schooling?) can lead to teachers losing their sense of why they came into the profession in the first place. Teachers, it goes without saying, want their children to do well. Seeing them succeed is the ultimate purpose. Leaders must always keep this human element to the fore.

Mastery is clearly applicable to teaching. For me, mastery in the working world means being able to do the job in hand, and doing it to a standard that pleases the individual. We must ensure teachers are set up to succeed at work. This mastery can be undermined by a weak behaviour system: if teachers cannot control their class, it is incredibly difficult – if not impossible – to feel like you are succeeding in your job. If you never receive any feedback, other than an annual high-stakes observation, it is almost impossible to improve your practice – a key element of mastery. And if you do not have the requisite subject knowledge or the support of a strong curriculum, it is hard to plan superb lessons.

Autonomy might be the most challenging of these three pillars in the school context. Daniel Pink notes that: 'human beings have an innate inner drive to be autonomous, self-determined, and connected to one another. And when that drive is liberated, people achieve more and live richer lives.'[3] In some schools, autonomy is automatic – in my first year of teaching, for example, I had complete autonomy over every single one of my classes. I could teach anything I wanted to years 7, 8 and 9 – as long as we had copies of the books, or I could print them off the internet – and year 10 were the only class taking a new specification for GCSE, so again I had total autonomy to teach and plan what I wanted for them.

As a brand-new teacher, you can imagine how that went.

On the other side of autonomy, I've heard of highly successful schools who dictate every single slide of the teacher's PowerPoint, and monitor which slide teachers are on to ensure 'consistency.'

I think there is a happy medium between these extremes, where teachers can be supported to teach to a mastery level, but with enough autonomy to find fulfilment in their work. In *Simplicity Rules*, I advocate for a booklet-based curriculum, for example.[4] PowerPoints are open to endless tweaks from teachers, which can ultimately result in a radically different learning experience across classrooms. The simplicity of the booklet resource means that you have total curricular alignment on what is being taught and in what order, while giving teachers the autonomy to decide how these lessons will be communicated with the children in front of them.

A large aspect of autonomy is also reliant on leaders' approach to feedback, which we explore in more depth later in this chapter. If leaders are genuinely open to feedback, teachers can make some incredible contributions to whole-school policy, which has the dual benefit of hugely benefitting the school and making all teachers know that they can seize autonomy and have impact if they choose that.

I once had the privilege of being deputy to a headteacher who was the last word in humility. In the face of praise for the school she had turned around, she would refer to herself as 'the conductor of the orchestra', always seeking to praise others and give credit to anyone but herself. At one point in the final year of her Headship, a middle leader went to her with a suggestion to change the school's detention policy completely. She listened, asked questions, and got the middle leader to flesh their ideas out in more depth. Having consulted her SLT, we went with the new plan for detentions, and when the headteacher announced this plan she gave full credit to the middle leader whose idea it had been.

Everyone is a winner under such leadership: the middle leader knows their voice is heard and they can have a whole-school impact; every member of staff hears this and recognises that they too can have such an impact if they choose to; the school improves because the people who live the day-to-day of a (nearly) full timetable are shaping the systems.

Shoring up purpose

I believe it is on the 'purpose' part of Pink's trinity that school leaders might focus most of their efforts. There is a fashion among school leaders to diminish the importance of a whole-school vision, or school mission statement – perhaps the more pressing to redress years of promoting abstract leadership qualities. In his excellent post on school leadership, Tom Rees makes a strong argument against the genericism of leadership:

> I want to argue that our conception of school leadership and the narrative that surrounds it has its roots in the theory of transformational leadership, a term first referred to in Downton's *Rebel Leadership* (1973), and then separately described by James MacGregor Burns in 1978. I think that this narrative has become unhelpful ... School leadership as a 'transformational' activity puts the emphasis on change being the driver of success and the main purpose of leadership as creating a vision, motivating people through relationships and influence towards change. Is this really the optimum way to run a school? ... I think school leadership shouldn't be a club reserved for the charismatic, the extrovert and the dynamic. We need to think harder about the specific problems that school leaders face and how we can help them to tackle these issues. In particular, we should place greater emphasis on the domain-specific knowledge that school leaders need so that they can make decisions and solve problems from a position of expertise.[5]

Rees makes some salient points here. It is undeniable that charisma is not enough to make a great school leader. It is clear that many people who are not 'charismatic' in the traditional sense run phenomenal schools and are loved and respected by their staff. The best leaders, according to Rees and many others, have strong domain knowledge: they know a lot about how to run a school.

Do you need a vision at all?

And yet there is space for vision setting within this framework of knowledge. I always used to joke about school visions that they were all the identical same: 'we want our kids to do better than they would have done if we did not exist'. But this was before I witnessed school visions executed well. Visiting Dixons Trinity Academy, I saw how leaders set their vision ('to get students to and through university so that they thrive in a top job and have a great life') and make it something that lived in every classroom. Every decision they made ultimately came down to this vision. At Becky Curtis's school, Ark Elvin, where the vision is 'to ensure that every pupil leaves Elvin confident, articulate, and culturally aware; able to pursue careers they are passionate about, contribute to society and live happy, healthy and fulfilled lives', this forms the basis of a series of annual strategic meetings at many levels. They pick it apart each year and re-commit to what they are doing; they ask challenging questions of themselves as leaders: where are we not yet meeting this vision?

At my first Trust meeting for Ark Soane, I shared my vision and received the brilliantly honest feedback that 'This could be any school.' I accepted this as absolutely true, because this tallied completely with exactly how I viewed school visions – that they could work for any school.

When I redrafted my mission statement, I spent a significant amount of time on it. It went through no fewer than twenty iterations, and I sought feedback from everyone whose opinion on school culture I really respected. By the end, though, I was so sure this was right for my school that when someone suggested I change some of what I saw as the non-negotiable words, I suddenly realised I could not change it – I had finally crafted something I could believe in, that I wanted to spend time making a reality.

Eternal redrafts

Abandoning version 53 of the vision for Ark Soane for the succeeding leader was challenging having spent so long considering it, and as I redraft this chapter I feel a slight nausea that I will have to go through the same torturous, soul-searching process again for Ark John Keats. Our vision for Soane at that time was that we wanted our students to go on to lead happy and fulfilled lives as the drivers of their own destiny.

I started to see the value of this vision when I had thought deeply about the wording. I saw 'fulfilled' as linking to curriculum, and careers: without an academic curriculum and great academic results, you can't do the job you love (or change career to something you might like more). I saw 'happy' as helping children to understand and turn around negative thoughts, focusing on gratitude and counting their blessings, and contributing to society in a meaningful way as a track to true happiness in comparison with pleasure or mindless acquisition. Driving their own destiny linked to self-reliance and autonomy, as well as the ability to take responsibility and see mistakes as learning opportunities.

Once I had unpacked the vision, I knew I would need to do this with all of our teachers. Just asking teachers to say what that vision meant for them and which parts they felt especially drawn to revealed a great deal about their alignment, and we discussed this in all of our teacher interviews. I felt sure we had got this right when, addressing a group of our founding families, I said the vision and a parent in the front row shouted 'YES!' with a fist-pump. To find something people could rally around and believe in made what we were doing feel incredibly special.

Drawing from examples of some of my excellent colleagues at Ark, you can't set a vision and ignore it: you must revisit and refine your mission as the years go on. In this revisiting, you can ensure it still aligns to your purpose and your organisational values. You can then, if you are happy it is still right for your community, check you are on the road to fulfilling it.

Communicating your vision

For school leaders, every time you communicate with teachers is an opportunity to front the culture. Consider every opportunity the team is together – staff briefings, whole-staff emails, staff CPD, the Christmas party, end of term gatherings – what are you saying to people? How do you fire them up? How do you make them feel like what they are doing is special? Because, of course, it is special: in every single school in the country, adults are changing children's lives. Taking every opportunity to remind people what an amazing thing they get to come to work to do, and what an impact they have on the young people in their care, is always time well spent.

Line management

Creating a culture where people don't want to leave requires careful planning and consideration of all the interactions between adults in an institution. Line management is a clear example of something which, if neglected, can become patchy or variable in quality, and no one's priority. Yet most of us know how beneficial a truly great line manager can be, and most of us will have stories of how our favourite ones grew, challenged and nurtured us to become the professionals we are today.

Start with outlining the basic expectations of line management. It is important to meet regularly. I have rarely found weekly meetings to be excessive, especially as these allow people to cancel the odd one without it becoming too long between meetings, or the flexibility of running frequent meetings which are shorter. Check it is happening, chase it to ensure it does, and prioritise it when the life of a school inevitably gets in the way.

Plan out your meeting. When I was managing a large team, I would keep post-it notes of everyone I managed on my planner, and add anything I thought of to the post-it. I'd then review this before the meeting, prioritising checks and carefully phrasing larger discussions. This also helped me to give others a heads' up if they needed it – I'd say what I'd like their thoughts on, but also qualify that I didn't expect them to bring anything – I just didn't want them feeling blindsided by being asked for their ideas cold. If I wanted people to prepare something, I'd ask them in person for it at the next line management at the earliest.

Generally, I would advocate asking the person you line manage if they have anything pressing. It's good to get the urgent, little things out of the way early on, as otherwise people can be distracted by thinking about these. How much you choose to allow your line managee to determine the scope of the meeting is a personal matter – I was surprised to read Kim Scott's advice to allow 'reports' to 'set the agenda' for line management meetings, with the reasoning that 'when your direct reports own and set the agenda for their 1:1s, they're more productive, because they allow you to listen to what matters to them'.[6] I've never experimented with this in schools, but it's perhaps something to bear in mind in terms of the proportion of our meetings we allow our 'reports' to dictate.

One aspect that was always on the line management template of one school I worked at was 'professional development': we had to ask every session whether our report wanted professional development, or else about their career progression or hopes for the future. I always enjoyed this part of the discussion greatly – though having this conversation weekly was possibly too much, unless you managed seriously motivated individuals (I think only one of the people I line managed would have an education book she wanted to discuss, conference she had gone to, part of her Master's she was completing or blogpost she had read to discuss every single week, and she truly was exceptional in every way).

This part is illuminating because we often assume we know people's career ambitions. It is human nature to assume others are more like us in their hopes and dreams than they actually are. Often, of course, people (including ourselves) don't actually know what they want. It's great if you can have the relationship where your reports bounce their current thinking off you in confidence, not least because you can be sure they will be honest when the time comes that they are seeking to apply for other positions.

It is vital we plan for our line management meetings, if for no other reason than this forces us to think about the people we are managing. What are their strengths? Where would they benefit from support? Where are they aiming to go with their career in the coming years? What do they need to learn, read or do in order to meet their career aspirations? Seek out things that would benefit them – conferences, blogs, books, and people who you can put them in touch with to improve or develop their practice.

Largely, there are two types of reports: those who require more stretch, and those who require more support. Both come with their benefits and challenges. For colleagues who need stretching, there is a balance of granting earned autonomy and exciting projects and over-working people, or making people feel their job does not map with their pay, for example. For those who need more support, ensuring this genuinely does feel supportive is a constant challenge for line managers everywhere.

It is down to headteachers to set an agenda for line management that guides managers to the most important things, without constraining unnecessarily. In the school where line management was most effectively done in my experience, we were given a pro forma and told to 'edit it as you see fit'.

In the first year of Ark Soane, I drafted the following advice to line managers:

Agenda: the items below must be discussed *at least every other week* (you may wish to split these two and two, or run one LM for your managee and one for these questions).

1 Teaching: discussion of the classes taught, resources, planning and delivery.

2 Outcomes: who is not on track to pass this subject? What needs to be done to catch them up? (Consider: teaching, planning, resources, parents).

3 Leadership (if relevant): how are the people you line manage getting on? What have you changed with their feedback? Who are you supporting and how?

4 Line manager feedback: What could I do to support you? How am I making your job harder and what could I do instead? What could I do differently?

5 Items for discussion sent by managee.

We will come back to point 4 later in this chapter, which I've taken from Kim Scott's *Radical Candour*: build in opportunities for leaders to model taking feedback. Line management is a great time to ask people for advice on how to better support them. Asking for feedback, as we will discuss, can feel incredibly awkward for individuals, and putting this on a framework makes it easier for individuals to do it ('well, if this piece of paper wants me to say it, then I'll say it').

The main thing in line management, as in all aspects of school life, is to always remember the human: don't over-plan every interaction. Have some key questions, but ultimately leave some freedom to respond in the moment to your people, to have that free conversation where you genuinely seek to understand and then support action.

Another useful insight is to be aware of how often your line management meetings happen: 'If people who report to you cancel 1:1s too often, it's a sign your partnership is not fruitful for them, or that you're using it inappropriately to dispose of criticism you've been stockpiling.'[7] Any time my reports cancelled with me in my last school, I took it as a sign I wasn't being helpful enough, and re-invested more time in planning for our meetings and asking for direct feedback on how I could make the sessions most useful for them.

The final piece of the line management puzzle is what happens with the minutes. When I've been a line manager with difficult relationships with reports, I've frequently had minutes sent back to me with notes and clarifications. Clearly, it is important that the minutes are an accurate record of the meeting that has taken place, particularly if things are going to become tricky later on. But it is also difficult to balance active listening with note-taking. (One of my more impressive colleagues shared with me that she would make only brief notes with a pen during the meeting itself, and afterwards type up her notes. She did also admit she was quite behind in sending minutes out as a result.) I'd try and type as we went, especially if there are quick and easy 'sign-offs' to get through, and then for longer discussions stay present and afterwards just write: 'year 11 intervention strategy – discussion'.

The headteacher asked for all line management minutes to be sent to the individual with her copied in. This was great for ensuring she had minute oversight of all areas of the school. I knew she read all of the minutes, because not infrequently she would write back a comment or question about something in them. The knowledge of her oversight made me up my game in terms of what we discussed and how, and like all great management systems it challenged me to do a better job while never feeling oppressive or controlling. I've adopted this at Ark John Keats, and a number of people have reported that they actually like knowing I read the minutes – it is especially useful for sending quick clarifications, or offering support when things look like they are getting tricky.

Overcommunicate clarity

In *The Advantage*, Patrick Lencioni emphasises the importance of clarity. Indeed, he says that the way you build a strong team is:

1 build a cohesive team;

2 create clarity;

3 overcommunicate clarity;

4 reinforce clarity.[8]

It is obvious that we cannot communicate too much (an old boss of mine used to say: 'no one ever left a job because there was *too much* communication'). Ensuring people stay happy in our organisations is built to a large degree on having clear systems and making sure people use them. This means simplifying, where possible, how things are done, and not being afraid to tell people this over and over again, as well as checking the system is being used correctly by all stakeholders. We could do worse than testing people – after all, we use the same system to help children remember what we tell them! In our September induction at both Ark John Keats and Ark Soane, I tried to model this insistence on memory by starting every session with a recap do now that ranged over the systems we were teaching people to use.

Just as the best schools revisit core routines regularly (and I would advocate thinking about setting aside time at the start of every half term to do this effectively), so the staff bodies with most clarity and coherence invest time in revisiting these systems.

Keep it simple

Having simple systems means people are more likely to understand and use the systems. The more layers you add, the more complication, the less likely people are to use the system. And, as Becky Curtis is fond of saying, 'a good school is an organised school.' A school without systems, or with systems no one uses, cannot function as effectively.

I remember a conversation early on in the planning of Ark Soane where my colleagues were concerned about a system for students to catch up on work missed after an illness. After about ten minutes of suggesting various possibilities, we'd come across so many minor differences to account for – how long the illness was, how able the student would be to catch up on work as well as do current work, how supportive their family may or may not be, and whether students might become anxious about the pile of catch up work they had on their return and find it harder to come back. In the end, our system was so complex we realised nobody would be able to remember it, so we scrapped it. We decided that for occasional sickness, we wouldn't worry about catch-up work. If students asked for it, teachers could give it. For students off for long-term issues, we would have a bespoke system run through their head of year that would suit their particular needs. Although this may not be the optimal system, it's the one that ensures most clarity.

Similarly, we looked early on at including a wider range of subjects in our timetable, but that too proved incredibly complex. After working on forty minute lessons (too many lesson transitions, too little time to really immerse themselves in the work), split lunches (too few breaks, too little down time), getting rid of tutor time (we decided this would be crucial for supporting our students in succeeding in school), running assembly after lunch and having five periods in the morning (making lunch incredibly late), and running a two-week timetable for people to have to remember, we realised that any timetable with that many subjects would involve complex choices we weren't prepared to make. We chose instead to keep the curriculum and timetable simple. Though students would not experience as broad a breadth of subjects, the timings of the school day made more sense from a pastoral and care perspective and, crucially, were easier for everyone to remember. (In October I remember visiting a school that had recently changed its timetable to a mix of forty-five- and fifty-minute lessons to ensure the curriculum stayed broad. I was struck by no one being able to tell me what time the next lesson would begin. This might have been understandable, but when in February an extremely competent senior leader was still getting the lesson timings wrong, it seemed clear to me that this was too complex to be effective.)

Holding people to account

'People want to be held to account' was the theory of one of the best headteachers I have worked for. 'They want to do a good job, and they want to be pushed to do better.' Having taken over and turned around multiple schools, this had been what she had found: good staff were frustrated that low standards were permitted to permeate.

I have also found this to be the case: nothing frustrates good people more than seeing those less effective remain in positions of power, seemingly getting paid more to do less.

If you want advice on how to have difficult conversations with people, Kim Scott's *Radical Candour* is the best book available.[9] At the start of the book, Scott uses an anecdote which exemplifies the importance of this approach: using the anonymised 'Bob', Scott paints a picture of an employee who came with excellent references, but who hopelessly underperformed. Instead of holding

'Bob' to account, Scott describes how she made countless excuses for his poor performance:

> I liked Bob, and I didn't want to come down too hard on him. He had looked so nervous during the meeting when we reviewed his document that I feared he might even cry. Because everyone liked him so much, I also worried that if he did cry, everyone would think I was an abusive bitch. Second, unless his résumé and references were bogus, he'd done great work in the past. Maybe he'd been distracted by something at home or was unused to our way of doing things. Whatever the reason, I convinced myself that he'd surely return to the performance level that had gotten him the job. Third, I could fix the document myself for now, and that would be faster than teaching him how to rewrite it.'[10]

Scott goes on to describe the effect of underperformance on a team:

> And of course, the impact of my behaviour with Bob didn't stop with him: others on the team wondered why I accepted such poor work. Following my lead, they too tried to cover for him. They would fix mistakes he'd made and do or redo his work, usually when they should have been sleeping. Covering for people is sometimes necessary for a short period of time-say, if somebody is going through a crisis. But when it goes on too long it starts to take a toll. People whose work had been exceptional started to get sloppy. We missed key deadlines. Knowing why Bob's colleagues were late, I didn't give them too hard a time. Then they began to wonder if I knew the difference between great and mediocre; perhaps I didn't even take the missed deadlines seriously. As is often the case when people are not sure if the quality of what they are doing is appreciated, the results began to suffer, and so did morale. As I faced the prospect of losing my team, I realised I couldn't put it off any longer. I invited Bob to have coffee with me. He expected to have a nice chat, but instead, after a few false starts, I fired him. Now we were both huddled miserably over our muffins and lattes. After an excruciating silence, Bob pushed his chair back, metal screeching on marble, and looked me straight in the eye. 'Why didn't you tell me?'[11]

This story brilliantly depicts the way good people want to be held to account. Almost no one, and no one I have ever worked with, goes into teaching to do minimal work badly. The job is simply too hard for this to be an option. If someone wanted an easy life, it is impossible to conceive of them thinking: 'yes, teaching's for me'.

Scott's central message is: tell people the truth, and do it kindly. In a talk, Scott uses the example of her own interaction with her boss at Google to illustrate this. Following a presentation Scott felt had gone well, the boss asked her to go to her office. Her feedback? 'You said "um" an awful lot – were you aware of it?' Scott brushes it off as 'kind of a verbal tic – no big deal really'. The response: 'I can see I'm going to have to be a lot more direct with you. When you say "um" every third word it makes you sound stupid and insecure.'[12] As a result of the directness,

Scott raced to a speech coach and in telling the story in retrospect cites this as a turning point in her ability to give presentations. The feedback was honest, perhaps painfully so – but it had the impact of making her much better at her job.

There is no single blueprint for having difficult conversations, but I will share what I've learned from having many of them.

Don't delay

The sooner you can have the conversation, the better. Ideally, aim for the same day or the next day. Choose your moment – I'd pick the end of the school day. Definitely don't give someone a tough message when they are about to teach. (Once, I was called out of a lesson midway through to be told I had not been shortlisted for a promotion I'd applied for. It was my first rejection in teaching, and I'm still not sure how coherent the second half of my lesson was.) When thinking about your timing, make sure you ask: is this best for me, or for them? If you're delaying because you don't want to deal with it, that's an issue. If you're delaying because they've just told you their mother is in hospital, that's keeping their best interests at heart.

Prepare

Ensure you have all the facts. Don't make any assumptions. If someone has shared information, ensure you present the information as just that: the subjective observation of another individual. If you need to have information from multiple other sources, ensure you've gathered that swiftly, reiterating the need for discretion with all parties. If your feedback is based on data, understand the data fully. If you don't understand it, script your questions. In fact, script a list of questions to ensure you get everything you need. Asking questions isn't weak – it's essential to get to the reality of issues which will often be dominated by personality or subjectivity.

... but don't over-prepare

Be ready for the conversation to go in an unexpected direction. Steeling myself for my first difficult conversation with an operational manager I'd hired, I asked my questions only to realise that the issue was not at all what I had assumed it was. All my preparation was for nil, and I just needed to find out more.

Know the options

For serious issues like capability or suspension, be crystal clear on what the possible outcomes are following the meeting. People need and deserve clarity at this point. Tempting as it might be to fudge this, have a quick conversation with someone you trust in HR prior to your difficult meeting and run through possible scenarios and likely outcomes. Even if you can't give a definite answer, having clarity around timescales and when you will be able to make decisions can be reassuring.

Do your HR homework

It is well worth, especially as a headteacher, having a robust understanding of HR systems, including dealing with union issues. Most of the HR training I have received is very specific, but the true essence is this: if in doubt, definitely don't say it.

Less is more

A piece of advice that has stood me in good stead in all parts of my life is that when you are in a difficult situation, never give more information than you are asked for. If a conversation is becoming contentious or, even worse, litigious, the worst thing you can do is to blurt out inaccurate and unnecessary information that could be used against you in the future.

Stay compassionate

Scott's matrix of radical candour shows that being overly compassionate leads to 'ruinous empathy', the trap too many leaders fall into.[13] In our need to protect the feelings of the people we work with – an entirely human one – we think we are protecting them by withholding feedback. According to Scott, though, this has disastrous consequences, as poor performance cannot be addressed if it is not known about. We have to be compassionate to those we work with, but we cannot use compassion as an excuse to not be direct. We have to both be direct *and* stay compassionate. It's an almost impossible line to walk. I think listening and empathising as people share their fears and worries is crucial. Make sure you're genuinely committed to finding a solution together, should one exist. Agree the terms that you can both be happy with, and agree when you can revisit these. Listen, and let people talk about what scares them. But don't use that information to excuse any poor performance. Adults are just like the children in that way: you wouldn't excuse a child performing poorly – you'd put in supportive measures to help them to achieve. Teachers deserve the same compassion.

Let people leave with dignity

The hardest part of a difficult conversation normally comes after a string of other difficult conversations, when it is ultimately decided that this simply is not the right school or right role for the individual. If significant support has been agreed, put into place, and reviewed frequently but problems persist, you have to ask: if this a competence issue, or a conduct issue? *Can* they not do the job? Or are they able to do it but wilfully are not doing it?

In both cases, find an out for them. I've worked with colleagues who are great teachers, but couldn't manage behaviour in a very challenging school. Such people can usually improve their behaviour management if they are committed to this – but they may not want to. Have the difficult conversation: is this the right kind of school for you? I've worked with other colleagues who have been hugely unsupportive of a new SLT's position – they've felt the new behaviour system being imposed was unjust, for example, and so wilfully did not use it, undermining their other colleagues. It can be tempting for leaders to think such individuals are simply wrong and do not deserve to be in education. But all schools are different, and plenty of schools value restorative justice in place of strict discipline. Where possible, have conversations around alignment as well as competence. There can be nothing worse for a great teacher than to be doing a bad job. Show them it does not have to be this way.

Group norms

One of the most important ways to make your school a place people won't want to leave is to cultivate strong group norms. When I first joined Ark, one of the first things my then regional director, Jerry Collins, asked me to read was a document entitled *Ways of Working*. It was incredibly short. In less than a page, the document outlined the ways all the principals in the region were expected to relate to one another and support one another, and how we would work together as a group to move our schools forward together.

Inspired by this, when I was asked to outline the ideas that would guide our school, I set aside a part for our school's ways of working together, and here is what it reads:

> **We are honest with each other, support and respect each other, constantly seek to improve, and use time effectively.**
>
> Ark Soane Academy employs a culture of respectful honesty. We talk about others as if they are in the room. We address all concerns to the individual in the first instance or seek support from our line manager in advance if guidance is required. We never raise a problem without also suggesting at least one specific and actionable solution. There are no lengthy meetings, only professional development and strategic planning. Operational and logistical briefings are shorter than 15 minutes and frequent, so everyone knows what is happening and when. All staff members operate an 'open door' policy in their classrooms and offices. Leaders support teachers 100% of the time in front of the children, never undermining colleagues publicly and addressing concerns rapidly and privately.

This statement begins by foregrounding respect: we always talk about others as if they are in the room. Our ideal is that people raise issues with one another in the first instance. Such choices create clarity and trust: nobody is talking about anybody behind your back. I remember feeling uneasy when a previous Headteacher saw something they didn't like in one of my English teacher's classrooms and directed me to address this with the teacher. Going to a teacher to say something you have not yourself seen is dubious feedback; having that teacher know the Head has spoken to your line manager about you doubly so.

We do recognise, of course, that saying: 'just tell them!' is easier said than done. Plenty of people are anxious about having such conversations, and it is our job as an organisation to support them. So we say, do tell your line manager if what you are doing is seeking confidential advice on *how* to address your concerns. Have someone who you completely trust with whom you can role play a tricky conversation.

In this statement, we go on to talk about being solutions-focused: you may not have the right solution, but we always want people to approach issues with this in mind. We build something together, we don't tear down without thinking through a better solution. I will talk more in Chapter 4 about the importance of short and purposeful meetings to ensure staff buy-in, but the policy of leaders having open doors is, I hope, self-explanatory (and I myself have benefitted from the open doors of countless senior leaders in my career – my apologies and thanks for allowing me to melt in your many offices along the way).

Finally, the notion that we support one another publicly is hugely important. As far as the school is concerned, as a staff body we are an impenetrable fortress. Our colleagues may get it wrong, but it serves no one to say: 'Yes, Sir shouldn't have done that.' Teachers want to know leaders will support them no matter what.

Feedback: asking for it

My feedback idol, Kim Scott, is clear that it is up to leaders to set a culture of feedback.[14] By modelling asking for feedback, we safeguard against many difficult conversations. If people are constantly asking how they are doing, this opens the door for feedback to be given, and normalises an attitude of constant improvement. That way, when someone gives you feedback, you don't feel picked on – it is simply 'the way we do things here'. As outlined above, we build this into our weekly line management sessions to prompt leaders at all levels to model asking for ways to get better, and hold them to account to ensure they act on it.

At one extraordinary school I visited, the principal and their senior team would craft and send out just one question to all staff each week. It would be something like: do you feel SLT support you with behaviour appropriately? This question will be tailored on the current issues facing the school, or prompted by any concerns from members of staff. Every teacher had to respond with either yes or no; and if they responded with no they had to give a reason for their answer. Leaders then followed this up with an email explaining to teachers what they have done or will do to address this feedback using the eminently helpful: 'you said … we did …'.

Feedback: giving it

Giving feedback, even when someone is asking for it, is intense and difficult. I'll always be grateful to the senior leader who gave me feedback on an unsuccessful interview. In the interview, the Headteacher had said: 'you've walked the school a lot today. What do you see that needs to improve?' I had gushed about how great the school was and how much I longed to work there – both of which were true.

In my feedback, the senior leader (who I hear is by all accounts now a stupendous headteacher herself, and unsurprisingly so) said: 'The principal asked for feedback on the school. You need to give that feedback. You need to be strong enough to speak truth to power.'

It was a revelatory thing to say to me, as an aspirant senior leader myself, and I have never forgotten it. But giving feedback is hard – particularly in the absence of a relationship.

For feedback to be a learning process, it must be underpinned by genuine care for the other person's development. If I had done the right thing in my interview, it would have been to point out how the school could improve, but the intention behind this would have been important. If I had nit-picked in order to make myself or my own school seem superior, that would not be genuinely helpful feedback. But if I had thought: these children and adults deserve the very best education has to offer. What could the school do differently to improve learning and working for everyone in the building? If I had looked for ways the school could improve because I genuinely cared about the school, that feedback would have been (or could have been – I mean, it's hard to hit the nail on the head after a day's visit) useful.

Having said above that we should give direct feedback where we see it is needed, schools are full of humans, and humans are incredibly complex. Some leaders may say that no matter the individual's personal circumstances, you should always put the learning of the children in the school first, and continue to tell people to improve.

But let's think. Terrible things happen in a school. I worked in a school where a colleague, tragically young, died. His closest friend worked in the school, and *continued to come into work* in the aftermath of the tragedy. He did, as he always had, a remarkable job. But let's imagine he missed a deadline, or had a terrible lesson. Would it be right to give such an individual feedback at that difficult and emotional time? Absolutely not, in my view.

When colleagues are handling tough situations and coming into work and doing a less than perfect job, we have to decide. Ultimately, the children deserve the best education – but we have to balance this with the real human emotions of our adults, and the long-term impact. Long serving members of staff may very well have a term where they aren't their best. Keep the long term in mind. By all means, do all you can to support that individual: could their teaching load be temporarily reduced? Could you remove their tutor group, or take them off duties? Do they need compassionate leave?

All these are possibilities, but we cannot anticipate what will support people. In one school I worked in, a member of staff came back from paternity leave feeling hurt and upset that they hadn't been contacted for two weeks – they *wanted* to be kept in the loop. But the assumption had been made that they would not want to think about school.

Of course, there is the argument that some people don't know what they want – for example, I have often found myself advising young, ambitious teachers to take the weekend off or stop taking work home. I related this to a friend who works in the private sector, and their comment surprised me: 'isn't that what you did? Work hundreds of hours – evenings, holidays, weekends?'

'Yes,' I replied, 'I want to save them from what I did.'

'But haven't you been promoted so quickly *because* you did that? And you want to deny that to others now?'

It was a fascinating perspective, and perhaps contained some truth. Of course, I continue to work hard. My choice has always been to work hard, although not knowing when to stop has, for me, resulted in some avoidable mid-week meltdowns.

I now have this conversation in a different way. I talk about workload, and how we can ensure this is manageable. I try now to genuinely listen to what the person I'm managing wants. When someone is hugely ambitious, I normally know that, because they now confide in me what they want from their career and how soon they want it. And then I try to say something more like: 'life is long, and you will get there in time. If you want to get there quickly, don't work hundreds of hours marking books. Let's find you a project instead.' For people who are ambitious and want to work hard, burdening them with unrealistic working conditions is not the answer. Keep working conditions reasonable for all teachers, and for those who want more, find meaningful projects where they can contribute to the whole school, building value for both the organisation, the children and their CV simultaneously.

Team building

I've worked with a range of headteachers now who all had different approaches to building an esprit de corps in their staff bodies. Ultimately, you will never please all of the people all of the time.

I have worked for headteachers who plan what I term 'organised fun'. Team trips, team away-days, games on the last day of term. And when I have complained about these activities, I have found people fall into one of two camps: they totally hate them, or they totally love them.

I have also worked for headteachers who put on a glass of champagne at Christmas in the staff room and some nibbles, but don't specify that people *have* to attend. Such end of term celebrating ultimately does feel a little underwhelming.

We do need to think carefully about how we build a team. My preference has always been to have a meal and some drinks together, and let the bonding occur naturally. But to do this might exclude those teachers (who are, in my experience, a very significant minority), who find social situations with a large group quite intimidating.

To provide a balance, I think it's worth thinking through ways to build in 'forced communication' time between teachers. Top performing teams tend to be those that can see each other in person frequently, and this is a challenge in large organisations. To safeguard against people working alone in their silos, we need to build in time for people to work together, including working with individuals from other parts of the school. At Ark John Keats, we have some CPD sessions focused on taking a part a school priority and working out new solutions as a team. This forces people to work together, talk and listen to those they do not see every week as part of their subject or year group teams.

Ultimately, giving people space to bond is important. Having some non-negotiable staff socials everyone has to attend is important to build a sense of camaraderie and team-spirit, whether it is gathering ten minutes before a carol concert to come together and celebrate something, or mandating that all subject teams do a meal a term. Team bonding doesn't have to mean paint-balling (for me, one of the most stress-inducing hyphenates in the English language). Indeed, it is my view that the best way to bond with others is to do the work with them.

Take-aways

▨ Create a work culture of autonomy, mastery and purpose.

▨ Great systems of behaviour make for happier workplaces.

▨ Overcommunicate the why.

▨ Use line management to support and challenge.

▨ Train everyone in how to be compassionately candid.

▨ Ensure leaders model asking for feedback, and act on feedback.

▨ Create opportunities for the team to bond.

Notes

1 Retrieved from https://schoolsweek.co.uk/assaults-in-schools-soar-by-72-in-four-years and www.independent.co.uk/news/education/education-news/teachers-pupils-violence-classroom-behaviour-nasuwt-teaching-union-a8877776.html (accessed 27 July 2021).

2 Daniel H. Pink, *Drive* (Canongate, 2011).

3 Ibid., p. 73.

4 For more detail on this, please see Chapter 4 in Jo Facer, *Simplicity Rules* (Routledge, 2019), particularly pages 43–46.

5 Retrieved from www.ambition.org.uk/blog/helping-leaders-keep-getting-better (accessed 9 March 2020).

6 Kim Scott, *Radical Candour* (Macmillan, 2017), p. 77.

7 Ibid., p. 79.

8 Patrick Lencioni, *The Advantage* (Jossey-Bass, 2012).

 9 Scott, *Radical Candour*.
10 Ibid., p. x.
11 Ibid., p. xii.
12 Retrieved from www.youtube.com/watch?v=yj9GLeNCgm4&t=2s (accessed 28 July 2020).
13 Scott, *Radical Candour*.
14 Scott recommends a series of helpful questions for managers seeking feedback, most of all: 'what could I do or stop doing that would make it easier to work with me?' (Scott, *Radical Candour*, p. 205).

3 How can we develop teachers?

Along with a positive working culture, teachers want to feel like they are getting better. It is very rare to find a teacher who considers themselves to be the 'finished product', perhaps because of the nature of the job: our entire trade is learning. We are invested in the idea that children are always learning, and therefore we automatically carry this expectation into our own lives. A friendly and happy staff culture where people are held to account for what they are expected to do is therefore not enough: we must also help teachers to develop. In this chapter, we're going to explore the many facets of teacher development and how we can ensure our school are places where people can grow year on year.

Teacher development tends to be thought of in two main ways: promotion and professional development. For a significant proportion of teachers, 'development' and 'promotion' become synonymous. ('I left because I couldn't see any development' is a frequently cited reason for leaving, but what most people actually mean is: 'I want to be promoted, and no one is leaving'.)

'Development' (promotions)

And of course, succession planning is a vital part of school leadership. I've worked with leaders who, desperate to keep bright sparks, have invented near-meaningless teaching and learning responsibilities (TLRs) to entice them to stay. If those TLRs are carefully considered, and that individual goes on to fill a genuine gap and add value to the school, then this can prove a win–win for all parties. But too often, small TLRs are invented for, frankly, absurd things (I was once granted one for 'oracy', which my spell checker does not even recognise as a word). I've met with too many new headteachers now who have spent years unpicking a trail of nonsense TLRs, the awarding of which has undermined their importance.

It can, moreover, be tempting to recruit a large leadership team, because the best people often want to be leaders, and don't we want the best people in our schools? Unfortunately, what starts out as common sense can soon leave those on a large extended leadership team feeling shut out and ignored. I vividly remember being a part of a leadership team of nearly twenty, and feeling like I had no more say about running the school than when I had been a head of department. Working on leadership teams of 7, 5 and 6 in subsequent schools did not feel the same way.

We should not have a surplus of many leaders. Leaders want to forge a path, and the chances of twenty people wanting to forge the same path are vanishingly small. To assuage the fears of those who wish to develop, I'd suggest making a big deal of pay progression (being clear up front: it's a big deal when you progress to the next rung – very well done, you've grown this year and proven yourself), making an enormous deal of those who pass threshold and enter the heady realms of the upper pay scales, and letting those who want to develop in the promotional sense go wherever they need to and do that – supporting them all the way.

Keep your leadership team lean, and you'll find it easier to lead. A large middle leadership team, properly managed and fully aligned to your priorities, can provide good capacity to make that vision a reality – it doesn't have to be leaders doing everything. But the decision makers should be a small group, and it should be clear who they are. If, as we said in the previous chapter, you are constantly asking for feedback, then people should feel their voice is heard at all levels of the school.

Continuous professional development (CPD)

In my eleven years of teaching, I can think of absolutely no whole-staff continuous professional development (CPD) that I could genuinely say has transformed my teaching practice. Granted, for around the last five years I've worked in schools I tended to be the person inflicting whole-staff CPD on others, but I couldn't say whether anyone actually found it useful, because the only people who gave me any feedback on it said it was great at the time. (I've got better at both asking for feedback and at following up on training in the interim – though this is still something I need to work much more on.)

The issues of whole school CPD sessions are well-known to teachers. A large school staff is the ultimate mixed ability class. Bringing together veteran teachers, trainee teachers, teachers of PE and teachers of maths and serving them all something that they will find useful to their practice is an inescapably tall order. It might be argued that it is rarely appropriate to run professional development with the whole staff body, but I tend to disagree.

First, there is the undeniable benefit of coming together. Some of my warmest memories of colleagues I didn't spend nearly enough time with happened when thrown together making tea in the back of the hall, or sitting on another department's table by accident, or bonding over the excitement of free biscuits. There are times when you want to bring everyone together: for unavoidable operational briefings (before the first day of school; on a trip day; before student induction begins), for celebrations (the end of term, a colleague getting married, someone being promoted in the school), for crisis communication (an act of God such as schools all around the world have had to deal with a surprising amount in recent times).

But I would argue there are still times when every member of staff benefits from training. The most obvious example of staff training which everyone needs to attend is a change in behaviour policy training. In such circumstances, everyone in the room needs to know and be able to apply new rules, and face to face mass training makes sense.

Similarly, if a school is moving towards a blanket curriculum policy – for example, every lesson should have a recap do now activity, or every lesson should include reading and here is how you read with children, or we're moving away from marking and to whole class feedback and here is why – again, whole-staff CPD may be appropriate. In such scenarios, it is advisable to consider every member of staff – for example, when running a training session on reading I excused the maths department (or rather made it optional for them to attend) as we did not want the maths team focusing on literacy when they could instead be focusing on extended practice, which made far more sense for them. (In the end, the head of maths ran his own CPD session tailored specifically for maths.)

When delivering whole-staff CPD, consider members of staff who may already know a good deal about what you are about to present. For example, when delivering a whole-staff CPD on writing in one school, we identified members of the English department who had already done a lot of reading and work on this area, and they worked to co-present with SLT. This helped to ensure those who were 'most able' in our staff team were able to feel like their time was being used wisely, though by contributing to the development of others and sharing good practice rather than by learning.

Where does whole-staff CPD fit in?

Despite the drawbacks of whole-staff CPD outlined above, I do think there is a place for ensuring that all teachers have training on the core aspects of schools. A lot of this will depend on where your staff body is and the focus on your school's improvement needs, but in general I would advocate ensuring you have everyone trained in some way on the following:

- **Behaviour**. The most important thing in a school is that the children behave. Managing behaviour should be returned to again and again to ensure all teachers have clarity, and that the systems are applied consistently by all. It is also worth thinking about when and where behaviour slips – is it in the canteen, at the beginnings of lessons, during the fire drill – and addressing those specific moments with a new approach or additional student practice.

- **Reading**. Children read in every single lesson, but it's not always obvious how to get them to the point where they will read aloud confidently.

- **Writing**. Children write in every single lesson, but is their writing always accurate and coherent? There are lots of small tweaks we can make to our practise to help children write more effectively.

- **Questioning**. I think questioning is the absolute most important thing a teacher does. The best teachers I have seen pepper their explanations with multiple questions asked to as many students as possible to check they understand, and then to see if the students can apply their understanding to new scenarios and begin to think more deeply about the content. It's not obvious and it's never perfect – we can all always get better at questioning.

- **Explanation**. Subject departments should be talking in their CPD time about the best way to explain tricky concepts, and thinking about the common misconceptions children have. This is best delivered by subject experts, however, as they key to a great explanation is content-specific.

- **Booklets**. Rather than using PowerPoints or photocopying multiple sheets, departments should focus on pre-producing booklets and then planning how to deliver them. Those responsible for resourcing should be trained in the best and fastest way to produce booklets under the inevitable time pressures of any school.[1]

- **Knowledge organisers**. Good knowledge organisers force teams to consider what they want students to learn for the long term. CPD on making them as effective and clear as possible would be helpful, especially in the early days of adopting them.

- **Recaps and quizzing**. Understanding the science of memory, the power of overlearning, and the simplicity of recapping prior knowledge would go a long way to helping children retain knowledge for the long term.

- **Deliberate practice**. Not all practice is as helpful as it could be. Helping teachers discern the most important skills for children to practise and then supporting them to make activities that ensure children are undertaking deliberate practice is invaluable.

- **Feedback**. Rather than laboriously marking every book, teachers can give whole-class feedback. But it is not always obvious which aspects to focus on to make the feedback as effective as possible.

Coaching

It is clear, and the research evidence supports this, that the most effective form of teacher development is individual coaching. Sam Sims outlines in his excellent blog the evidence for this:

> In February 2018, a team of researchers from South Africa published the results from a ... randomised controlled trial ... they compared a control group to (A) a group of teachers trained on new techniques for teaching reading at a traditional 'away day' and (B) a group of teachers trained on

the exact same content using coaching. This type of A-B testing provides an opportunity to isolate the active ingredients of an intervention. The results showed that pupils taught by teachers given the traditional 'away day' type training showed no statistically significant increase in reading attainment. By contrast, pupils taught by teachers who received the same content via coaching improved their reading attainment by an effect size of 0.18. The coaching was therefore a necessary component of the training being effective. A separate A-B test in Argentina in 2017 also found coaching to be more effective than traditional training on the same content.[2]

I first read about instructional coaching, by which teachers are coached as individuals by individuals to improve their practice, in the book *Leverage Leadership* by Paul Bambrick-Santoyo.[3] I was so struck by the method, I immediately sought to introduce it as a middle leader in a department who already weren't crazy about my leadership (which was in its embryonic stages, and dubious at best). The level of resistance to the thought of me, a manager, coming into people's lessons each week for a short period of time and providing feedback in the form of a single action step that I judged would improve their practice, was significant.

In the end, only three of the teachers in my department agreed to weekly coaching. They all gave glowing feedback on this process – but of course, they would, as I was their manager. What is more important, perhaps, is that I saw dramatic improvements in their classroom practice, even in a very short period of time. Again – this isn't research evidence; you might argue that I was bound to see improvements of a scheme I personally believed would work and that I was driving forward.

When applying for my first senior leadership role, I was halfway through an intricate explanation of instructional coaching when the headteacher leaned forward and said: 'you can stop there. I know what coaching is; we run a full coaching programme here.'

What is coaching?

The model of coaching I've used is that delineated in Paul Bambrick Santoyo's *Leverage Leadership*. Bambrick Santoyo argues that 'teacher feedback is not about the volume of observations or the length of written feedback; it's about bite-sized action steps that allow a teacher to grow systematically from novice to proficient to master teacher'.[4] In this ideal coaching model, 'every teacher is observed and receives face-to-face feedback every week'.[5] Nowhere in this model are teachers *judged*: as we know, it is, after all, almost impossible for external observers to judge teacher quality.[6] Bambrick Santoyo posits: 'The primary purpose of observation should *not* be to judge the quality of teachers, but to find the most effective ways to coach them to improve student learning.'[7]

In stripping away performance appraisal or formal observation procedures, we free leaders up to do the most important thing: help teachers make marginal gains every single week to transform their classroom practice.

The method is simple: schedule time to drop into lessons for a short time period – five to fifteen minutes is usually enough. Decide, from that short observation, the action step – the thing that teacher could do – that would have the highest impact on improving the class's learning. Meet the teacher in person and give the feedback. The final step is the one many teachers, myself included, find the most cringe-inducing: practice.

At Uncommon Schools, where Bambrick Santoyo still works as chief schools officer for high schools and K-12 content development, and the founder and dean of the Leverage Leadership Institute, they believe in teachers practising their craft. Like actors, much of what we do in pedagogy is physical rather than cerebral, and the rehearsal matters more than we want it to. In the practice part of coaching, coaches should model what they want to see – role playing as student and teacher, usually – before switching over so the coachee can practise their action step. The coach should then give feedback on the performance of the action step. While this might sound time consuming, in practice if you limit yourself to a single action step, you can do this surprisingly rapidly. When I was coached by a phenomenal vice principal, our meetings rarely lasted longer than 25 minutes, and when they did it was usually because I wanted to ask her for help or advice after the coaching, which she was always very generous to provide.

Who should coach?

Who you choose to coach your teachers is the difference between an extraordinary piece of professional development that has a genuine impact on improving teachers and improving student learning by proxy, and a tick-box waste of time that no one wants to be a part of.

In short, you have to make sure your coaches know what great teaching is and are able to help people get to great. The quality of the coaching participants receive is almost entirely due to their coaches.

And choosing the right coach will be different for different individuals. Arguably, for great teachers, there is little a non-specialist will be able to add to their practice. While it is relatively easy to give feedback on the basics of pedagogy and the fundamentals of behaviour management to new teachers, once professionals have mastered keeping good order and have a strong understanding of the ways to deliver information and ensure children understand it, what they benefit from most is someone in their subject nit-picking their explanations and questioning.

I was convinced of the need for subject specialism when watching an interview lesson with my head of maths. While I was blown away by the teacher, the head of maths was less so. While what I saw was children behaving well and answering questions, she was far more fixated on the times the teacher skipped over student misconceptions and the way they could have drawn out more depth of understanding through their questioning. Such aspects were not easy for a non-subject-specialist to see.

I don't believe it is impossible to give great teachers feedback, but if we are looking to develop teachers in the best way possible, then there comes a time when we have to submit to subject specialists and allow them to give curriculum feedback alongside pedagogy.

In planning out the first year of coaching at Ark Soane, we were working with fourteen teachers, a number of whom were the only teacher in their department. Choosing coaches for the NQT and the unqualified teacher was not challenging – we thought about areas of their practice they would want to develop, and matched them with a member of staff who was strong in that area. For the experienced and sole music teacher, we made sure her coach had deep subject knowledge and a depth of experience to match her own. In almost all other circumstances, we allocated coaches within subjects – so our two science teachers would coach one another, as did our maths and English teachers.

At Ark John Keats, despite having a teaching staff of over a hundred, we retained the school's founding commitment that every teacher would be coached. As resources and time are not infinite, something had to be compromised: either more people would have to be coaches, or some teachers would have to not be coached every week. For us, we opted for the latter. If you have too many coaches, and you have compromised on the quality of those imperfect coaches, and you are not therefore able to have the detailed oversight of so many people to bring them to your high bar, the programme will not have the desired impact. Instead, we ensured new teachers and trainees would have weekly coaching, and other teachers would be coached every two or three weeks by an exceptional coach.

It is important to us to keep the lines of coaching clear: particularly where a coach was a line manager, protecting the time and divorcing the feedback from any kind of performance appraisal remains crucial to retaining our commitment to teacher development. At Ark John Keats, the line management framework does not mention teaching: that conversation happens purely with the coach, and line management is about everything from outcomes to additional responsibilities. In a more ideal world, I'd advise having coaches separate to line managers, unless the choice is between out of subject or line manager, in which case I'd go for the latter.

The more (feedback), the merrier

Short, sharp feedback is the guiding principle for teacher development at many Ark schools including mine, and with a strong staff body we decided the more feedback the better. Like many schools, we institute and uphold an open-door policy, where we strongly encourage everyone to get out of their room and see as many of their colleagues as possible, sending a line of action-step-style feedback and/or a key takeaway when they leave.

In fact, when this kind of observation becomes normalised, it is important to remember common courtesy. I remember being a little early to observe a colleague, and deciding on a whim to pop into one of my favourite Science teachers to see the end of his lesson. As always, he was using every minute, the children were responding, and his questioning was at a high level. I spent five enjoyable minutes at the back of his room and left.

An hour or so later, this wonderful teacher popped me an email: 'you came in earlier – what did you see? Is there anything I could be doing better?' This individual's proactive approach to seeking feedback reminded me I needed to do better for him. Unfortunately, I'd been focusing on enjoying his lesson rather than working out what he could do better – and I had to honestly tell him that. But this was a learning point for me to never walk into someone's room without sending, at the absolute minimum, a one-line email saying how much I'd enjoyed their classroom in that short time.

In one school I worked in, we were explicit about the expectations around these kind of 'pop-ins'. The thinking was that our best teachers should *always* aim to give an action step, every time they popped in. For our new or struggling teachers, their job was to email the teacher (copying in their line manager) saying something they had learned, or a take-away they would apply to their own practice.

This is absolutely appropriate in some circumstances. In general, for schools needing to improve rapidly, I'm in favour of more direction, because in general such schools lack control and clarity, and so the more things SLT can be clear on and control in those schools, the better. This is not, of course, the way to run a great school in the long term – teachers, as mentioned in the previous chapter, thrive on autonomy. Such militant expectations ought to be a temporary step to build habits.

Stop tracking everything

At the same time, even in the most strained of circumstances, I always advise against documentation. By documentation, I mean pieces of paper that explain things that people do, which are created by individuals but read by absolutely no one except the individual's line manager. In my experience, the vast majority of documentation is a pointless waste of time and paper, and you'd have been better off not writing it down but investing that time in training and communicating what you're doing. That's not to say I ban people from writing things down – often people will *choose* to outline what is happening because that is the way their minds work, and of course it would be nonsense to stop people doing something they found helpful to their work.

But open-door observations are not about paperwork. They are about culture.

When I began at one school, each learning walk conducted by SLT had to be entered into an Excel spreadsheet. A member of the SLT would email frequently, imploring people to fill the spreadsheet in. At an SLT meeting, they raised their concern: 'no one is doing any learning walks.'

After a brief discussion, it was clear that the concern was somewhat founded: people were seeing lessons, but not systematically. Why? For some of us, it was not prioritised – we simply weren't visiting lessons. For others though, it was about filling in the spreadsheet. 'I've got all my notes,' said one of the more assiduous vice principals, 'I just haven't filled it in yet.'

Perhaps worse, at another school SLT had a period blocked out on their timetable to conduct learning walks, which again had to be logged on a spreadsheet. Not only did they have to be logged though, but you had to grade the individual out of four (those of you familiar with Ofsted's much bemoaned grading system can probably guess what the grades were), and submit that judgement each time. The teacher would not receive the feedback – it would be 'anonymised' so we could understand the 'general issues arising around the school'.

The problem was, anyone with eyes knew the issues around the school: lessons weren't planned well enough, and the behaviour system wasn't being implemented consistently. We knew this. Everybody knew this. Everybody on the SLT knew this; the NQT and trainee teachers knew this. Filling in grades for ten-minute drop-ins, aside from being data so meaningless it was clearly pointless, was time-consuming and would certainly damage staff morale if they ever discovered it.

In both of these schools, documentation was getting in the way of genuine feedback. Luckily, when concerns were raised, sensible leaders saw through the need to gather numbers and move instead towards a culture of feedback and improvement.

Instead of filling in spreadsheets, we would conduct the learning walks and always give a short email of feedback, to which we would copy in the SLT. It was a workload killer: one short email that served the purpose of letting the teacher know what was good and a possible action step, and the SLT could both see what the issues were different teachers were facing with different classes, and be nudged to complete their own learning walks by the knowledge that everyone else was doing theirs.

Just as in your line management interactions with others, as leaders we need to model asking for feedback and be the first to welcome and act on it. Just as that excellent science teacher had nudged me, so I knew it was incumbent upon me to ask anyone who popped into my classroom: 'what did you notice?' I'd usually follow this by pointing out something I was working on, as it can be easier to give feedback 'upwards' if you are invited to do something specific. With my sixth formers, for example, I would ask the head of English who often popped in to give back homework or give work to those who had been absent in her lesson earlier that week: 'what did you think of the group task? I'm never sure about group work but I think they can handle it and I'm not sure of a better way to get multiple views on their coursework.'

Courses and conferences

It is rare to find yourself in middle or senior leadership and to not be bombarded with flyers advertising external CPD courses, often ranging in the hundreds of pounds and always run on a school day. I would strongly urge caution when it comes to courses and conferences.

After all, we have surprisingly few days in a school year with the children. Teachers in England are required to work 195 days a year, and depending on the number of inset days schools choose to have (which in my experience can be anything from three to fourteen), this leaves less time than we might imagine to be with our classes. I would posit that the days we spend with the children in our schools are the most important thing that we do, and that the one-day CPD course that can have a greater impact on our overall practice than just being there for those children is rare indeed.

Now, I have colleagues who I greatly respect who will fiercely disagree with me. In particular, everyone I know who has ever done one of Doug Lemov's professional development days would argue that the enormous impact this day out had on their practice since makes it more than worth missing a day with their classes. But few CPD courses are as well thought out, both in terms of content and ability to 'stick' and change practice, as those run by Lemov.

The balance of one person attending a one-day course means that up to six, or maybe seven (or even eight if you have a tutor group and it was your duty day) professionals have to change their work schedules to cover for you. If your school employs teachers from cover agencies, they will spend £100-£220 for that individual for that single day (rates vary across the country). With the best will in the world, even the country's best supply teachers cannot possibly know the school or its behaviour system as well as those who have been expressly and deeply trained in its permutations, and so the children will be extremely unlikely to have lessons as good as they may have had with their regular class teacher.

But the loss of learning for one lesson, though grave, is not the worst impact a day's supply can have on a school. Far worse is the impact it has on culture. The best schools invest heavily in ensuring all their teachers are aligned on the school's culture: they are hired, as explored in Chapter 1, because they align to that school's culture; they continue to embody that culture in every micro-interaction they have with the children.

To expect a stranger to the school to pick that up straight away is just not going to happen. So what you get, over the course of those six lessons, is six lessons where culture has been subtly undermined: an off-the-cuff comment, a behaviour routine executed incorrectly, a misconception accidentally embedded – all these things chip away at children's belief that schools will transform their lives.

Now of course one supply teacher one day in 195 will not destroy a school's culture. But if you think about every day of supply as chipping away at it, little by little, it should give school leaders pause to think about whether they could or should grant that cover request.

This is especially true because leaders will have multiple requests for days out that they probably *should* honour: a family wedding inexplicably held on a weekday, a child's nativity play, a child's first day at school, a child's parents' evening, a funeral – and no doubt many other important family events that leaders will want to grant time out for. They must balance this against every external course on offer.

There is, in addition, a wealth of professional development offered in evenings and weekends: the best events I have attended have been 'Teach Meets' held after school, or the Research Ed conferences on Saturdays. While it is a lot to ask teachers to give up their free time to attend such conferences, offering to pay for teachers' tickets is a great way to endorse attendance at these without giving up valuable teaching time in school.

The innovators

As discussed in Chapter 2 of this part, an important aspect of leadership – listening to other people's ideas and feedback – links to teacher development. By encouraging and rewarding innovation, you allow people who are self-starters to innovate.

When I first opened applications for our founding staff at Ark Soane, I was struck by the three or four people who asked: 'how will you develop me?' Although I firmly believe that schools have a responsibility to develop their staff and that teachers deserve that development, I also believe that teachers must have the freedom and autonomy to largely direct this themselves. Answering 'how will you develop me?' was impossible at the stage before interview – I didn't even know these people! I tended to say that teacher development best worked in a bespoke way, and that we would get to know each other through line management, and co-create their development plan together.

By encouraging innovation, you are more likely to retain your most motivated members of staff. Just as in the earlier chapter, the leader who listened to the feedback of a staff member, adopted his plan, and then flagged to the whole staff that what we were doing was not imposed by SLT but rather the brain-child of a respected teacher in the school, encouraged other members of staff to come forward with their ideas in the future. Although it is of course the job of an SLT to set the strategic direction of a school, this balance must be struck to ensure teachers are able to drive their own development as well as contribute to the improvement of their school.

Initiative-itis

At the same time, we need to beware of initiative-itis. With a talented and enthusiastic staff body, encouraging innovation may easily lead to this. Having welcomed ideas, how can a senior leader bear to crush the new initiative of the bright young teacher who has spent so much time and care on something?

Yet crush we sometimes must. It is not enough to hire great teachers and encourage them to lead. Direction is the crucial ingredient of successful leadership, and individuals will rarely find the same direction independently. It is the job of a leadership team to set a direction and to filter any new ideas to ensure that they align to that direction.

More than that, though, it is the job of a senior leadership team to manage the whole staff's workload – which we will go into in much more detail in our next chapter. For any new initiative, an SLT must review the impact it will have on staff workload – and this is not always immediately obvious. Ask specific questions of the initiative: who will do this? When will they do it? How long will it take? What will the impact be? Is that impact worth the combined hours of staff time we will be investing in this?

I learned much from my executive principal, Becky Curtis, who spends a great deal of time weighing up the effort to impact ratio of all new proposals. Curtis works on the assumption that her staff are working at 100%, so when a new idea is tabled she asks: what do we need to stop doing in order to have time to do this?

The question is a vital one for leaders to add to their agendas up and down the country. Surveying your staff team right now, can you honestly say that there are members of staff who are not working at full capacity? Find the teacher who arrives at 8:15 a.m. and leaves at 3:15 p.m., and if there are a large number perhaps start considering what new initiatives might stretch such a staff body. Usually, this will not be the case. To make room for something new, we need to scrap something old – if we do not do that, we run the risk of burning out teachers.

The final challenge to welcoming new initiatives is to be mindful of change management. All new systems, no matter how exciting, involve some degree of change. Senior leaders should think carefully through the mechanics of any change: who will need to do what and when? This must be done while remaining aware of how rapidly you are bringing staff with you: a small team who know one another well can usually move more rapidly than a large or disparate team, or a team who have not worked together for very long.

A piece of advice I learned from great leaders is to go at the pace of your school. If you are turning around a troubled school, choose only a few key things to introduce and embed. It is better to do three great things well than to do a hundred things poorly.

Take-aways

- Be alert to the limitations of whole-staff training.

- Coaching is the best way to develop teachers.

- Don't be tempted by high-stakes observations.

■ Limit paperwork.

■ Encourage innovation – in moderation.

Notes

1 For much more on how to make booklets, see Jo Facer, *Simplicity Rules* (Routledge, 2019), pp. 43–46.
2 Retrieved from https://samsims.education/2019/02/19/247/ (accessed 25 March 2020).
3 Paul Bambrick Santoyo, *Leverage Leadership* (Jossey-Bass, 2012).
4 Ibid., p. 61.
5 Ibid.
6 Prof Rob Coe writes: 'the recent Measures of Effective Teaching Project, funded by the Gates Foundation in the US, used five different observation protocols, all supported by a scientific development and validation process, with substantial training for observers, and a test they are required to pass. These are probably the gold standard in observation (see here and here for more details). The reported reliabilities of observation instruments used in the MET study range from 0.24 to 0.68. One way to understand these values is to estimate the percentage of judgements that would agree if two raters watch the same lesson. Using Ofsted's categories, if a lesson is judged "Outstanding" by one observer, the probability that a second observer would give a different judgement is between 51% and 78%.' Retrieved from www.cem.org/blog/414 (accessed 29 July 2020).
7 Santoyo, *Leverage Leadership*, p. 63.

4 How can we reduce workload?

The current crisis

In October 2014, then education secretary Nicky Morgan launched the 'workload challenge', which was billed as an initiative to: 'reduce unnecessary bureaucracy and paperwork in schools and support teachers to get on with what they do best – inspiring young people to reach their potential'.[1]

The initial fact-finding part of this 'challenge' was to find out how bad workload in teaching was. Having promoted this initiative to schoolteachers, who we know intuitively work long hours at comparatively low pay (compared with other graduate professions, that is) in sometimes stressful situations, the Department for Education received 43,832 responses.[2] This represented, at the time, around 10% of all teachers in the UK.

The results of this survey remain interesting, and give us a helpful snapshot of the issues of teacher workload in the early 2010s:

- 63% of respondents stated that the excessive level of detail required made the tasks burdensome

- 45% stated that duplication added to the burden of their workload

- 41% stated that the over-bureaucratic nature of the work made it burdensome

Other factors noted by respondents included:

- the volume of work that they needed to get through in the time available (particularly in relation to marking books)

- unrealistic/very short deadlines

- long meetings, or meetings not thought to be relevant to their role/Key Stage

- too many sources of information to manage (e.g. email, virtual learning environment, bulletin)

DOI: 10.4324/9781003097075-5

▓ poor/unreliable Information and Communication Technology (ICT) equipment and lack of software training

▓ lack of clarity with observation requirements

The most frequently mentioned tasks contributing to unnecessary and unproductive workload fitted within the category of lesson planning and policies, assessment and reporting administration (82% of respondents mentioned tasks which fitted into this category).

There were two specific tasks that were reported as being burdensome for the majority of sample respondents:

▓ recording, inputting, monitoring and analysing data (56%)

▓ excessive/depth of marking – detail and frequency required (53%)

Six other tasks were reported as adding unnecessary burden to the general workload by at least 20% of respondents:

▓ lesson/weekly planning – detail and frequency required (38%)

▓ basic administrative and support tasks (37%)

▓ staff meetings (26%)

▓ reporting on pupil progress (24%)

▓ pupil targets (setting and continual review – including target culture) (21%)

▓ implementing new initiatives/curriculum/qualification change (20%)

Respondents most commonly said that the burden of their workload was created by:

▓ accountability/perceived pressures of Ofsted (53%)

▓ tasks set by senior/middle leaders (51%)[3]

How we create the crisis

In 2018, I attended a talk by Norfolk headteacher Peter Bloomfield, where he memorably called to mind the feeling of a class when a wasp flies in the room. Every teacher in the audience laughed in recognition – not one of us had escaped the swirling hysteria such a tiny insect will evoke in children. When our laughter had subsided, he said: 'Well, sometimes SLT *put the wasp in the room.*'

That phrase has haunted me since I heard it. Bloomfield went on to describe every time an SLT member interrupts a lesson to take out a child, or turns up and starts chatting to the students, or stops the class for an 'important announcement', they disturb the class just as a wasp does. But more than that, every time SLT adds to the teacher's workload, they run the risk of preventing them from being the inspiring individual we know they can be. When we create excessive workload, we stop children from learning as well as they might: we put the wasp in the room.

Those reading might wish to shield themselves from such an accusation ('I would *never* make teachers' lives harder!'), but we do it without thinking. I'm going to quote three senior leaders, each of whom I thoroughly respect and admire, and each of whom run wonderful schools. But each of them make a dangerous assumption we need to begin to challenge:

- 'Working in a school is just hard work. If you want to do it right, it's just hard.'

- 'Staff morale was highest and workload was best when results were worst.'

- 'Taking PIXL resources and tweaking them is just lazy teaching.'

The first senior leader is not wrong. Of course working in a school is hard work. But there must be a recognition that *given* how hard it is to work in a school, senior leaders must do all they can to minimise excessive workload. To this leader's credit, they spend their time doing exactly that, and teachers at their school have, in fact, reported a dramatic decrease in workload over the past years.

Nor is the second senior leader wrong. I know their school, and this is categorically, depressingly, true: the results were worst when workload was lowest. But correlation is not, we know, causation. We must find a way forward where we can deliver great results for children *and* reduce workload (plug time: I suggest such a way is possible in my book *Simplicity Rules*[4]).

And the final senior leader – well, I'm not sure about the quality of PIXL resources myself, and I would never advocate taking poor resources and delivering them untouched. But the issue is in the expectation: if you have a resource and it is good, to deliver that resource is not 'lazy teaching'. It is pragmatic. Why change something that does not require change?

The influence of the Charter Schools

It is undeniable that working harder results in gains – educationalists have often spoken of 'marginal gains' and 'low-hanging fruit', which normally means artificially boosting year 11 results by simple things such as running targeted intervention sessions, whole school walking-talking mock exams, reworking the end of the course to squeeze the most we can into their brains prior to the exam, changing the amount of subjects they are studying to maximise results. All of this results in higher teacher workload.

Moreover, when we talk to teachers at England's highest performing schools, they admit to working extremely long hours – many were routinely working from 7 a.m. to 7 p.m., along with the occasional evenings and weekends. A glance through the educationalists on Twitter around mock season (or, truthfully, any time from March to May) reveals just how hard some teachers are having to work.

We also have the examples from America: the US Charter schools. Chains like KIPP, the Success Academies and Uncommon Schools blaze a trail for others to follow – and yet workload is high in the top performing American chains. In Robert Pondiscio's book *How the Other Half Learns*, where the author spends time in Success Academies, he describes the preference to teachers serving short tenures where they work extremely, almost unconscionably hard:

> If you are in your twenties or thirties, there's a fair chance that at least some of your elementary school teachers are still at your old school … They serve for life … If Success Academy students visit just a few years from now, they might not see even a single familiar face. The de facto model that has evolved is more like the US Army or the Marines: a small and talented officer corps, surrounded by enlisted men and women who do a tour, maybe two, then muster out, with new recruits reporting for duty. Teacher turnover, and lack of experience and continuity, is widely assumed to be a problem … But it's never suggested that our military would be better if only soldiers stayed in uniform longer. So far, the relative inexperience of Success Academy teachers hasn't seemed to compromise their effectiveness.[5]
>
> In Jay Matthew's *Work Hard Be Nice*, in telling the story of the hugely successful KIPP schools, the author writes that 'KIPP teachers are paid extra for the more-than-nine-hours-school days, the required four-hour-every-other-Saturday sessions, and the three week summer schools, but they know how much easier their working lives would be if they chose jobs in regular schools.'[6]

An esteemed colleague of mine often says that the UK is 'five or ten years behind' the US in terms of education. From the American Charter schools, we know that extraordinary results are possible. But what that means is that we know that excessive workload yields great results. What we don't know is whether we can get great results without burning out teachers.

At what cost?

In 2015, as an on-paper 'successful' Head of English with some great looking results behind me, I began to question what I was doing, both in terms of workload and also in whether it was garnering genuinely great results. My thoughts were threefold: marking, intervention and activities. On marking, I wrote:

> I mark every student's book every week, unless they are ill when I take them in. In addition to this, I mark any essays or assessments students have done, whether for a pre-decided mock exam or assessment point, or simply exam practice. When I made the change from fortnightly marking to weekly marking, I saw a dramatic improvement in my students' progress.
>
> But at what cost?
>
> I have marked, for the last five years, constantly. I have marked in free periods, before and after school, at home, during the weekend and even on flights. Some might say this is the inescapable fate of the English teacher.

Yet now I am on a very light timetable, with very small classes, and my marking load appears undiminished. Although what I do works, would I want it to be replicated by every teacher in my team on a full timetable? Absolutely not. If I were to continue in this way, would I remain in the profession? Absolutely not.

If the cost of student progress is teacher burnout, it cannot be worth it.

The intervention culture thrives in many schools, in particular those who have experienced disappointing results in recent years. My school experience is exclusively in schools which serve a 'challenging' intake: ones where social deprivation levels are high. I had come to rely on a rally of intervention in year 11 to pull out results in August. It seemed as if my entire job was orchestrating year 11 intervention, with a short six weeks at the end of the year when they had left and I could think about something else. On intervention, I wrote:

> Last year, as head of English, I checked student data weekly for exam classes. That is because it was constantly changing, what with redrafted coursework, completed speaking and listening exams and constant teacher-assessed mock essays and exams. Using this data, I picked out students and created personalised intervention plans. I would confidently estimate that there is practically no year 11 student who was not in some way 'intervened' with.
>
> I have given up before school time, after school time, lunchtime, Saturdays, half-terms and Easters over the years. I have altered entire holidays to fit in with a schedule of revision, to the point of cancelling and re-booking flights.
>
> Our students achieved phenomenal results; only King Solomon Academy achieved better in English the year before last for schools in London with comparable amounts of students receiving free school meals.
>
> But at what cost? If I knew I would have to run intervention in this way until retirement, would I stay in this profession? Absolutely not. Do I want to stop running intervention and instead delegate it to my team, asking them to similarly give up weekends and holidays? Absolutely not.
>
> And what of the students? Tired, stressed, but well-prepared; what happens to these students at sixth form? At university? Learning there will always be 'extra' put on for them can't incentivise them to make the most of lesson time.
>
> If the cost of student progress is complacent students and teacher exhaustion, it cannot be worth it.

Coupled with marking and intervention, two well-acknowledged creators of excessive workload, I cited 'all the activities' in this post as a third driver of workload. In 2015, I was moving towards simple planning, but was still teaching nowhere near as simply as I now advocate. Even so, I noted the difference:

> I used to spend hours lesson planning. I would research existing plans and resources, cross-referencing with other teachers' and TES resources, and trying to make every lesson an individual snowflake, never repeating the same

series of activities. I would ensure there was something for everyone, and plenty of opportunities for students to talk together, research independently, collaborate and postulate together. I would review their 'learning' and value the 'ideas' they came up with, however ill-founded; however misunderstood.

I have had students carouselling, moving, making, standing, dancing, clapping, acting, advocating, laughing, enjoying and even learning while they did this.

And those students did achieve good results.

But at what cost? How many Cs could have been Bs, Bs As, if I had stopped cramming in activities for the sake of engagement and fun, and started simply telling students what they needed to know, and then testing to make sure they had learned it?

At this point, it must be added that of the students who scraped Cs, and particularly those who managed to achieve Bs, they struggled immensely at A level. I remember having a disagreement with an A level economics teacher who had inherited one of my year 11s on the strength of her B grade in English. 'She can't write a sentence,' the teacher informed me. 'Her writing is totally incoherent.'

'But she got a B!' was my argument. My assumption, though I did not share it then (thank *God*) was: the problem is you. I got this student a B; you can get them an economics A level.

The reality, of course, was that our curriculum had crammed this student ready to score her B at GCSE. I'm proud that she can have that grade on her CV for the rest of her life, but if the cost of that grade was her ability to actually *write coherent English*, it's definitely not good enough.

My 2015 post continues, acknowledging the weak subject knowledge of my students, and not quite accepting that this was actually *my* fault:

> Would I have still been addressing classic misconceptions after 3 years of teaching the same class – no, Shakespeare was not a Victorian; no, that's not where you put a comma …
>
> With my year 10 intervention class last year I tried something different. Shocked by their lack of knowledge and understanding, their lack of retention, I relentlessly talked to them, got them to write independently and then quizzed them. It was a massive uphill struggle, but that struggle was as much against preconceived expectations of what their lessons should look like and the expectations I should have of what they were able to access as it was about changing what they remember. And while I struggled on, students knew more, could explain articulately, and could remember and apply challenging concepts. It was far from perfect, but I haven't seen better progress previous to employing these methods.
>
> If the cost of student engagement is student learning, it cannot be worth it.[7]

Ultimately, the 'low-hanging fruit' sought by senior leaders in turn around schools is just that: a short-term boost in results. This is easily justifiable in the early days of turnaround: the argument is that school leaders need to prioritise those children entering external exams because their futures hang in the balance, which is absolutely true. It is also the case that schools posting poor GCSE results year after year will find they have fewer children choosing to attend them, which has serious financial implications for running a school. It is also true that eventually, no one will choose to attend such schools, and they will cease to exist. So of course results must be boosted. But schools ignore long-term results improvement at their peril: to do so risks alienating teachers with excessive workload. And where once it could have been argued that teachers could be burned out and leave and replaced, that is no longer quite the case.

The challenge of recruitment

Teacher recruitment has become steadily more challenging as the years have gone by. The impact of the recent coronavirus on the economy, and therefore on teacher recruitment, has yet to be seen,[8] but in late 2019 newspapers everywhere carried the phrase 'teacher recruitment crisis' as if such a state of affairs were a given. In November 2019, Schools Week were pointing to a 4.6% rise in teacher vacancies; the fact that in 2017 more teachers left the profession than entered it was coupled with the point that a boom in secondary age pupils meant even more teachers were needed.[9]

This puts school leaders in an extremely challenging position. Particularly where there is pressure for improving results rapidly – from government, a local authority, an academy trust, Ofsted, or just the genuine feeling of wanting to serve their children more effectively – leaders have to balance everything they ask teachers to do with the questions: 'Will this add to workload? Will our teachers potentially leave because of this?'

(Some) teachers love work

The additional complication of the issue of workload is often teachers themselves. I have worked with many, many teachers who complain about workload, but who also refuse to do things that would decrease theirs. For example, I've argued with teachers drowning under their marking that they could just *not* mark and instead complete whole-class feedback, only to have them refuse and say: 'my children *need* me to mark their books', and then look at me as though, given this immovable fact, the only logical option would be to reduce their teaching load by a class midway through the school year, perhaps reallocating classes to one of the many members of staff we've got on the teacher bench who have empty timetables currently. I've discussed whether teachers *need* to re-plan the centrally planned lessons which are already very good, only to hear them say: 'it helps me if I put what is in the textbook onto PowerPoint slides', and again give me the same 'what other option is there?' look.

I visited one high-performing school which had identified workload as its number one issue – each year they were losing great teachers who cited excessive workload. I spoke to a few of the teachers identified as most 'at risk' of leaving to discuss how their workload might reduce. My opening question was: 'What are you doing right now that is not essential? What *could* go?' Every single one replied: 'Everything I do is essential.'

When I arrived at Ark John Keats, workload was similarly cited by most of the individuals I met with as a challenge: while I would speak of workload reduction in the general sense and get enthusiastic nods, the second I suggest cutting something specific I was met with reasons as to why we should not or could not cut that particular piece of work. Early on, I enjoyed a robust argument with senior leaders over Saturday detentions, during which it emerged that one senior leader had held almost every single Saturday detention the previous year – and was willing to take on every Saturday this coming year rather than see these cut. Supporting their colleague, another leader said: 'If you go into leadership in schools, of course you're going to work weekends.' It seemed outrageous to suggest professionals might expect two days off a week.

To pre-empt these difficult conversations, I told the team on the first day of inset: 'you will hear me say "no" a lot this year … Unless you are asking to cut something.' We needed to do fewer good things to win ourselves the capacity to do the great things brilliantly – and make this a school where people worked and stayed for the long term.

I'm not suggesting teachers and leaders are all like this, but in my experience there is a hardcore out there of teachers who are making their lives harder. It comes from a good place – it comes from a great place: these people are truly driven to give children an amazing academic experience. It is, therefore, often the job of leaders to stop good people doing good things so they have the energy to focus on the very most important things, and the energy to remain in teaching for the long term.

One tremendous 'experiment' Becky Allen and Sam Sims describe in their superb book, *The Teacher Gap*, is to institute working hours of 8 a.m. to 4:30 p.m. for a limited period of time – a week, two weeks – and have teachers reflect afterwards: what did they not have time to do that really was essential?[10]

I think this is a marvellous idea. Rather than tackling issues individually, why not see if teachers can actually work out for themselves how to continue being superb professionals while not working all the hours in the day? In such an experiment, books could not be taken home, access could not be granted after 4:30 p.m. to shared areas or emails, and teachers would see how well they could do their jobs.

Clearly, this would not work if it were just a blanket policy – let's be mindful of the well-documented challenge of managing change – but if sold as a time-limited experiment, with time built in to reflect on how teachers adjusted their practice, this could have far-reaching implications for long-term workload. Give a prepared time where teachers can feedback, and script questions to shape the discussion: which aspects of your teaching suffered? What had you been doing that you found was not essential? How did the shorter hours impact your life beyond work? What changes did you notice in yourself when you were in work? What differences did the children notice?

Email

Email is one of the chief time drainers in the modern school. Where we have much to celebrate in being able to communicate over long distances with far-flung friends and relatives, schools are not big places, and email makes them feel bigger than they need to be. How far away are people, actually?

One of the many great pieces of advice I've learned from a great line manager was to stop sending emails. He made me count how many I'd sent in a day, and then told me to halve it 'at least.' (I think everyone who has line managed me since will smile at this – please know that I really am trying to send fewer emails.)

Instead, this teacher told me that I needed to find a system to see people in person. It shouldn't have been hard, since I shared an office with the entire team I managed. Yet it somehow was. Getting messages to people became the mainstay of my job. I had a system to organise my day: a post-it note, where I numbered my tasks in order of importance, and crossed them off when I had finished. The post-it was divided into two, and in the right-hand column were just names. Names of people I needed to talk to. I never went anywhere without my post-it, and on a good day I had ticked off everyone I needed to talk to (in the literal pen-on-post-it sense. I didn't go around telling people off, I promise).

In another school there was an acknowledged issue with email. The school was the largest I had worked in, in terms of pupil numbers and also the sheer size of the site. It was split across different buildings. In my first week, I clocked up thousands of steps to speak to the people I needed to speak to, and wasted hours trying to locate people who never seemed to be where I imagined they would be. 'Just send an email,' my line manager advised me. I explained what I had been taught by my previous line manager. 'Forget that – you'll waste hours doing that. Just send an email.'

Perhaps it was the subtle difference between managing a department and managing an area: where once all my seven people had taught in predictable, close classrooms, and shared a workspace, my whole-school role involved people from every department of the school.

And yet the school did have a problem with email, and I had free reign to contribute to that problem. Indeed, the problem was so acute and so roundly recognised that the school instituted a termly 'no email day' to assist with 'well-being.' I have two memories of 'no email day.' The first was the email that dropped into my inbox at around 7:30 a.m. from the attendance officer, celebrating 'no email day' and reminding everyone that the exception to this joyous day would be her emailing us the attendance update later that morning. The second was a minor emergency involving the individual with whom I shared an office. When instructed to 'fix it', he responded: 'but it's no email day.' I'd never seen that particular senior leader more apoplectic, and indeed never heard him raise his voice, but he did then: 'I don't care if it's no email day! Send the email!' he raged.

Email is fraught with difficulties, is unreliable, is ineffective in communicating tone, and undoubtedly increases workload. At the same time, putting extensive curbs and limits on people's emailing in a culture of email causes tension and stress.

In my view, it is crucial to place some limits on emails, but to do so in the absence of a culture shift is to invite rage and stress. Just like the *Teacher Gap* shorter school day experiment, leaders must clearly signpost the issues and work together with teachers to find a solution, while also bearing in mind that some teachers really do need saving from themselves. (I am one such teacher; given free reign I will email anyone anything anytime. And I have. I apologise now to everyone I have ever worked with, and indeed everyone I now work with. You just need to tell me off every time).

First, reveal the issue. Find out how many emails your main scale teacher receives in a day. Find out how many of these should have been conversations. Find out how many of these were urgent, and how many should have been saved up for your regular, in-person check-in. Get concrete examples of this from a range of people, and then anonymise these stories. (You'll need to change a lot in the process – that's fine. Better to not name and shame in this case.)

Hold a staff meeting, or ask through line management for teachers to share the issues, and listen to people speak about how they find the email culture in the school. Genuinely listen. Do they find it a problem? Who does and who doesn't? How much time do they spend on their emails each day? If they don't know, ask them to time it for a few days. I assure you, no one can fail to be shocked by the results.

Then, and only then, present the solution: limits to email times. I can already hear everyone who works flexibly screaming that this is a terrible idea. I hear you. As a profession, we need to get much better at understanding and working with those who wish to work flexibly. In part of your consultation, make sure you speak with your flexible workers to understand their particular working patterns. I would always advise making an arrangement with them which does not undermine the new policy, but which allows them to do their job effectively (anyone can time their emails to send at particular times; not everyone should be doing this).

I've worked in a school with 7 a.m. to 7 p.m. limits; I've worked in a school with no start time stipulated but a firm cut-off at 6 p.m. Both worked well. In both, the policy also stated you could not send emails on weekends or during school holidays, and both had the exception of safeguarding concerns. In both, the SLT were exempt from this policy – and yet in both, as a member of the SLT, I found I received very, very few weekend emails – and there was never an expectation I would answer them.

At Ark John Keats, we stipulate emails may only be sent until 6:30 p.m., Monday to Friday. Of course those who leave work long before 6 p.m. and wish to spend precious time with their children may have serious and valid issues with such a policy. My suggestion is that for these people, and only these people, you enable the capacity for them to reply to their emails when they choose, and to schedule that reply to fly out at 7:30 a.m. the following morning. I suggest you train people in how to do this so there is absolute clarity. I would not, however, advocate allowing anyone to time-send their emails, or you will find a morning traffic jam of emails. It is also crucial you help teachers to manage their workload, and as mentioned above, many will *want* to work late into the night. We have to help people to not do this in any way in our power.

Sharpen the saw

In Stephen Covey's *The Seven Habits of Highly Effective People*, his seventh habit is 'sharpen the saw'. It is vital that everyone in schools – including senior leaders and including the headteacher – takes time out. No matter what we imagine about ourselves, we simply are not as good at our jobs when we work all the time.

Covey writes that taking time for ourselves 'is the habit that makes all the others possible', and he uses a humorous story which many teachers may see themselves reflected in:

> Suppose you were to come upon someone in the woods working feverishly to saw down a tree.
>
> 'What are you doing?' you ask.
>
> 'Can't you see?' comes the impatient reply. 'I'm sawing down this tree.'
>
> 'You look exhausted!' you exclaim. 'How long have you been at it?'
>
> 'Over five hours,' he returns, 'and I'm beat! This is hard work.'
>
> 'Well, why don't you take a break for a few minutes and sharpen that saw?' you inquire. 'I'm sure it would go a lot faster.'
>
> 'I don't have time to sharpen the saw,' the man says emphatically. 'I'm too busy sawing!'[11]

This wish to work excessive hours comes from a wonderful place which we can celebrate. Yet we will be much more effective in the hours we spend at school if we have lived lives of balance and joy in our non-working time. We must get teachers to see that teaching is a marathon – we don't want to run schools that rely on people leaving after three or five years and leaving this wonderful profession. We must be working for the long term.

Pointless work

A common thread in the workload report is this idea of 'pointless' work. Teachers seem relatively content with even excessive amounts of lesson planning and book marking. They have less time for the other aspects of workload. Aspects of the job that are regularly dismissed as pointless are:

- CPD – with which I sympathise, as it is clear so much of it is probably pointless for many teachers. (See the previous chapter for more on this.)

- Marking assessments – particularly those that seem to be at stupid times, for example a mock paper before students have finished the course, or exams right before a half term with a deadline for data right after the half term.

- Meetings – I have rarely attended a meeting that could not have been a well-worded email, and so sympathise with this also.

- Paperwork – risk assessments (which in every school I have worked in have included a pro forma already filled out, which has required minor changes and zero thought), request forms, back to work forms, student report cards – if you are also marking, teachers probably write the equivalent of *War and Peace* in their paperwork and student books over the course of five years.

In the staff survey of one school I worked in, one of the questions was always: 'is there anything you have to do as a part of your job that does not have an impact on improving the learning of your students?' The responses to this were fascinating, and the headteacher would ruthlessly cut anything that appeared there from our policies.

Data

I will focus in on data, both because this is a particularly large source of excessive workload and because I had to good fortune to sit on the Department for Education's data workload committee[12] and have spent an inordinate amount of time thinking about data in schools. Teachers, with the general exception of the maths department who usually have degrees in this stuff, hate data.

When I was first asked to join this group, my initial (foolish) thought was: why do people hate data so much? It doesn't take five minutes to enter grades on a spreadsheet. How is this a driver of workload?

After I had thought about this for five seconds, I realised that data is so much more than this. Entering data may well only take five minutes – but everything that sits under that data drives workload. Designing assessment, administering assessment, marking assessment, moderating assessment all takes hours and hours of teachers' time in an academic year. Which would be almost acceptable, if what resulted from these hours of work gave us a helpful insight into where our children are right now and how likely they are to get the grades we want for them in external exams some years down the line.

When I ask at conferences: 'how many assessment points does your school have each year?' the number of schools with six is quite terrifying. Some even report more than this. The follow up question I always ask is: how far do you trust the data you are entering for those assessment points?

Is the data valid?

Since the government removed levels, which could provide only spurious accuracy across a school, let alone across the country, schools have scrambled to create an assessment system that is meaningful, and have, largely, failed.[13] For most if not all teacher-designed assessments, all we can actually tell is how well the child is doing compared with the other children in their year group on that particular test – and that is only if you've invested time moderating year 8 January assessments (anybody?).

Even for the most carefully moderated Key Stage Three assessment, we can't use this to make inferences on how well they are doing compared with their cohort, because we don't know how well the cohort would do on that test. So we cannot use these assessments to decide whether a child is 'on track' for future success.

The national assessments which schools can buy in from large assessment companies promise comparability by ensuring large numbers of children are sitting the same test across the country. Yet here we come unravelled with the curriculum question, especially now more schools are academies, and academies do not need to follow the National Curriculum (and though in my experience most schools, academies or not, *do* follow the National Curriculum, in, for example, English departments I have visited schools almost never choose the same texts to study from the billions of possible books; in History departments you almost never have schools studying the same material and so on). Though these bought-in assessments, we may think we have more valid data on a cohort of children, but because we don't know the extent to which other schools have aligned their curriculum to suit the assessment, we still can't reliably compare our school with others.

Having recognised the Herculean challenge of making an assessment that will give us data that has some meaning, middle and senior leaders across the country are then charged with breaking down that spurious data into sub-groups, one of the most critical wastes of time we can employ.

How useful is data analysis?

In my first year as a head of department, I was charged in week three with writing my exam analysis report. Thankfully, I was given the previous head of department's report to use as my model – otherwise I really would have had no idea what to do – and it ran to fourteen pages. That was for English language. There was also one for English literature. And another one for media studies.

This report was my first experience of what I would come to encounter in almost all subsequent schools. We broke the data down by gender. We broke it down by ethnicity. By whether the child was on free school meals, or looked after. We analysed which groups had made the grade and which hadn't, and made inferences about this.

This was almost impossible for me to do without the context for the children themselves. With two looked after children in a cohort of 120, it seemed madness to draw inferences – surely someone knew these two children? The reason that one massively exceeded expectations and one failed would surely be clear to their teachers and the school. What possible lesson could be drawn from these two wildly dissimilar trajectories?

Conversely, what about the 54% of the cohort who were on free school meals? Overall, they had done slightly worse than those who were not on free school meals. But that was 65 children – somehow this seemed like too many children to say one sweeping thing about. And they hadn't *all* done worse – there was immense variation – this was just the average. To draw singular learning points from this large cohort seemed misguided.

And yet this is what we did: used old data about a cohort that had passed to inform what we would do for the next set of 120 children this year.

At one school, a member of staff was charged with raising the attainment of the lowest performing group – those of black Caribbean ethnicity. They organised an event and invited only those students and their families. There was something uncomfortable to me about this homogenising of a group. I wondered what the parents might feel, being corralled into sessions just because of the ethnicity of their offspring?

No teacher has ever said: 'oh yeah – all my kids on free school meals have identical problems.' I would argue it is unhelpful to see a child with white skin and immediately think: 'white British children on free school meals underperform across the country – this child will likely do the same.' Even if we can reliably identify underperformance (after the event, which is not that helpful), how can we reasonably know how to put this right for the next cohort of children? Children will have wildly different needs, and these needs will not tend to group themselves comfortably into economic or ethnic groupings.

Instead, I would argue for thinking about the child individually. What do they struggle with? These are the trends we should be looking for. Let's find all the children who struggle to memorise dates. What intervention can we give these children? What about all the children with illegible handwriting – let's split them off and do something different with them. How about the children who can't yet decode? Let's organise a special reading group with an expert member of staff.

Where data becomes meaningless

We come into even more messy territory when we try to mimic Progress 8 – a measure so complex it takes months to be accurately produced after external exam results are out – in our own schools. Judging the progress children are making is a fool's game. Most predicted grades are inaccurate to say the least.[14] The time teachers spend entering data of this kind is therefore highly questionable.

Though perhaps no data entry is of more questionable value than target grades. It is achingly difficult to set a target grade that both challenges the individual child and that they think they might ultimately have a chance of achieving. Set a target grade too low, children despair and give up; set it too high and they do the same. The thing is that we're talking about humans – there is no algorithm that can spit out the perfectly pitched target grade. It is nuanced.[15] While teachers may know some children well enough to determine what target grade will have the magical effect of spurring the child to work harder and feel more motivated, this is by no means the case for every child. I would advise leaving target grades until you can ignore them no longer – for example, when sixth form colleges begin to ask for them, or when students are choosing their next steps and need to be guided towards the most appropriate direction.

Indeed, the power of assessment itself is questionable. I was once at a meeting with a renowned education professor who asked a room full of teachers: 'who here has ever changed what they were doing because of what the data said?' Not a single hand went up. (For me, this was as revealing a moment as when a colleague asked: 'how many times has a parents evening had a transformative impact on a child?' and I could think of exactly none. At the time of writing I can think of two appointments at individual parents' evenings. Is that worth it for the hundreds of teacher hours invested?)

This is not to say that assessment can't give us new and important information on where a child is – but that sheet of data is not the bit that makes our teaching and the children's learning better.

Furthermore, the extent to which grades impact a child's performance is questionable. It has long been an educational truism that a visible grade makes children much less likely to take on board feedback to improve.[16] In a series of blogposts, Professor Rebecca Allen delineates the multiple issues with how data can impact on students' beliefs of their potential to improve, as well as their motivation to do so. For example, Allen writes:

Where a mark or grade received simply confirms our prior view of how well we were doing, the act of receiving the feedback might have no impact because we have no need to adjust behaviours to close the gap between our current performance and the internal standard we had in mind for ourselves. This was demonstrated in a nice experiment, albeit one on undergraduates, which provided students with their position in the grade distribution every six months. The researchers found that giving this grading feedback actually LOWERED academic outcomes more frequently than it raised them! How can this be? Well, it turns out that, in the absence of knowing their rank, many of these students had actually underestimated how well they were doing. When they received the good news they were doing better than they thought, their (self-reported) satisfaction increased and they ramped down the effort they were putting into their studies. There was a smaller group for whom the reverse was true – they had overestimated their position in the year and so receiving the bad news of their true ranking caused them to increase their effort.[17]

The entire series of posts is worth reading, and is referenced with the robust research you would expect from a leading voice in education research.[18]

Could it be possible then that data actually *detracts* from student improvement? I would argue that the most valuable and important 'data' is not numeric at all – it is the subject specificity of knowing precisely what children need to do to improve. In short: what are they getting wrong? This is what we need to focus on. The more energy we spend testing and marking and formulating numbers, the less we have to think deeply about where our children struggle and how we can help them improve.

A watershed moment in educational leadership for me came with the idea of being 'data driven.' Having spent my early years in education floating around the classroom encouraging children to explore what was inside their own heads (not nearly as much as you would hope), I and many others latched onto the idea that we could be data-driven about our work. I would therefore analyse my imperfect data capture, ignorant of the imperfections of my teacher-designed test and total absence of moderation that rendered it entirely spurious, and home in on the children who had failed to master one of the millions of assessment focuses on the imperfect grid we used before the government realised how pointless it was and told us to just make it up ourselves.

In 2014, Dylan Wiliam's paper offered valuable clarity around data. We were simply collecting far too much data to do anything with. In the midst of all the numbers and percentages, what could we actually do? In perhaps the most helpful phrase written about assessment, Wiliam writes: 'it is more productive to focus on decision-driven data-collection, rather than on data-driven decision making'.[19]

Instead of taking the results of various tests and then working out what to do, begin with the decisions you want to make and work back to decide what data you will need to collect to make this work. For example, if you test everyone's reading ages and then realise there are far more children in need than you have capacity to do anything with, you have spent an awful lot of time and money testing children to just find something out. Instead, if you decide: we can do targeted phonics intervention with our weakest 12 year 9 students – you know who to test. It's probably not top set year 9.

Lauren Thorpe, the director of strategy at Ark Schools, speaks clearly about this programme of working backwards. By starting from the general and moving to the specific, she illustrates clearly how we can use data in a more effective way. If we begin thinking: I want students to do better at biology, we then need to ask: what do we need to know for this to happen? We need to know what topics students struggle in and what we need to re-teach. We need to know which students therefore have done poorly and in which topics. This means the data we need for our purpose is a question level analysis of the biology we need students to know.

Frequency of assessment

How many times a year *can* we meaningfully collect data? It is telling that Ark Schools have moved from six times annually (very many years ago) to three, and in very recent years to two times a year.

But just because we are not collecting data does not mean we are not assessing. Of course, we need students to get better at what they are doing. This is the fabric of teachers' planning and delivery of excellent lessons, as well as the feedback they give to students. But none of this needs to be prepared, moderated, inputted and analysed in numerical form.

Workload can be reduced if we reduce data input, and continue to hone teachers' craft in questioning and lesson planning for student misconceptions. The most important thing for teachers to think about when it comes to assessment is what you as a teacher will do differently in response to what the students say, write and do. That happens multiple times, every single lesson. Not six times a year with numbers on a spreadsheet.

Feedback, not marking

Ask any teacher what takes the most time, and they will almost always reply (with a groan) 'marking.'

There was a time that I loved to mark. In my first year of teaching, I was absolutely awful at it. The only thing I could control was the words I would write in the students' books, and so, inspired by Phil Beadle's advice (which I can assure you is correct):

> You can turn up hungover every morning, wearing the same creased pair of Farahs as last week, with hair that looks like a bird has slept in it, then spend most of the lesson talking at kids about how wonderful you are; but mark their books with dedication and rigour and your class will fly.[20]

Or, in my case, you can be a novice teacher with tenuous control of the class and a lesson plan fully flawed, but you can speak to every child individually via the medium of writing comments of questionable use in each and every one of their books, and they will at least not go backwards.

Our school policy dictated we mark books every other week; I marked double that to be doubly sure the children in my classroom might learn something. I persuaded myself it was useful, even though I tended to write the same things over and over ('use more ambitious vocabulary', something one child engaged with by writing: 'like what?' and helping me to recognise that if they knew more ambitious vocabulary, they probably would have used it).

The interaction that sealed the knowledge that 90% of my marking was in vain was when a colleague interviewed a section of my class to find out what they thought of my marking. One student candidly told my colleague: 'I don't read

Miss's comments.' When asked why, she followed up not with 'I can't read her writing' as I would have expected (I have the handwriting of a general practitioner) but 'I can't *be bothered to* read it.' The second prompt was: 'how can Miss make her marking more helpful to you?' To which this wonderful child (who I taught for three years – three years' worth of painstaking comments in that girl's book which I am in no way resentful about) suggested 'read it aloud to me?'

Marking works, just like intervention works – but it is not the right choice in the long term. The addition to workload is simply unsustainable, and it will make teachers leave – the school and ultimately the profession.

Instead, I advocate SLT asking for whole-class feedback in place of marking. Instead of expecting to see marks in individual children's books, the teacher makes notes on the class set of books on a separate piece of paper. I would advocate making notes of:

- The most impressive student books to award merits or house points to.

- Any scrappy work to give warnings about (two teacher book looks in a row of scrappy work should result in a sanction).

- Superb work to be showcased, ideally under a visualiser, with the rest of the class.

- High-frequency misspellings, especially if multiple students are getting these wrong.

- One to four misconceptions for reteaching.

- Names of students who have particular mistakes.

The last bullet point is important: the biggest critique of whole-class feedback is the students who are making different mistakes to everyone else. In reality, this number is far smaller than anyone ever imagines, but it is not normally zero. After delivering whole-class feedback, go straight to that one or those two children who did something different, and explain in a whisper what *their* focus needs to be for green-pen-editing their work.

It is important to look at books frequently because if you save this up and do it every two weeks, you will have so many misconceptions to reteach your children will never take in all of that information. In my experience, four is about the most the students can reasonably take in before you ask them to redraft their work. With the most crushing misconceptions and the groups who struggle the most, focusing on just one thing can really help them to master that element. Less is more in my experience.

Keep this feedback handy. When teaching, I always have a clipboard that has three things: a class list so I can tick who deserves merits (and who, conversely, I need to log detentions for), the lesson pack itself and the feedback sheet from a previous lesson. That way, when I set students off on their next task I can remind them of the mistakes they made last time and what they need to do differently this time.

Spellings are important and I am told by too many teachers that 'there aren't any marks at GCSE for spelling in my subject'. Spelling accurately will be important far beyond school examinations, and we must work as a team to get children to produce more accurate work. I'd advocate between three and ten spellings for your class and never more. You will notice over time students becoming more and more accurate, and even finding three spellings can become a delightful challenge for some classes. When it is hard to find a spelling more than one student has got wrong, lower your bar: if a single student writes 'repitition' instead of 'repetition' it is worth assuming this is a mistake others might make at some point. They can over-learn this to the point of automaticity: everybody still benefits.

We know that testing helps new knowledge to stick, so I would suggest teaching the spellings students got wrong and testing them either immediately or at the end of that very lesson. Their (hoped) success should boost their confidence. The next lesson, test them again. The time between lessons should prove a good break for them to do some forgetting. I would probably do one or maybe two further tests of these spellings, after which it is probably the signal that it is time to look at the books again.

It is important to be led by curriculum experts in the amount of feedback students are given, however. In English, if you have five lessons a week, looking at the books every three or four lessons seems sensible to me – after all, you're probably only looking at a double page or two for each child. Your feedback might be focused only on the last paragraph they have written – indeed, I would suggest it *should* be focused only on a single piece of writing. Depending on your curriculum, you might check books more often if they are practising extended writing every lesson, and if they are simply doing comprehension questions which you have marked in class (see below), you might do a book check less frequently looking for neatness, effort and spellings only.

Teachers can be surprisingly resistant to whole-class feedback. Many will, like I did, have spent years marking, and to move away from that is almost an admission that those hours have been wasted. Many will have felt their children did better when they marked more. Both of these things are more true than is convenient in a policy change. Acknowledge the marginal gains that come through marking, but have conversations around workload and prioritising. With younger teachers, talk about how teaching is a marathon, not a sprint. Would they want to do this for the next ten years? Perhaps share stories of great colleagues you have known (I'm sad to predict there will be many) who have left the profession due to workload.

If they aspire to middle leadership, ask them whether, if they were head of department, they would want everyone to be doing what they are doing. Talk about equality of provision for children, and how we don't want to set teachers up against one another. (I visited one school and watched an amazing English lesson where the children were rocketing along. At one point, a student said: 'Sir, can you buy us chocolate because we've been so good?' The teacher sagely replied: 'Your success is your reward.' 'But Miss Collins buys us chocolates,' came the riposte. 'Miss Collins doesn't have a family to feed,' was his.) For anything we do, we have to think: should everyone do this? If not, you shouldn't do it. If so, you should ensure everyone can do it, wants to do it, and has the means to do it.

Of course you do want teachers to write in student books when needed – just not after the lesson in a Sisyphean pile that never ends while their family and friends slowly forget what they look like. Tell all teachers to carry a red pen as they circulate, and mandate the children to do silent extended practice for at least twenty minutes in most lessons. As the students write, the teacher can make a bee-line to those who are most struggling, or perhaps to those students you noticed had specific issues on your last look at their books. I had a student in a very high-ability class who struggled with even the most basic spellings and use of capital letters. I sat him on the end of the row so it would be easiest for me to 'get' to him in circulation, and made sure I gave him specific spellings to master separately from his peers.

Paperwork

One of the most hated additions to workload is paperwork and documentation. For every piece of paper you are thinking of asking people to produce, ask yourself: who actually uses this document? If you're not sure, ask. I have yet to find a teacher who uses the scheme of work, for example (they normally clicked onto it once, saw it didn't provide them with what they wanted, and clicked out again forever). Why spend hours writing detailed schemes of work, especially now that Ofsted have finally, and explicitly, told us they don't expect to see this kind of documentation?[21]

And while I would expect every teacher to make a seating plan (first: to learn the children's names; then, to seat them away from people who will distract them), why this needs to be written down and updated constantly is beyond me. I change the seats of my classes every few weeks, swapping someone with someone else if I needed to put someone easily distracted at the front, or move to the aisle someone who had missed a lot of school and needed extra attention. To constantly update this document would take time, and who would ever use it? (There is an argument for having a seating plan for cover lessons which I do appreciate – if I was going to be out, I would leave an updated seating plan – though other teachers found it just as effective to say when covering a class: 'I'm jotting down where you're seating today and if it's not your correct places your teacher will give you a detention when they're back. Does anyone wish to move right now?')

The practice of marking a seating plan with a child's learning needs – whether special educational needs or English as an additional language – is also a pointless data exercise no one will ever need or use. (Show me the teacher who doesn't know who needs additional support in these areas.) The even more objectionable practice of recording a child's *financial* situation (pupil premium or in receipt of free school meals) seems actively unhelpful, if not outright harmful.

I say harmful, because there is some evidence that teachers, however good their intentions, can lower their expectations for certain groups of students due to unconscious bias.[22] While there is little teachers can do about some causes of bias – those visible – apart from be aware and check their thinking, those invisible causes like family background can easily be pushed to the back of teachers' minds. And let's be blunt: do you teach a child differently because they are poor? *Should* you treat a child differently because they are poor? Replace 'poor' with 'black' or 'female' or 'Jewish', and you see just how offensive such a sentiment really is. If you do not treat a child differently because they are poor, then spending the time making plans which highlight financial disparities between children is nothing but an exercise in paperwork, and a waste of teachers' time.

The only thing you need to know about the children in front of you is who is struggling and how, and what you as a teacher need to do to help them. *Why* they are struggling is cause for speculation, and not worth your time thinking about it.

Planning

When I started teaching, planning took up the majority of my time. I would jot notes on what I wanted to teach, type these into a lesson plan pro forma, and then make a PowerPoint and series of worksheets as the lesson the students would experience. It took me a really, really long time to plan every lesson.

There was a time, not so long ago, when PowerPoint was not omnipresent in classrooms. When I trained to teach in the summer of 2010, Teach First placed us in pairs as trainees in someone else's school. We had to teach a twenty-minute lesson together, and we were given four hours on site to plan that lesson (I remember thinking how brief that time was…). In her break, the class teacher found the other trainee and I and explained some information about the class and what they were studying. Before she ran off to teach, she said: 'oh, and of course you'll want to make a PowerPoint.' We nodded, but when she had gone I said: 'I've never made a PowerPoint,' and the other trainee replied with: 'I think I used it for a presentation at uni once?'

So we sat at the staff room computer and spent an unreasonable amount of time trying to open the programme and put some information onto the slides. We didn't know how to make pictures come from the internet into the presentation (it was a simpler time), so we filled the slides with a lot of unmatching clipart. The result was not very pretty.

When it came to teach the class, we trainees took to the front. The class teacher was at the back. There was a teaching assistant hovering around the most challenging child. We were never more surrounded by other professionals while teaching.

The lesson was awful. The children were unsettled, and our PowerPoint was more hindering than helpful – we would move around the class briefly, then realise we needed the next slide, and shuffle back behind the teacher's desk to click the arrow. At one point, a clipart decision horribly misfired, and the children found something side-shakingly funny about it, and we had our first taste of the horror of losing a class.

First impressions aside, I'm nothing if not a fast learner; by the end of my first year of teaching, I was creating and delivering thirty slide monstrosities for fifty-minute lessons. Planning was taking hours upon hours – I'd not taken a two-day weekend all year (consoling myself that 'work in pyjamas' counted as rest); I arrived at work at seven or just after and I'd not left work before six pm (when the caretaker threw me out) on any day.

As a teacher, I came to find PowerPoint guilty of a series of flaws. As we reduced text to bare minimum bullet points, student literacy suffered. Children's attention was split between the slides, their book and the handouts. To use a PowerPoint meant drawn curtains and lights off, which meant children complained they couldn't see the book or their book, so you spent the lesson in a cycle of – blinds down, lights off; lights on blinds up; blinds down again. Then, of course, came the inevitable failures of technology and feeling like you were teaching in freefall when the board wouldn't turn on, or the slides wouldn't move on.[23]

As a middle and senior leader, though, my focus has changed somewhat. I've had experience of working in challenging schools, and sometimes some of the best teachers are working well in difficult situation with a PowerPoint that they themselves have created. In a challenging environment, it seems misjudged to have a blanket ban on something that an individual is using without any actual harm to learning.

My new concern with PowerPoint is how hard it is to share. I work with more and more schools which share curriculums, and I have yet to see a shared area that doesn't have five or more iterations of the shared PowerPoint (one for every teacher). Concerns of middle leaders about 'plug and play' are no less common where teachers are delivering 'Lesson 5 CTO WITH EDITS.pptx'.

When we drill down into these endless iterations, we find anything between minor tweaks to total rewrites, making us question what the workload alleviations of a shared curriculum actually are. And sometimes, teachers are making it worse.

I visited a trainee teacher and was surprised to see a card sort activity, for example. The academy trust I work for has pleasingly evidence-informed ways of planning the curriculum, and I'd not seen one of these in our shared curriculums. When we discussed the lesson, she explained that she had changed the PowerPoint and resources to include the card sort. We discussed why this might not have been the best task to get the students to learn difficult material rapidly,[24] and she learned quickly. My concern remains that sometimes brand new or trainee teachers do not know the best way to improve lessons, and inadvertently spend a lot of time and effort making those lessons worse.

The reason some teachers make PowerPoints worse is not because they have bad intentions or poor subject knowledge. It's my belief that the medium itself discourages teachers from putting in the right kind of intellectual preparation to making their lessons better. With a PowerPoint, the core knowledge is presented so thinly – almost equal to the tasks set – and is simplified to seem so obvious to all, that there doesn't seem to be much to prepare intellectually. It misrepresents the depth of knowledge we want teachers to have, and what we want teachers to communicate to students.

Booklets

The workload argument is the biggest argument in favour of booklet teaching. I covered a lesson in my last school where I was given a PowerPoint, a textbook, a YouTube clip and a worksheet. I was amazed at the level of detailed planning that had gone into a cover lesson, and wondered how much effort was being put into their day to day lessons. And it's great if teachers want to spend time planning their lessons – I'm just not sure that creating PowerPoints and photocopying is the right use of teachers' time.

A booklet is simply a two page per lesson restraint you place on yourself. Everything for the lesson is contained within these two pages. It is like a textbook you have created for your own class: every child has it and every adult has the same one. There is total clarity over what the class is learning and how, as well as what they have learned previously. Heads of department have total clarity on what is being taught in every lesson. The consistency that can be achieved through this is unreal. Another benefit is that new teachers and new students have clarity on exactly what has been learned, and you can give them the exact lessons the class has done, packaged in a portable format.[25]

In the case where you have a great textbook already, of course use that. In my experience, it is rare (but not unheard of) that a textbook has the exact tasks you want, and I have never seen a textbook with recap questions (certainly not questions that recap previous units). If you have a textbook you like using, my advice would be to script your recap questions and tasks and put these into booklet format to sit alongside the textbook. Don't reinvent the wheel, but do keep it simple so children have one booklet they take out (and teachers have one load of photocopying for the term).

The greatest benefit of textbooks or teacher-made textbooks is the ease with which teachers can then engage with the crucial subject content to be taught. Having text in front of you focuses the mind, and annotation is second nature to almost every teacher of the humanities, and many of our maths and science colleagues.

At West London Free School, annotation is the clue to lesson excellence. Louis Everett describes how heads of department review annotations as a team, as well as following up, if a learning walk has revealed explanations or questioning to be a point for improvement, by looking together at how the teacher has annotated the lesson to support them in developing their subject knowledge:

> One way of clearing time for staff to focus on the quality of their teaching is by creating high-quality centralised resources. As a head of department, I achieved this by giving responsibility of resource creation to different subject experts within the team. This empowered them, freed up my time to quality-assure, and meant staff could concentrate on what they were teaching rather than fiddling around on PowerPoint. Lesson planning became a process of purely annotating the text you were reading from and thinking about the pupils in front of you. I have included an example of my annotations of a double page spread in preparation for a year 8 lesson on the English Civil War. As a department we were clear before beginning to design resources about what were high impact activities and what resources should look like/consist of. This made quality assurance easier and ensured teachers could concentrate on communicating their subject-expertise rather than spending hours creating complex activities. The result was high-quality resources available for teachers to concentrate on teaching.[26]

The planning we want teachers to do is not making resources or PowerPoints. The planning we want teachers to do is the intellectual preparation to teach. How do we teach *this* content to *these* young people? Rebecca Boomer-Clarke refers to this stage as the 'final foot':

> One of the common criticisms of formal curriculum programmes is that they seek to turn teachers into robots. It is true that we expect our programmes to generate high-quality resources for teachers and students, and that we believe this provides a big opportunity to reduce the planning burden on our staff, but we have no expectation that teachers would follow these unthinkingly. Indeed, we expect … that teachers will engage intellectually with the subject content of the lesson before they teach it … We believe that teachers can be supported and resourced strongly enough so more of their focus can be on that final foot, on how this material will get into the heads of these particular children.[27]

Done is better than perfect

One of my favourite phrases to apply to what we do is 'done is better than perfect'.[28] Too many teachers are hamstrung by a driving need for perfectionism, and too many people in all walks of life fail to provide something good for fear of it not being the best. There is a minimum standard, above which improvements can be made year after year. Having planned like a maniac for two years in the absence of a sensible amount of sleep and a comforting amount of seeing friends and family, I can attest to the fact that an under-planned lesson with a happy, rested teacher will always be better than a perfectly planned lesson and a teacher who is tired, grumpy, lonely, ill, and leads a life of limited experience.

With this maxim in mind, absolutely do not go and tell teachers they need to convert all their lessons to booklets immediately. This will result, quite obviously, in an increase in workload. Instead, I'd be letting teachers use what they have, and asking them to plan their future lessons using the two-page method. If we can wean teachers off PowerPoints slowly and get them to see how much quicker and more effective their lessons are by fronting the core content in this way, that is our aim. It doesn't need to happen tomorrow. Anything that increases teacher workload in the short term should be avoided if at all possible.

When Becky Curtis at Ark Elvin plans with her team, she uses the 'togetherness principles' learned from *The Together Leader*.[29] Building in diary time to SLT meetings, she asks what leaders need to stop doing in order to do whatever new idea or policy they are looking at. There is an upfront recognition that time is limited, and frequent discussion around what teachers are being asked to do.

Continuous improvement

Done is better than perfect, but it's not the ultimate aim. While resisting perfectionism in the initial stages of planning, build in time for departments to come together and review their resources prior to the next teaching. Again, booklets lend themselves well to this. It is hard to remember individual PowerPoints, and time consuming to click into each one to make changes, but it is straightforward to scribble your thoughts on a booklet (even *as you teach* – 'kids struggled with this'; 'badly worded'; adding a new question you found your students responded to) and revisit this as a team. In once school where time was pressed, I would ask teachers to simply hand me their scribbled-on booklets and I would then comb through these and add in their improvements.

Behaviour

Poor student behaviour is draining for teachers. The more time teachers spend dealing with poor behaviour, the less time they have to plan, teach, respond, and generally help their children academically.

While student behaviour can be draining, what can be more infuriating for teachers is the logging of behaviour data and the administration of detentions. In my first school, in the absence of a detention system, we would all organise our own detentions. I would start at ten-minute detentions and double them each day they were not attended.

I think very few of my detainees sat only ten minutes.

I had a notebook that I kept purely to log detentions, and then that became two: one for my tutor group (who were late, without equipment, with unsigned and forgotten and lost planners, in addition to the normal chattiness and occasional backchat) and one for all the classes I taught. At the end of any given day, there would be between seven and fifteen names on my list, and maybe five would turn up to a detention. The rest I would move over to the next day.

The upshot of this was that behaviour did not improve very much in my lessons. If anything, standards started to slip.

After a term of chaos, I stopped setting homework I needed to take in, for example. I grew fond of 'read this' or 'learn these spellings for a test' or even more embarrassingly: 'think about' or 'perform your presentation for your family'. This cut down a significant amount of detention chasing. Right for my work life balance, wrong for my children – especially the 60–70% across my classes who *always* did their homework. In upper year groups, I continued to set decent homework for the most motivated, and simply narrated what would happen if they didn't do it: 'it's your future, it's your exams – if you don't do it, the only person who misses out is you'. I'll leave you to imagine how effective this speech was at eliciting homework from my most disaffected children.

When children came to my classroom with make-up on, they got a make-up wipe instead of a detention; when they came without a pen I gave them a pen. I must have spent hundreds of pounds over several years on make-up wipes and equipment to give away (in addition to the chocolate I bribed them with towards the end of term when they were most liable to misbehave).

There are education professionals I hugely respect who would argue that that is actually the right approach – when someone doesn't have something, give them it. My argument against this is two-fold: it costs nothing for a child to wear their uniform correctly instead of incorrectly, or to refrain from putting make-up on their face and nail polish on their hands. A Bic biro costs less than 50 pence, and it is rare that children do not have that within their means (rare, but not never; it goes without saying that we must be on high alert for those truly in trouble).

The other issue is one of values – I value personal responsibility deeply. I think it is one of a few very important qualities we should actively seek to develop in children. Children who take responsibility feel their lives are in their control (a powerful need for most adolescents) and can forge their futures. Not all adults have my values, so I won't ask you to share them. I simply ask you to consider the impact of a child who does not take that responsibility in school when they are surrounded by people who care and want to help, and what happens to that child's prospects in the cold and unforgiving world of work.

But actually neither of these approaches needs to differ in terms of workload, because ultimately when something in a behaviour policy calls for a detention, the best way to reduce teachers' workload is to centralise that detention.

Centralised detentions

Centralised detentions means a teacher logs it – whether on an impressively complex system, or by sending an email, or by giving a form to someone, or by giving a list of names to someone – and the detention is run in one place by one or more people. The system is crucial. When all the children are in the same place, there can be no excuses for not attending. Everyone respects the system. Teachers don't ask students to wait behind after the last lesson – if the student is in detention, they are in that detention and the teacher can speak to them there. Everyone must be on board for this to work – if you have teachers running their own private detentions at different times or in different places, you don't allow the benefits of a team approach – which are manifold.

When all the children in the school with a detention are in the same place, this provides Heads of Year or form tutors or teachers with an opportunity to have restorative conversations somewhere where other members of staff are on hand to support them. It allows multiple detentions from multiple individuals to be clocked up centrally and sat there. It means there is clarity on who attended and who was missing.

The system of what happens when you miss a detention is best to keep out of the teacher's workload where at all possible. The missing of a detention is an administrative task. If the system of escalation is clear – you miss a detention, this happens – it can be built into an automated system to communicate with parents (by now, most parents have access to email and almost all have access to text messages) to ensure the child sits the next level of punishment the following day. A centralised administration support can be used to collate any valid excuses for missing detentions.

There are those who argue that the crucial part of behaviour management is rebuilding the relationship between the student and the teacher, and I don't actually disagree with that. Giving a child a detention is a necessary evil: it is the right thing for their character development, but will almost always strain your relationship (parents across the country denying their non-vegetable-eating children dessert know this to be true).

That said, if a child is late, or ill-equipped, arguably there is not the same need for a restorative conversation. I would be pushing for teachers to attend detentions to speak with students who have been poorly behaved. One school I worked at only mandated this for teachers who had sent a student out of their lessons, which I think is absolutely fair: if a child has disrupted the class to such an extent that they have been removed, a conversation does need to take place. Where possible, over-staff your detention with trusted middle and senior leaders to mediate difficult conversations between teachers and pupils. This is a time investment, but a meaningful one: teachers are our front line and most important resource in schools, and effort put in to support them is never wasted.

The stress of a school with poor behaviour can be upsetting and emotionally draining, but it doesn't have to add as much to workload as it currently does in so many schools. A centralised system with administrative support frees teachers up to do what they do best: support young people's learning in the classroom.

Take-aways

■ More is more, so be prepared for high teacher turnover if you choose that route.

■ Some teachers need saving from themselves – tell them not to work and make it OK to not work sometimes.

■ Create rules around email use.

■ Rest makes us all better at what we do.

■ Scrap pointless work and don't collect meaningless data.

■ Focus on feedback, not marking.

■ Set up systems of planning which are simple.

■ Done is better than perfect.

■ Centralise detentions.

Notes

1 Retrieved from https://teaching.blog.gov.uk/about-the-workload-challenge (accessed 4 April 2020).

2 *Workload Challenge: Analysis of Teacher Consultation Responses*, research report, February 2015, retrieved from https://assets.publishing.service.gov.uk/government/uploads/system/uploads/attachment_data/file/401406/RR445_-_Workload_Challenge_-_Analysis_of_teacher_consultation_responses_FINAL.pdf (accessed 4 April 2020).

3 Ibid., pp. 7–8.

4 Jo Facer, *Simplicity Rules* (Routledge, 2019).

5 Robert Pondiscio, *How the Other Half Learns* (Avery, 2019), p. 294.

6 Jay Matthews, *Work Hard Be Nice* (Algonquin Books of Chapel Hill, 2009), p. 2.

7 Retrieved from https://readingallthebooks.com/2015/11/28/at-what-cost (accessed 7 April 2020).

8 As of July 2020 the *TES* reported an increased proportion of early career teachers staying in schools: retrieved from www.tes.com/news/glimmer-hope-teacher-shortages (accessed 28 July 2020).

9 Retrieved from https://schoolsweek.co.uk/schooldash-research-teacher-job-adverts-rise-recruitment-retention-crisis (accessed 8 April 2020).

10 Rebecca Allen and Sam Sims, *The Teacher Gap* (Routledge, 2018), p. 103.

11 Stephen Covey, *The Seven Habits of Highly Effective People* (Simon & Schuster, 1989), p. 287.

12 Making Data Work, November 2018, retrieved from https://assets.publishing.service.gov.uk/government/uploads/system/uploads/attachment_data/file/754349/Workload_Advisory_Group-report.pdf (accessed 13 April 2020).

13 Daisy Christodoulou's *Making Good Progress* (Oxford University Press, 2017) is the best read on this phenomenon.

14 This small-scale project found predicted grades to be accurate an average of 29% of the time. Ben White comments: 'Our ability to accurately and reliably predict the future

is highly questionable. These 'predictions' were essentially made at the last possible moment (two months before the actual exam). Interestingly almost a third of the teachers involved in this challenge are required to provide predicted outcomes for pupils in year 8 onwards. Some data use in schools can produce work for teachers without providing clear returns for pupils in terms of improving their learning. Time spent producing, analysing and responding to wobbly grade predictions can easily fall into this category. Furthermore, some school data systems are premised on this predictive data being highly accurate and reliable. Based on this little experiment, it doesn't seem to be' (retrieved from www.waldeneducation.org/grade-prediction-project, accessed 16 April 2020).

15 Dawn Cox's 2019 Research Ed talk explores a multiplicity of ways target setting is flawed, including citing many different studies to support this (retrieved from https:// researchschool.org.uk/public/docs/Dawn-Cox-Why-are-you-using-marks-and-grades-rEDIpswich19.pdf, accessed 30 July 2020). Target grades are particularly troubling when applied to students who struggle most academically, according to the Education Data Lab: 'The predictability of progress and attainment as children pass through schools is particularly poor for those with low levels of attainment at Key Stage One. For children achieving a Level 1C, B or A at this stage, their development is so unpredictable that most will either outperform or underperform any Key Stage Two target that might be set. It would seem important that these children are not unthinkingly receiving curriculum restriction through placement in lower ability teaching groups or given low targets for attainment, because many of them will go on to achieve success later in their school career' (retrieved from https://ffteducationdatalab.org.uk/2015/03/why-measuring-pupil-progress-involves-more-than-taking-a-straight-line, accessed 30 July 2020).

16 Dylan Wiliam comments in his seminal 2011 text *Embedded Formative Assessment* (Solution Tree Press, 2011): 'Most teachers are surprised to learn that the effect of giving both scores and comments [when marking a piece of student work] was the same as the effect of giving scores alone. Far from producing the best effects of both kinds of feedback, giving scores alongside the comments completely washed out the beneficial effects of the comments; students who got high scores didn't need to read the comments, and students who got low scores didn't want to.'

17 Retrieved from https://rebeccaallen.co.uk/2019/04/25/grading-game-part-ii (accessed 17 April 2020).

18 Part I of the series can be found at https://rebeccaallen.co.uk/2019/04/24/grading-game-part-i (accessed 17 April 2020).

19 Dylan Wiliam, *Principled Assessment Design*, SSAT 2014, retrieved from www. tauntonteachingalliance.co.uk/wp-content/uploads/2016/09/Dylan-Wiliam-Principled-assessment-design.pdf (accessed 18 April 2020).

20 Phil Beadle, *How to Teach* (Crown House, 2010), p. 214.

21 The May 2019 handbook lists exhaustively on pages 13–15 what schools *do not* need to supply for Ofsted. Some relevant highlights are: 'Ofsted will not … create unnecessary workload for teachers through its recommendations; advocate a particular method of planning (including lesson planning), teaching or assessment … Ofsted does not require schools to provide evidence in any specific format, as long as it is easily accessible for inspectors …, curriculum planning in any specific format … individual lesson plans … Ofsted does not specify how planning (including curriculum and lesson planning) should be set out, the length of time it should take or the amount of detail it should contain' (retrieved from https://assets.publishing.service.gov.uk/government/uploads/system/ uploads/attachment_data/file/843108/School_inspection_handbook_-_section_5.pdf, accessed 3 August 2020).

22　Pran Patel writes eloquently of the risk of teachers' unconscious bias: 'There is an enduring body of evidence which indicates that teacher assessments are subject consistently to a large and significant level of error (Brookhart, 2013; Eckert et al., 2006; Harlen, 2005) … and, more importantly, research also indicates that some of this error may be systematic (Harlen, 2005; Robinson and Lubienski, 2011) (Campbell, 2015, p518). Burgess and Greaves (2009) look at the teacher assessment versus actual attainment of external exams of 11-year-olds across 16,557 schools, 3 subjects and 4 years. This showed that the past performance of a specific ethnic group directly impacted on the current teacher assessment' (retrieved from https://theteacherist.com/2020/03/29/teacher-bias, accessed 31 July 2020).

23　I've ranted a lot about PowerPoint, so please see Facer, *Simplicity Rules*, pp. 41–43, or my 2017 blogpost at https://readingallthebooks.com/2017/03/25/powerpoint, for further details of why I hate PowerPoint.

24　There is a growing convergence in the education community that varied activities do not result in exceptional student learning, explained brilliantly by Jennifer Beattie, who writes: 'Experience as a teacher has shown me that telling pupils the rule about the past tense in French gets you better results than making a game of it. Experience has shown me that telling the pupils what a word means gets you a quicker result than making a 'card sort' game … We cannot allow more trainee and NQT hours to be spent trying to create 'perfect' lesson resources. The best resource, for any lesson, is the teacher' (*Research Ed* magazine, September 2018, retrieved from https://researched.org.uk/wp-content/uploads/delightful-downloads/2018/09/researchEDMagazine-Sept2018-web.pdf, accessed 31 July 2020).

25　For a more detailed explanation of how to make and use booklets, please see Facer, *Simplicity Rules*, pp. 43–46.

26　Retrieved from https://justonethingafteranotherblog.wordpress.com/2019/12/26/what-makes-a-good-head-of-department (accessed 31 July 2020).

27　Rebecca Boomer-Clarke, 'The Final Foot', in Roy Blatchford (ed.), *The Secondary Curriculum Leader's Handbook* (John Catt, 2019), p. 160.

28　Sheryl Sandberg, *Lean In* (W. H. Allen 2015), p. 126, describes this as one of many aphorisms adorning the walls of Facebook.

29　Maia Heyck-Merlin, *The Together Leader* (Jossey-Bass, 2016).

Part II
The children

It is a fact widely accepted among educationalists as well as the general public that children are under more stress and pressure than they have ever been before. The thornier question is why this is the case. After all, our society is wealthier than it has been at any point in history. We have many more safety nets for those out of work or ill than are found in even other developed nations. We are not embroiled in active conflict on our doorstep, as so many nations of the world are.

So why do we have some of the unhappiest children in the world?[1]

There are some challenges that are particular to modern society, of course. Chiefly, social media has an unhealthily consuming role to play in all of our lives, and this affects those whose personalities and characters are in their formative phases most of all. All adults are, to some extent, both moulded and marked indelibly by their adolescence; imagine how much harder it might have been had every awkward move been documented day by day, or the seemingly perfect lives of others been live streamed into our houses – into our *bedrooms* – twenty-four hours a day?

And what is the manifestation of this unhappiness? One of the clearest signals that a child is in crisis is that they stop coming to school. The reasons for their reluctance are manifold, and no two cases in my experience have mapped onto each other perfectly. Schools that put effort into tracking attendance and dealing with the root causes when it is poor, and who work proactively with families to get the children in, are well-placed to read into individual cases improvements that can be made for the whole student body. Our basic aim as professionals should be to ensure school is somewhere our children want to come every day.

Some theorists have begun to posit whether our focus on finding happiness might, ironically, be the thing that is making us so unhappy. In *The Power of Meaning*, author Emily Esfahani Smith charts the rise in the publication of 'happiness' literature: in 2000, just fifty books were published on happiness; by 2008 it was four thousand.[2] Esfahani Smith writes: 'there is a major problem with the happiness frenzy: it has failed to deliver on its promise. Though the happiness industry continues to grow, as a society we're more miserable than ever.'[3] Indeed,

DOI: 10.4324/9781003097075-6

happiness alone is not enough: this is clear in Aldous Huxley's *Brave New World*, where adults take 'soma', a drug that cures all unhappiness. No reader would suggest the individuals under this drug's influence are happy.

Ultimately, we know that happiness is not pure pleasure: our society is strewn with examples of celebrities who appear to 'have it all' – who have the means and access to every stream of pleasure – and who are also desperately unhappy.

Happiness, according to Esfahani Smith, comes not from pleasure but from meaning. She quotes the philosopher John Stuart Mill, who cautioned in his autobiography:

> Those only are happy (I thought) who have their minds fixed on some object other than their own happiness; on the happiness of others, on the improvement of mankind, even on some art or pursuit, followed not as a means, but as itself an ideal end. Aiming thus at something else, they find happiness by the way. The enjoyments of life (such was now my theory) are sufficient to make it a pleasant thing, when they are taken en passant, without being made a principal object. Once make them so, and they are immediately felt to be insufficient. They will not bear a scrutinizing examination. Ask yourself whether you are happy, and you cease to be so. The only chance is to treat, not happiness, but some end external to it, as the purpose of life. Let your self-consciousness, your scrutiny, your self-interrogation, exhaust themselves on that; and if otherwise fortunately circumstanced you will inhale happiness with the air you breathe, without dwelling on it or thinking about it, without either forestalling it in imagination, or putting it to flight by fatal questioning.[4]

A focus on making children 'happy' is misguided. The things which make children happy in the short term are all but damaging in the long term: ice cream, video games, skipping school to watch a film – all these things might be more immediately pleasurable to most than maths period 3.

I grew up, as I am sure so many people did, in a household fixated on happiness. My parents only had one child (a fact which, when I share it, is usually mortifyingly met with: 'Oh! Now I understand'), and they were determined it would be a happy one. 'Are you happy?' my mother would ask anxiously throughout my childhood – she still asks it now. My grandfather, the original Facer philosopher, always says: 'love everyone; be happy'. It's his motto, and I can't imagine a better one. For me, though, it has become shorthand for a series of things we can do; if it were as simple as 'be happy' then we could deliver Grandad's message in assembly on the first day of school and be done with it.

Ultimately, schools do not own the full lives of the young people they serve. Families, friends, communities all play a part in raising our children. Our children come to school tired, hungry, upset from arguments at home, upset from arguments with friends. Many of our children come to school teenage, and are by default not happy.

I have come to the sad conclusion that no matter how hard we try, schools cannot make children happy. But we can make children learn.

If happiness is more complex than we have been brought up to imagine, while schools shouldn't indulge in creating short-term happiness, they certainly have a major role to play in ensuring children lead happy lives – eventually.

In this chapter, we're going to look at the role schools play in building a culture which makes children want to come to school every day, and the things we might do to set our children up to go on to lead fulfilled and, yes, happy lives.

Notes

1 A *Guardian* article from December 2019 notes: 'The OECD tested children in 79 countries, and found that British 15-year-olds ranked 69th out of 72 countries in the world for life satisfaction, with boys in particular among the least satisfied with their lives' (retrieved from www.theguardian.com/education/2019/dec/03/british-schoolchildren-among-least-satisfied-with-their-lives-says-oecd-report#:~:text=The%20OECD%20tested%20 children%20in,least%20satisfied%20with%20their%20lives, accessed 1 August 2020).
2 Emily Esfahani Smith, *The Power of Meaning* (Ebury Digital, 2017) p. 10.
3 Ibid.
4 John Stuart Mill, *Autobiography of John Stuart Mill* (The Floating Press, 2009), p. 142 (partially quoted in Esfahani Smith, *The Power of Meaning*, p. 16).

5 How can we help our children lead fulfilled lives?

Schools can't make children happy

Why can't schools make children happy? The same reason well-meaning parents and adoring friends can't make children happy. Happiness that relies on things that are external is fragile and liable to break. Intuitively we know that when our happiness depends on externals – other people, things, our jobs – it can be easily lost by the random unfairness of the world.

Schools won't make children happy by giving them loads of praise and merits and prizes and badges: at best, we can elevate their mood for a short time, before the feeling wears off and they once again seek recognition and praise. This is no bad thing to incentivise learning, but it is not the solid foundation on which happiness can thrive.

Schools won't make children happy by making lessons 'fun'. In my early career I both taught and observed some of the most 'fun' lessons imaginable; lessons in which almost no learning was taking place. The children enjoyed such lessons, at least in the short term. But when one of my most insightful and wise year 8s said plaintively to me: 'I don't feel like I'm learning anything,' the other shoe ought really to have dropped. (In reality, I replied – in my first year of teaching naivety – 'it's not about *learning*! It's about *discovering for yourself.*')

'Fun' lessons are like ice cream: delicious in the moment, but you know you probably shouldn't be eating it all day. Children know this, even when we adults don't.

Finally, schools can do everything in their power to prevent bullying and unkindness, and they should. But we are fools to think we will ever catch and sanction every instance of bullying that occurs. It would simply be impossible. Small unkindnesses and thoughtless actions will happen every day unnoticed, and while social media makes some aspects of bullying easier at least to prove, to be masked by a screen, and often anonymity, means unkindness can proliferate in a way unimaginable when most teachers were in school themselves.

DOI: 10.4324/9781003097075-7

And while we can sanction and do much to prevent bullying, we can't dictate friendship groups. Friends will cause children all manner of pain and heartache, and what can a school do about two people not liking one another?

The job of a school is not to make children happy. That is not even the job of the parent. That job is reserved for Santa, for a short, seasonal period when the normal rules of engagement are suspended.

A parent's job is to make sure their child becomes a good person. A school's job is to ensure children learn.

Academic success

A good many people argue that academic success is too narrow a prism to judge children on. There's more to life, we have all heard people say, than grades.

This is of course true. And yet when you ask parents what they want for their own children, they almost always include academic success in their wish list. When you ask middle class parents if they would be satisfied if their child left school without qualifications, few are brazen enough to say they would.

'There's more to life than grades' contains sometimes a sinister lowering of expectations for those most vulnerable in society. At one time, British society segregated children on a mass scale. Those thought to be 'smart' went to one type of school, and those who were not thought to be smart by virtue of having failed a single test at a single point in time in their eleventh year went to a very different type of school. The grammar school and secondary modern divide exposed some hard facts about what our society actually values. 'Some kids are just better with their hands,' was the lie people told themselves. The fact that those who were the 'smartest' in society were overwhelmingly the most financially privileged should surely trouble any professional in education.[1]

I think we should challenge the assumption that some children are destined for academics and some children are not. I can't count the number of times someone has told me: 'university isn't for everyone,' but every time they are the kind of person who completely assumes that university *is* the place for *their* children.

I believe that every child is academic. Worst case, if I turn out to be wrong, is that this is a helpful delusion. If you start with the premise that school is for everyone, you organise your systems, curriculum, teaching and culture around the assumption that all children can achieve.

One parental perspective to draw on in this assumption is Amy Chua, who in *Battle Hymn of the Tiger Mother* explores the cultural differences between American and Chinese parenting. To those who may argue that not all children can be successful, Chua cites her sister Cindy, who was born with Down's syndrome: Chua's mother spent 'hours patiently doing puzzles with Cindy and teaching her how to draw. When Cindy started grade school, my mother taught her to read and drilled multiplication tables with her. Today, Cindy holds two International Special Olympics gold medals in swimming.'[2] For Chua, there is no such thing as stupid – anyone can become academic, if they only work hard enough, a sentiment expressed in this tongue-in-cheek passage:

> If a Chinese child gets a B – which would never happen – there would first be a screaming, hair-tearing explosion. The devastated Chinese mother would then get dozens, maybe hundreds of practice tests and work through them with her child for as long as it takes to get them up to an A. Chinese parents demand perfect grades because they believe that their child can get them. If the child doesn't get them, the Chinese parent assumes it's because the child didn't work hard enough.[3]

To many, this may sound overly harsh. But perhaps we might investigate our biases here. We are offended by the thought that we might label someone 'lazy' who, in fact, struggles academically. The fear here is that we cause offence, which is not insignificant. I would argue, however, that the counter-possibility is worse. If we call someone 'academically unable' or 'not academic' or 'challenged', then we are writing off the possibility that they might achieve. We assume they *cannot* do it, rather than assuming they need to just work a bit harder at it.

Hard work is the key, and getting children to invest in this is one of our core jobs as educators. This job is never straightforward – I remember meeting children in an elite boarding school who had taken a battery of tests to get in, who described themselves to me as 'dumb' because they were in the third of eight sets for a subject.

Indeed, any setting which makes extensive use of selection testing opens itself up to letting children believe there are some who can and some who can't. Working in a comprehensive school in Kent was eye-opening for me: on entry, our children's academic profile was as mixed as you would expect any comprehensive school to be, with a strong top end and a small weaker end. Yet even in the top sets the prevailing opinion was: 'I failed the eleven plus. I didn't get into the grammar school. I am stupid.'

A test at eleven, you don't need me to tell you, is not a robust indicator of a child's intelligence. We know that so much about testing is affected by test conditions. A friend of mine who is a parent noted at one Kent primary school she visited, the headteacher said proudly: 'We don't do any preparation for the eleven plus test, because we don't believe in that.' For her, as a parent, she could only compare this to the private school primary headteacher who said: 'We know many of you hope to get your children into the local grammar schools, and we have a comprehensive testing programme in year 6 to support that.' For those parents with means, they can afford to spend money on private tutors to ensure their child is in the best possible position to get into the grammar school.

Why is there such a disparity in economic status between children who go to grammar schools and children who do not? A government report notes that:

> In 2019, pupils at grammar schools were much less likely than pupils at non-selective schools to have Education Health and Care (EHC) Plans or

Statements (0.3% compared to 1.7%), have Special Educational Needs (SEN) support (4% compared to 11%) or be eligible for free school meals (3% compared to 15%).[4]

While we might argue that children with Special Educational Needs are inherently less likely to be academic (though this is not an argument I would personally support), we must take issue with the financial disparity. Why are children at comprehensive schools five times more likely than their peers in grammar schools to be in receipt of free school meals?

What we must recognise now is that wealthy children could not logically be more inherently intelligent than poor children. It is clear that the system disadvantages the poorest in society. That private schools exist feels unfair – why can some parents pay for something others cannot? – but largely, in a capitalist society, we accept this (though plenty will argue that the charitable status of such institutions is unfair).[5] What should strike us as more egregious is that the state funds schools that poor children struggle to access, for whatever reason.

But even if grammar schools were to, say, accept children in receipt of the pupil premium to the same percentage as lived in their catchment area (though this may help but little, as parents with means may sometimes move homes to be closest to the highest performing schools),[6] I would still argue that such schools are damaging.

These schools are damaging because to be told you have failed is no way to begin your secondary education. We know that children's minds are still forming; that they are deeply impressionable, and that it is difficult to unform the ideas of youth. I have yet to meet an adult who failed the eleven plus who does not still speak about it with despair and longing, long after they have had successful careers and families of their own.

It is hard enough to get children to believe that they are capable: adolescence, in particular, is a time of deep insecurity and lack of self-belief for many, many young people. To have to first unpick negative beliefs about their abilities is an added obstacle to getting children to believe that they are capable.

In all schools we have an obligation to over-communicate the message: you are as smart as you work hard. Nobody is innately smart or born intelligent. The harder you work, the smarter you will be. The purists might quote some inconvenient research on IQ at birth, but you can argue against this. Even if it is true, and it is far from conclusively proven that some children just *are* brainier, it is highly unlikely that extreme intelligence would flourish particularly where wealth flourishes (which you would imagine given the economic profile of children at grammar schools and elite universities). Moreover, it is an unhelpful line to pursue. If we as teachers believe intelligence is fixed, we might as well all go home now and let nature and families take their course.

We teach, surely, because we believe we *can* help to make that difference; we can help to unlock intelligence and grow it. It is there, we just need to help it to shine.

Results aren't everything

But does it even matter if some children don't do well academically? Some of the best people I know have few or no academic qualifications; some of the *smartest* people I know did poorly in school and went on to have great careers. Some of the best people in the world are unqualified – if we learned anything from the recent Coronavirus lockdown period, it was to appreciate the shelf-stackers, hospital cleaners and rubbish collectors, who were exposed as the heroes they truly are, going into work in the hardest of conditions with a patient smile for the rest of us and making our lives so much better.

Of course results aren't everything. Of course you can be successful without results. Of course you should measure success in other terms. Of course it is more important to be a good person than to be well qualified.

The thing is, that's not really the business of schools.

Ultimately, practically all parents are capable of bringing their children up and helping to form their character and morality. Practically no parents have the capacity or capability to teach their children to a GCSE standard across nine or more subjects. While schools have an undeniable role to play in supporting parents in their work – and we will go into much more detail on this later – their chief role is to teach children subjects.

In a very real way, children deserve results. Children and parents are our stakeholders as schools, and I can imagine the result if we told parents: 'your child didn't get any GCSEs, but he's a really happy person so we think we've done a great job'.

Results are not enough – no. But great results open doors for the future. Those who believe otherwise might have always found such doors open to them.[7] Those with no qualifications but strong social networks may well find life equally as easy. But for those of you who know personally people who, while capable and brilliant, cannot find jobs they actually like, you know the story is different. The labour market is a crueller place than many of us ever have the misfortune of finding out. I think one of the stories I found most sad was of an acquaintance who had applied for hundreds of jobs and had been rejected, saying: 'I'd love to have a job. I'd love to do the checkouts at Tesco.'

Great results open doors, which means you have choices open to you. Teachers, by virtue of the bar of entry to this profession, all do have such choices: with a degree and experience in a professional field, if we were to decide teaching was not for us, we are safe in the knowledge we can do something else. Not everyone has such options. The ability to leave a job you hate is one we all take for granted, but it is a freedom I would wish for any human on this earth. As teachers across the country tell children everywhere: you're likely to be working for fifty years. Make sure you're doing something you like in those fifty years.

There are, of course, plenty of people whose educational trajectories are less straightforward. There are those who work between school and university – saving money, discovering options, living their lives. In university, I worked a number of part-time jobs, and was interested to hear from more than one New Zealander during this time that is was 'unusual' in their circle to go straight from school to university; they, and all their friends, were spending three to five years working and travelling around Europe before they planned to head home and 'start their proper lives'.

There is no greater exemplification, though, of the limitations of a life without choices than Willy Russell's *Educating Rita*. Russell himself left school early, going straight into hairdressing, and returning much later to go to college and then qualify as a teacher. Much of Russell's body of work explores class conflict and educational assumptions.

In *Educating Rita*, we meet Rita, a hairdresser, who has decided later on than might be traditional to go to university to complete a degree in English literature. When Rita reflects on her life and its limitations, she speaks some profound words on educational disadvantage as she seeks to find a new, intellectual life to fulfil her, as she describes her response to her mother's crying words: '"There must be better songs to sing than this." And I thought, "Yeah, that's what I'm trying to do, isn't it? Sing a better song."'[8]

Choice is the critical thing. I will never forget the meeting I had with a student and their parent: the student did no work and I had to harangue him lesson after lesson to pick up a pen. He had serious doubts in his ability, and my initial diagnosis was that he was in need of a goal to motivate him, as well as some reassurance to increase his self-belief. In the meeting, I rolled out a line I had used with success in previous meetings with other families: 'What do you dream of doing after school?'

Without even a moment's hesitation, he replied with just a single word: 'builder'. It threw me.

I tried again. 'But what do you *dream* of? You know, when you're thinking *big* about your life and what would make you most happy?'

Honestly, I would even have taken the dare-to-dream 'footballer' at that point, but the student simply looked me in the eye, nodded, and said: 'builder' again.

Maybe he really did dream of being a builder. He certainly looked up to his father, and craved his approval. His father was, he shared with me later in that meeting, a builder: 'and there's nothing wrong with that'. I was suitably chastised.

There is nothing wrong with that, if that is what you choose and if it is a genuine choice.

In Kiley Reid's novel *Such a Fun Age*, she provides a nuanced depiction of a university graduate working as a nanny for a small child. The central character, Emira, adores her charge and loves her work, but has complex feelings towards her employer, and worries constantly that she is not fulfilling her potential in the way her university educated peers are.

The ending of this character's work life fascinated me. She takes on an assistant role to a high-ranking government official, and deeply enjoys this work. She resists her employer's urging to move up the career ladder; she rejects opportunities to progress her career. This woman, with her intelligence and competence and care and university degree, inspired me with her devotion to a job she genuinely loved. When her boss, Paula, tries to talk to Emira about how she sees her career developing, Emira says: 'I actually think I'm okay', and the author follows up on this:

> maybe she wasn't by her girlfriends' standards ... but Emira really *was* doing okay. She'd gone to Mexico for Zara's birthday, all five days ... She had a savings account, which she dipped into often, but not so much that it didn't exist ... Her boss was fairly rude to everyone except for her, and Emira went to work feeling paid and protected ... She would stay on as Paula's assistant until Paula retired.[9]

Would that we all felt so content we never left, never looked for more or different or better.

There are many differences between these two interactions, not least that one is fictional. What I dream of for my students is that they make genuine choices. When I was about thirteen years old, my English teacher, whose word I came to see as gospel, asked me what I wanted to do for a career. I was the daughter of two people who had not pursued academics, who had left school at sixteen and joined the army, who had struggled to make ends meet and struggled to find jobs they enjoyed. My parents' social circle, like most people's, was made up of people just like them. I searched my mind far and wide for jobs of grown-ups I could possibly want to do, and came up with: 'I'd like to be a hairdresser.'

My teacher's response? 'Don't be so stupid.' And off he walked.

Some might call this harsh, but for me it was a turning point. The shame I felt was galvanizing. I was choosing the wrong path, and there was a right answer if I could only find it.

For children without a history of tertiary education in their families, the very prospect of university is terrifying: expensive and unknown. Looking around at friends and family, many of whom seem content and all of whom are socially accepted, it is natural for children to 'prefer' this way of life – after all, adolescents want few things more than to fit in. For such children, university represents the unknown – where will their place be in their families when they come back?

I too shared those anxieties. When I came back from university during the holidays (which, I'm sorry to say, was extremely rare – I tended to see the holidays as a chance to pick up extra shifts in each of the jobs I had to fund me through the process), I felt out of place. I talked at length about my part-time jobs, and not at all about university. (Also, I studied English, and it's hard to make people take: 'I read some books about imaginary people and things and write essays about them' very seriously.)

The reality is, these anxieties were created by me and existed in my mind. With time (and wine), each of my family members have said something along the lines of: 'we're so proud of you', without any hint that I'd betrayed anyone, and without any feeling that I was somehow superior to them now I had some fancy letters I could stick after my name if I wanted to be a real numpty. Indeed, no one acted as if anyone was better than anyone else – that's the beauty of family.

Regardless of whether such supportive families are the norm, I tell this story to illustrate that even with the greatest, most supportive families, children themselves can convince themselves that university is not for them. Occasionally, and in the very worst circumstances, they are aided in this delusion by professionals: I was advised to apply to only 'universities in the north' because 'it's cheaper to live there' (I'm from Suffolk, and the furthest north I'd ever been was Lincoln, so this seemed beyond comprehension to my geographically limited mind). The great Michelle Obama was told by a guidance counsellor in school that 'I'm not sure that you're Princeton material.'[10]

It is the job of everyone around our children to emphasise that they *can* go to university, and that they *should* go to university, because often we are arguing against inner demons. The reality is, university graduates earn more over a lifetime and have access to a wider range of jobs. This means university graduates have more choices and easier lives. Many children will resist university because it goes against their perception of their tribe. We have to make university non-threatening. But we also have to make it a real possibility for every child.

King Solomon Academy: the school that can

I trained to teach with Teach First in 2010, and I will always consider that to have been a fortunate year because of one two-hour, voluntary session held in a lecture hall at Warwick University. In that session, a principal named Max Haimendorf introduced the pupils of King Solomon Academy (KSA) to us, and explained what his school stood for.

Looking back, it is clear to me that this was a defining moment in education. Schools like KSA simply did not exist back in 2010 in the UK. It's hard, now some of us have visited and worked at the many, many trailblazing schools that followed in its wake, to remember a time when no children in England did 'two claps on three' and chanted 'you've got to read, people read.' Back when schools were just schools – they didn't grow from nothing; they occasionally changed their name or tragically closed – but that was that.

In 2010, as KSA's founding cohort were finishing their first year, the simplicity and scope of Max's vision was ground-breaking: if 97% of privately educated children go to university, why not 97% of the children we serve? If we accept 97% as a benchmark, why not make it 100%? At that time, only 16% of children in receipt of free school meals were going on to university. The contrast of these figures could not be more stark.

That session in 2010 marked the first time someone had put it to me in those terms. I honestly think before that moment I had somewhere thought that some children were smart, and some children were not, and schools had to do the best they could with that. Max and his team's beliefs completely changed mine.

What is so humbling about the KSA story is its sustained excellence. That first cohort of children came out with stunning results – 93% of children gained five GCSEs at A*–C including English and Maths. But as the years have gone on, the school has continued to wildly exceed expectations, and put its children on a path to university and genuine life choices: in six years of GCSE results, five of the cohorts have achieved progress in the top 1% of all schools in the UK.

I've been privileged to visit the original dream school many times since that day, and every time I've felt moved by what that team does – day in, day out. The belief and the vision are strong as ever; the behaviour and the respect for adults from the children is clear; the copious amounts of work in every lesson and the focus on an academic core of subjects are still strong. After 10 years the results are still impressive. And after 10 years, Max is still there. In a sector where people often move on rapidly, or see success as running many schools over a career, to stay with the ever changing and ever challenging school you first founded seems to me the most admirable choice one could make, and illustrates the total commitment to mission that founded the school in the first place.

I remember leaving that meeting in 2010 buoyed with the infectious enthusiasm of the KSA team. I remember my shock that not all my Teach First colleagues felt the same.

'The clapping was weird.' 'I didn't like the chanting.' 'I don't think they're right – university isn't for everyone.'

The clapping is weird. So is the chanting. But for me it is weird in the way Shakespeare is weird: it creates a new world –one of endless possibility.

School is, at its heart, a place for reinvention. School is the place where children come, independent of their families and their backgrounds – they leave whatever home they have come from, and whatever troubles or issues might be present there, and they sit side by side with their peers and learn from the same teacher. At school, a child can be anything they want to be.

KSA taught me that the job of a school is to believe the impossible is possible, and to know that getting there will look different and feel, at times, different or even uncomfortable. The promise of university necessitates difficult choices on curriculum, on pedagogy and on ethos. But for the schools that make that promise, the results are extraordinary.

How do we get them there though?

It's easy to say 'we want everyone to go to university.' It is harder to make this happen. There are tough choices to make on the curriculum. If you want university to be a viable option, what do you do with the children who arrive in year 7 with a reading age of 6? What do you do with the children who are flummoxed by even basic Maths?

For parents of children who struggle continually in school, it is only natural to begin to think: it's *not* possible. It was possible, but now it isn't. I have much sympathy with this view; indeed, one of my most revisited metaphors when I give assembly is life as a long corridor. When I speak to year 7 and year 8 students, I explain that all the doors are open – if they work hard, they can go through any of them. Their actions and their choices, however, begin to close doors. For some children, choosing to not complete homework and not focus in lessons in year 7 will close the Oxbridge door: they simply have too much ground to cover to get to the top 1% of students in the country by age 18. But for almost everyone in year 7 and most of year 8, every option is open to them. If we're honest and say: you could get there, but you'd need to do an hour and a half of extra homework a night – what would they say?

Most children would say: no. I wouldn't tell this to children – I would tell this to their parents. The most important thing we can do for those who are most behind is to be honest with families about what it would take for them to catch up, and then allow the families to make that choice. Parenting is hard enough without having to start monitoring homework that is above and beyond their peers, and some families may well decide: this isn't for me. But we owe it to families to be brutally honest on this, and say that very few children will choose pain in the short term for a long term payoff.

Children and marshmallows

The marshmallow test, whereby small children are put in a room with a marshmallow and told to not eat it, and told that if they comply they will receive two marshmallows, is not without its critics.[11] The test, if not one to illustrate scientific determinism, remains a helpful metaphor to explain student attitudes, and reveals familiar attitudes to most school teachers.

Telling children that they will get more later if they can only hold out on the fun stuff now is the essence of the teacher's job. We ask children to forego playing with friends, watching television, playing video games and the other things that are intrinsically 'fun', and to instead come, every day, to a place where they must go from classroom to classroom at pre-organised times, and learn subjects – most of which have no correlation to their current lives or interests, and some of which they find uninteresting and unimportant. We tell them that though this fifty-minute lesson on fractions might seem abstract, boring and difficult, it is important, because eventually (in three or four years' time) they will need to take a GCSE in maths, and success in that GCSE will determine the course of the rest of their lives.

It's a tough sell. Children, most children, live moment to moment. Many children find it hard to think long-term. They get better at this deferred gratification as they get older – those of you with very small children will know this to be the case – but it is imperfect by secondary school age. Some teachers would argue that success should be its own reward. That is logically true, but very hard to make work with young people. External rewards, particularly with younger children, are important to begin to cue positive behaviours and curb negative ones. The closer these can be linked to the event itself, the better. (I remember working at a school that instituted a weekly detention; the children in that detention were almost always a bit confused as to why they were there.)

Impact every day

But rewards and sanctions are extrinsic rewards. What builds pupils' buy-in to a school's culture is not generally whether they tend to get merits or detentions, though this helps. If we want pupils to have belief that they are on the path to academic success, they need to feel this every day.

The impact of repeated failure is well documented: in the seminal 2014 publication *What Makes Great Teaching?*, Coe et al. write: 'the poor motivation of low-attaining students is a logical response to repeated failure'.[12] Knowledge-rich teaching fulfils this need for success beautifully. Skills are improved incrementally and the road to greatness can be frustrating (as anyone who has learned to go running will attest to – three years of running the same track around my local path sees me only thirty seconds a minute faster than when I began – and I began *slow*); it is very hard to see an improvement over time for students, and not motivating in the immediate term.

A very long time ago I raised the issue that my children didn't feel successful with a trusted colleague. 'It's hard at secondary,' she told me then. 'In primary, you can't read and then one day you can. That's clear. But secondary … They just get a bit better at reading.'

We can build student motivation and confidence if we teach knowledge explicitly: in all subjects, we can mimic this impact: they didn't know something, and now they do. When, instead of planning our lessons around 'read some things, write some things, talk about some things' we begin to introduce: here is the new knowledge I will teach you and here is how I will check you have learned it, we make concrete something that usually feels quite abstract for children.

The first step is identifying the core knowledge you want to teach in each lesson.[13] Then it is a case of ensuring your pedagogy matches your purpose. There is no greater driver of student motivation than frequent, low-stakes quizzes that they do well in. Testing student knowledge frequently has the dual benefit of helping the knowledge to stick (the act of retrieving previously learned knowledge strengthens the neural pathways and so ensures we remember things for the long term)[14] and ensuring students have something concrete to hang their self-perception on. It is hard for students to feel 'stupid' or 'a failure' when they normally get 8 out of 10 in a quiz, and the things they got wrong they begin to get right in future lessons.

I say 8 out of 10 as a guide, influenced by Rosenshine's principles:

The research also suggests that the optimal success rate for fostering student achievement appears to be about 80 percent. A success rate of 80 percent shows that students are learning the material, and it also shows that the students are challenged.[15]

I tend to make quizzes shorter in my lessons, opting for five questions, with the aim that most children can get four right. Beginning every lesson with a mixed recap of five questions and then going on to an in-unit recap of five questions is transformative for student self-perception. They mark their own quizzes quickly, you narrate that learning is about making mistakes, and then you say: 'who got five out of five? Four out of five? Less?' Watch the hands in the air and edit your questioning accordingly.

To those who argue that making our quizzes easier is depriving children of difficult knowledge, I have massive sympathy. Of course we need all our children to be tackling the tough stuff, and it is wrong to keep using 'Mickey Mouse' questions with our weakest children for the sake of their egos. Yet knowing the date Charles Dickens wrote *Oliver Twist* or the date that World War I began and ended or the number of degrees in a right angle are within the capabilities of all children, and far from 'dumbed down' knowledge. By breaking down what children need to know into these tiny components, teaching them well and testing them frequently, children can begin to build a schema of understanding to enable them to access subjects at a higher level. These isolated facts are not the end of the story, but they are a necessary foundation on which to build.

Indeed, in the absence of knowledge-led teaching, a sense of accomplishment in children is hard to inculcate. Children would enter and leave my room in the first years of my teaching career having practised a lot of reading and writing (and a *lot* of talking), but would sometimes say things like: 'I don't feel like I'm learning anything' or 'what are we learning today?' The truth was, I had swallowed the orthodoxy of my teacher training unquestioningly. I was that teacher who said: 'I learn more from my students than they learn from me,' and it was true, because my students taught me who the 'cool' rappers were and I asked them what they thought things might mean and assured them 'you already know the answer!' when trying to unpick complex poetry (spoiler: they did not).

Knowledge-led teaching, while of course incorporating plenty of exploration and self-expression as is fitting to different degrees in subjects like art and English, ensures children have the satisfaction of adding to their bank of knowledge each lesson. They have genuinely missed out when they miss a day of school; it is clear what they need to catch up on because we have expressed this clearly and concretely.

Gratitude

Happy people are grateful people. Yet the correlation between these two poles is often mistaken. It would make logical sense that people who have more – more things, better jobs, more choices – would be more grateful for all that bounty. Yet this is not what research suggests. Indeed, the suggestion is that it is the precise opposite: the practice of gratitude is what makes you happy:

> In positive psychology research, gratitude is strongly and consistently associated with greater happiness. Gratitude helps people feel more positive emotions, relish good experiences, improve their health, deal with adversity, and build strong relationships ... Two psychologists, Dr Robert A. Emmons of the University of California, Davis, and Dr Michael E. McCullough of the University of Miami, have done much of the research on gratitude. In one study, they asked all participants to write a few sentences each week, focusing on particular topics.
>
> One group wrote about things they were grateful for that had occurred during the week. A second group wrote about daily irritations or things that had displeased them, and the third wrote about events that had affected them (with no emphasis on them being positive or negative). After 10 weeks, those who wrote about gratitude were more optimistic and felt better about their lives. Surprisingly, they also exercised more and had fewer visits to physicians than those who focused on sources of aggravation.
>
> Another leading researcher in this field, Dr Martin E. P. Seligman, a psychologist at the University of Pennsylvania, tested the impact of various positive psychology interventions on 411 people, each compared with a control assignment of writing about early memories. When their week's assignment was to write and personally deliver a letter of gratitude to someone who had never been properly thanked for his or her kindness, participants immediately exhibited a huge increase in happiness scores. This impact was greater than that from any other intervention, with benefits lasting for a month.[16]

Our modern culture has embraced this notion in its typical 'life hack' way: there are no shortage of people keeping 'gratitude journals' where they write down things they are grateful for each day. Some families even take on the American practice of thanksgiving all year round.[17] It is a short leap to transfer this to our schools.

I trained with Teach First, a charity that places graduates in schools it determines to be 'challenging', which occasionally means they get terrible results, but which usually means they get terrible results and are full of children from 'disadvantaged backgrounds', which means they are deprived. Much of the training focused on this level of deprivation. In particular, I recall being made to watch a documentary which followed two children living in an estate in the north of the country, and being moved to tears by the total lack of books, paper or writing implements in their home.

When I reached my South London school which served a deprived intake, I too found children without pens and paper or any means with which to take part in my lesson, and made the assumption that their homes were as bleak as these boys'.

But when non-uniform day arrived, I couldn't help but notice those same pen-less children wearing extremely expensive trainers.

Poverty is complex these days. Laura McInerney describes this wonderfully in a 2012 post entitled 'Things Rich People Never Understand':

> Okay wealthy-people-wearing-real-Ralph-Lauren, listen up. There are five ways this happens: (1) The designer gear is fake – quite likely, (2) The designer gear was acquired from 'the back of a lorry or a pub' – medium likely, (3) The clothing was bought by a parent who gave up eating for a week in order that their child wouldn't be the only one in the local area laughed at for not wearing designer clothes – happens more than you think, (4) They were bought before the person lost their job or bought with the money they got in redundancy – again, happens more than you think, (5) They are real and were bought at full price while on benefits – true about 5% of the time.[18]

There are several competing realities at play here. Many families struggle financially, that is true. Schools have a duty to ensure anything they make parents buy is (a) essential and (b) inexpensive: uniform, equipment and school lunches should be as cheap as they can be without compromising quality. A Bic biro costs 50 pence, for example. It seems reasonable to me that we should expect every child to have their own.

Even for the very poorest nations in the world, gratitude is the best route to leading a meaningful life. An influential 2014 study on happiness reported in *The New Yorker* noted:

> The first result replicated plenty of earlier research: people from wealthier countries were generally happier than those from poorer countries. To reach an average life-satisfaction score of four out of ten, people needed to earn about seven hundred dollars a year; for a score of five, they needed to earn an average of three thousand dollars per year; for a score of six, they needed to earn an average of sixteen thousand dollars per year; and to score seven they needed to earn an average of sixty-four thousand dollars a year. But if wealth fostered happiness, it appeared to drain meaningfulness. Between ninety-five and a hundred per cent of the respondents from poverty-stricken Sierra Leone, Togo, Kyrgyzstan, Chad, and Ethiopia reported leading meaningful lives. Only two-thirds of the respondents in Japan, France, and Spain believed their lives had meaning.[19]

A long time ago, I worked in a church school which served an incredibly deprived community. Every week, as a form tutor, I would have to do something called 'Mission Collection'. Having been raised outside religion, this was new to me, so I will explain it for the equally uninitiated. We were given a small cotton pouch and a slip of paper inside it. The paper would contain a few sentences about the charity we would be donating to that week. The pouch would then be passed around the classroom and the children would donate to it, if they could.

I felt uncomfortable at the time – deeply uncomfortable. How Claire would donate £1 every single week, no matter what the cause; how many would pass it on looking guilty and sad. How one girl's mum gave her money for the collection, but she would put one and two pence pieces into the bag, and I knew that was not the money she had been given for that purpose. I wondered if I might have done the same when I was twelve and in possession of a surprise pound coin.

Once the money was in, a volunteer would count it up and write the amount on the slip of paper. We would celebrate if we reached £3, which was probably our maximum. If Claire was absent we would struggle to reach £2, and once we weren't even on £1 and I pleaded with the class who searched their pockets and added more coppers to the mix, but felt horribly guilty and from then on ensured I kept a stack of coins in the classroom to supplement the collection each week, and felt angry with myself for not thinking of doing this before. Surely I, the teacher, should have been contributing the bulk of the collection.

But looking back, I wonder if that was the point. Indeed, a small church school serving a deprived community would not be the difference between a small charity existing and helping others and not. The value of mission collection was not, in fact, about raising money in and of itself. It was a lesson in the value and habit of charity. In making it normal each and every week to comb your pockets looking for coins to give away to others, the school repeatedly sent the message that others are worse off than you, and you can help them. No matter how grim your own family circumstances, things were never so bad that you couldn't put 2p into a pouch and feel like you had that power to make others' lives better. The habit of giving instilled, we hoped, over seven years, when our children flourished and found gainful employment, they would carry on that habit.

Looking back, I am ashamed I was so ashamed to ask the children for money. By the end of my time there, I barely looked at the amount; I would never beat the drum to encourage them to give more. I think that was a disservice to their experience of the world at that young age as a place they could make better.

Instilling the habit of gratitude

No matter how little you have, being grateful makes you happier. Counting every blessing you can does not alert people to the little they have, but to the abundance. Indeed, it is not a surfeit of things that makes any of us happy, no matter what advertisers would have us believe.

But it is hard to be grateful. The mind is drawn to darkness; that is why we find it hard to remember happy memories but somehow can't forget that time two years ago we embarrassed ourselves in front of a total stranger who has definitely forgotten all about it, if they even noticed in the first place. We spend so much of our time contemplating what we do not have and how we could get it, even though this makes us more unhappy.

If we went through every day noticing the great things in our lives (warm house! Warm water running for the shower! Hot coffee in my mouth! Tiny device that connects me to everyone I know and love, and the rest of the world! So many amazing things, and we haven't even left the house yet), we would surely be happier?

If adults could benefit from upping their gratitude, children certainly can as well. Luckily for children, they have far more malleable minds, and we can turn them towards gratitude early and start a life-long habit of being grateful.

Gratitude is even more important in a school setting, because it is easy for children to resent school for any number of reasons. School means they have to get up early, put on clothes they normally hate which make them look like everyone else, sit inside on warm days doing maths instead of playing video games. It is all too easy for children to focus on the negative and think they 'hate school'.

By making schools places of gratitude, we can make them much happier places to be.

It starts with modelling gratitude. Teachers can also slip into negative mindsets, particularly around certain classes. Instead, we need to keep in mind how lucky we are to do this, a job we have, after all, chosen. At Oasis Academy Southbank, every Friday morning staff gather for a free breakfast in the staff room and write one another gratitude postcards, building staff morale and making the school a happy place to work.

We need to weave in opportunities for gratitude frequently to make it a habit. Just as staff write their cards each week, schools can institute this practice for students. One school I worked at gave over two tutor time sessions each half term for students to write thank you cards to their teachers. Tutors would then disseminate the cards in teachers' pigeonholes, and an informal practice of teachers sitting in the staff room reading their cards to one another grew.

At the end of every lesson, how many children thank you for their lesson? Of course, it is wonderful when children give their thanks spontaneously – but many will simply not yet be in the habit of doing this. By instituting it as a habit in the early years of school, this makes those spontaneous and genuine thanks more likely in the later years. One colleague I worked with likened this to when you say to your toddler: 'say please' and the toddler says 'please' in that way that suggests that they have no idea what they are saying. Of course, it is meaningless to parrot the word at that point in time, but we might see this as a necessary hurdle on the route to genuine gratefulness. Standing at the door of your classroom and thanking your students is a good way to model what you expect to see back, but this is best enforced by a whole-school approach where form tutors and heads of year are continually narrating the need to 'thank your teachers after the lesson!'

Tutor time is a great opportunity to give gratitude. Asking students to think about who they are grateful to at home and at school every week makes them in the habit of looking for people to thank. Take care, however, that students do not use this as an opportunity to reinforce friendships and groups of friends. Schools can be lonely places, and while students thanking other students for *specific acts of kindness* is heart-warming and positive, students thanking students 'for being my friend' can have adverse consequences. Friendship circles are ever shifting and changing, and anyone who watches teen dramas or reads young adult fiction will be readily reminded of just how difficult it is to know who your friends are at any one time as a teenager. Gratitude cannot be 'just because': 'thanks to Mel, because I like her' is less sincere than 'thank you to Mel, who noticed I was really struggling to put all my things in my bag, and came and held my bag open so I could do it easily.'

Schools like King Solomon Academy in London and Dixons Trinity Academy in Bradford make gratitude part of set-piece events in the school day. At the end of lunch time, students have an opportunity to stand up in front of their whole peer group and say who they are grateful to and why. This is impressive for visitors, but it does not happen spontaneously. Students are encouraged to script their thanks and practise them with form tutors. This supports shy students with their oracy, but also ensures the gratitude is built on acts of kindness rather than the fickle search for popularity with the 'in group'.

While for many schools, having a silent dining hall for five minutes where every child is present to listen to such expressions of gratitude is logistically impossible, almost every school in the country assembles children at least as a year group at least once a week. Having the opportunity for two or three children to give their thanks at the end of an assembly is great for their public speaking experience and self-confidence, and also serves as another opportunity to be grateful. A word of caution: if you start doing this, begin with younger year groups. Students in years 7 and 8 are far more likely to be willing to do brave things like stand in front of their peers and say thank you.

Service

Many schools incorporate community service or citizenship into the fabric of their school to great effect. But service doesn't have to mean big, one-off showcase events. In fact, it shouldn't. By their very nature, ticking a 'service' box by sending ten of your best year 9s to the local care home to chat with the elderly once, while hugely beneficial for those students and those care home residents at that moment in time, does not impact every student.

We have to think broad and small: all students benefit from acts of service. In *The Power of Meaning*, Emily Esfahani Smith says: 'those who choose to pursue meaning ultimately live fuller – and happier – lives... they evaluate their lives as significant and worthwhile – as part of something bigger; they believe their lives make sense; and they feel their lives are driven by a sense of purpose.'[20]

Connected to this is a well-known trope of psychotherapy: turning one's attention outside, rather than inside. When we feel unhappy, what is better – to sit around in our pyjamas thinking about how bad things are, or to call up a friend who is struggling and help them through *their* problems?

With some notable exceptions (in times of severe grief or trauma, you probably aren't the best person to talk someone else down from the edge), it is almost always better to turn your attention to helping others rather than focusing on yourself. The same is true for our young people, who are (if we remember our own adolescence) sometimes struggling to find meaning. What is their place in the world? What role do they play? Our children live their lives under high levels of control: they can't choose where they live or where they go to school; they can't choose what they eat for dinner or where they go on holiday. Children, more than adults, are working out who they are in a world which feels both very small and alarmingly large.

Children are, understandably, often unhappy. If schools can facilitate acts of service with *all* children, at least some of the time, we can lend them an insight into purpose. To do that means thinking small.

Indeed, the conclusion Esfahani Smith comes to in *The Power of Meaning* is that finding meaning is not a great enlightening:

> purpose sounds big – ending world hunger big or eliminating nuclear weapons big. But it doesn't have to be. You can also find purpose in being a good parent to your children, creating a more cheerful environment at your office, or making a giraffe's life more pleasant ... That's the power of meaning. It's not some great revelation. It's pausing to say hi to a newspaper vendor and reaching out to someone at work who seems down. It's taking care of a plant. These may be humble acts on their own. But taken together, they light up the world.[21]

If we think about how every child can contribute something, we can begin to build service into our schools in a meaningful way for *all* children. Giving thanks in big group events is a small way every child can contribute something meaningful which is based on others. Writing a thank you postcard to a teacher every couple of weeks boosts their habit of gratitude. Having four or five class monitors who rotate around the class all year means everyone has the responsibility to help make the classroom work well. Narrating the importance of speaking to people who seem to be alone on the playground, and positively reinforcing this behaviour through assemblies or shout-outs helps to make the school community a welcoming one. In some schools, every student tours visitors around at least once in the year when they are in year 8, giving them a small opportunity to give back to the school community. Other schools use drop-down days for community service instead of trips, and organise for every child to take part in an aspect of making the community a better place.

By building in acts of kindness and gratitude into the fabric of the school, we can help children begin to find meaning in their lives, a piece of work they will spend the rest of their lives working on.

Take-aways

- We can't make children happy, but we can help them lead lives of fulfilment.

- Academic success is important, and we do our pupils a disservice if we pretend it isn't.

- Schools should make university a genuine option for every child.

- We build student motivation by making pupils feel successful.

- Gratitude makes people happy: build opportunities for gratitude into the school day.

- Service – the act of doing something for others – is empowering and fulfilling, so build opportunities for service into school life.

Notes

1 In 2018 the BBC reported: 'On average 2.6% of grammar school children received free school meals compared with 13.4% of children across all state secondary schools, according to the latest school census' (retrieved from www.bbc.co.uk/news/uk-44081733#:~:-text=On%20average%202.6%25%20of%20grammar,exam%20results%20are%20comparably%20good, accessed 1 August 2020).

2 Amy Chua, *Battle Hymn of the Tiger Mother* (Bloomsbury, 2011), p. 18.

3 Ibid., p. 52.

4 *Grammar School Statistics*, Commons Research Briefing, January 2020, retrieved from https://commonslibrary.parliament.uk/research-briefings/sn01398 (accessed 8 May 2020), p. 12.

5 There is no shortage of commentary on this argument. Here are a selection of commentators arguing that charitable status should be removed from private schools: www.civilsociety.co.uk/voices/john-tizard-private-schools-charitable-status-is-neither-in-public-interest-nor-that-of-other-charities.html; www.theguardian.com/commentisfree/2018/aug/16/private-schools-charitable-status-strip-benefits; https://schoolsweek.co.uk/private-schools-need-phasing-out-and-heres-how-it-can-be-done (all accessed 1 August 2020).

6 Again, this is well documented. See the following selection of articles: www.theguardian.com/money/2015/sep/20/parents-paid-thousands-live-near-better-schools; www.independent.co.uk/money/spend-save/uk-parents-move-house-school-catchment-area-quarter-best-education-a7908046.html; www.thisismoney.co.uk/money/mortgageshome/article-7873857/Five-tricks-parents-use-kids-school-risks.html (all accessed 1 August 2020).

7 I was struck by a quotation when reading Deborah Frances-White, *The Guilty Feminist* (Virago, 2019), p. 81, that 'we only notice the doors that are closed to us and not the ones that are open to us'.

8 *Educating Rita*, directed by Lewis Gilbert, screenplay by Willy Russell, 1983.

9 Kiley Reid, *Such a Fun Age* (Putnam, 2019), pp. 301–302.

10 Michelle Obama, *Becoming* (Penguin, 2018), p. 66.

11 A 2018 study (https://journals.sagepub.com/doi/abs/10.1177/0956797618761661, accessed 2 August 2020) commented that the original sample size was too small to draw significant conclusions. *The Atlantic* reported: 'In restaging the experiment, Watts and his colleagues thus adjusted the experimental design in important ways: The researchers used a sample that was much larger – more than 900 children – and also more representative of the general population in terms of race, ethnicity, and parents' education. The researchers also, when analyzing their test's results, controlled for certain factors – such as the income of a child's household – that might explain children's ability to delay gratification and their long-term success. Ultimately, the new study finds limited support for the idea that being able to delay gratification leads to better outcomes. Instead, it suggests that the capacity to hold out for a second marshmallow is shaped in large part by a child's social and economic background – and, in turn, that that background, not the ability to delay gratification, is what's behind kids' long-term success' (retrieved from www.theatlantic.com/family/archive/2018/06/marshmallow-test/561779, accessed 2 August 2020).

12 Robert Coe, Cesare Aloisi, Steve Higgins and Lee Elliot Major, *What Makes Great Teaching?*, retrieved from www.suttontrust.com/wp-content/uploads/2014/10/What-Makes-Great-Teaching-REPORT.pdf, accessed 20 March 2020), p. 23.

13 I discuss this in much greater depth in Jo Facer, *Simplicity Rules* (Routledge, 2019), pp. 66–74.

14 The finest exploration of the science of memory and its application in the classroom is to be found in Peter C. Brown, Henry L. Roediger III and Mark A. McDaniel, *Make it Stick* (Harvard University Press, 2014).

15 Barak Rosenshine, 'Principles of Instruction', *American Educator* (Spring 2012), retrieved from www.aft.org/sites/default/files/periodicals/Rosenshine.pdf (accessed 2 August 2020), p. 6.

16 Retrieved from www.health.harvard.edu/healthbeat/giving-thanks-can-make-you-happier (accessed 2 August 2020).

17 In Sheryl Sandberg, *Option B* (Alfred A. Knopf, 2017), p. 25, she writes: 'Dave [her late husband] and I had a family ritual at dinner where we'd go around the table with our daughter and son and take turns stating our best and worst moments of the day. When it because just the three of us, I added a third category. Now we each share something for which we are grateful.'

18 Retrieved from https://lauramcinerney.com/things-rich-people-never-understand (accessed 23 March 2020).

19 Retrieved from www.newyorker.com/business/currency/do-the-poor-have-more-meaningful-lives (accessed 2 August 2020).

20 Emily Esfahani Smith, *The Power of Meaning* (Ebury Digital, 2017), loc. 248.

21 Ibid., loc. 1149, 3278.

How can we help children cope with negativity?

When we think about teenagers, we think about that archetype of a teenager, Holden Caulfield. The character typifies the kind of angst and cynicism we quite often find in today's teenagers:

> If you really want to hear about it, the first thing you'll probably want to know is where I was born, and what my lousy childhood was like, and how my parents were occupied and all before they had me, and all that David Copperfield kind of crap, but I don't feel like going into it, if you want to know the truth.[1]

When I turned the first pages of *Catcher in the Rye*, I was fifteen years old. I did not stop turning pages until I finished, and it was the first book I read cover to cover in a single sitting. Finally, I remember thinking, a book that *gets* me.

I am very glad I did not have to put up with teenage me.

Like Holden, there was nothing very much wrong with my life when I was fifteen years old, in that I had two parents who loved me and treated me well, I lived in a warm house, I went to a lovely school where teachers cared about my progress and worked hard to give me help above and beyond what they were expected to do. And yet, I related to that teen angst vividly.

Adolescence is hard, and it has probably always been hard. Children are finding their place in the world, and, what is more urgent, their place in the social hierarchy of their friendship groups. Exclusion from a single trip to the cinema or ejection from the lunch table can lead to what any sensible grown up might describe as extreme reactions.

Coupled with this knowledge that growing up has always been tough, however, is a new preoccupation with social media. For all the columnists who tell us that social media doesn't have *that* much of an impact on us,[2] this just isn't reflected even in our own experiences. I've lost count of the number of friends who have deleted their presence on social media for their own mental health and balance. Likewise, I could not count the hours I have wasted away looking at pretty photographs of other people's cats. What a way to spend the fleeting time we have on this earth.

 DOI: 10.4324/9781003097075-8

Social media has, in the eleven years I have worked in schools, exploded our pastoral worlds. When I began teaching, most teachers used Facebook and most children didn't; some teachers had smartphones, but many (including me) didn't; no children I taught did. Today, it is a rare secondary school student who doesn't have a presence across three or four platforms, which they carry on their mobile devices on their person at all times. The bullying issues I have dealt with over the years have moved more and more into this online space. Where once, for those who most suffered at school, home could be a refuge; now they carry around that potential for harm at all times and there is no respite. (Of course, they could turn off their phones, but anyone who has spent even an hour in the company of a young person will understand just how unlikely that is.)

We can brush away this mental health crisis all we like as overblown nonsense, given that we live in a rich country at one of the richest points of its history, and are living through the longest major conflict-free period of human history.[3]

The reality is, the mental health of young people is a real and pressing concern for families and schools, and it probably should be:

> Children and young people's mental health continues to be a cause for concern at a time of reduced mental health service provision. Worryingly, suicide and self-harm rates continue to rise. An estimated two hundred children and young people lose their lives annually through completed suicide.[4]

For a small minority, adolescence is harder than for most. In my career, I can call to mind several children who have suffered more than seems fair in their short lives – children who have lost a parent, who are young carers, who live in hostels or refuges, who are fostered against their will and want to go back home, who face being deported for being illegal migrants. The children I have worked with respond to these heart-breaking crises in as wide a range of ways as you can imagine – some were so stoical I was surprised to hear what they had been through; others would fall apart daily and needed professional help urgently.

I am no specialist in mental health, and I don't pretend to be. For children coping with epic disaster, they can and should have access to mental health services which are trained to work with young people through such shocking times.

Schools cannot be expected to fix the complex issues listed above – we can only provide a safe place, an education to provide life chances, and a watchful eye to conduit necessary information and raise alarm bells with relevant authorities.

Yet we know from personal experience that we can fall apart as much from the big shocks of life's buffets as we can from something small. One of my closest and steeliest friends unexpectedly fell apart when their cat died, for example. Everyone was surprised, but it made sense in a way – we never know how we will rise or fall apart with different situations.

Moreover, as adults we know for a fact that no life will be lived without hardship – even those with the most loving families and comfortable existences will suffer pain and loss in life. The question is not, therefore, how can we shield children from pain, but how can we explicitly teach children to be able to cope with life's inevitable challenges?

The sheer volume of children who struggle in adolescence should probably not tell us that every child requires intensive support or counselling. In an ideal world, this would be marvellous; in a world of stretched resources, it is vital that the children most in need of specialist interventions can access them fast. As schools, we can play our role in helping the majority of students to understand how to cope with difficult times, so that those who really and truly are not coping can access that additional support through professional services.

In this chapter, we explore what such a blanket approach might look like in a school context.

Negative thoughts

Human minds are drawn to negativity. It is their very nature. When we wake up in the middle of the night unable to sleep, it is not our loved ones and happy memories that we think of. I am haunted by memories of a minor faux-pas I might have made a decade ago that in all likelihood barely registered with the other party.

Why do negative thoughts hold our attention so much more than positive thoughts? Why do we resist happiness when we have it, and fear its imminent departure? Why do we constantly plan for the worst-case scenario?

Partly this is the result of the negativity bias: negative experiences or influences, even when they are as intense as positive ones, are much more enduring in our minds.[5] This is evolutionary: humans needed to avoid risk more urgently than seek out pleasure.

It is clear, though, that seeking happiness is not the route to happiness. We think we can be happy if we get the next promotion or buy a house in a nice area, only to find that as soon as we have it, we want something else. Adolescents follow a similar pattern – obsessing over friendships and later boyfriends or girlfriends or the lack thereof; being certain the latest trainers will be not only a piece of fancy footwear to admire, but their ticket to social acceptance. We invest things with too much power, and are disappointed when they do not deliver the satisfaction we crave.

Johann Hari's *Lost Connections* explores some common cures for the negativity that can become overwhelming in all of our lives from time to time. Hari explores the connectedness and hope we can regain through meaningful work, connection with other people, connection with meaningful values, connection with childhood trauma (in order to deal with it appropriately), connection to status and respect, connection with nature and connection with a hopeful and secure future.[6]

But when negativity inevitably arises, what can we do? No matter how we orientate our lives towards these pillars of meaning, we cannot escape the reality of negative thoughts invading our minds. So much of what upsets all of us is not events in their reality, but our own minds. How often have we worked ourselves up thinking a friend is upset with us, when they just fell asleep before replying to the message we sent? Or when someone cancels at the last minute, how often do we reason 'something must have come up' rather than assuming we are not worth spending time with? Or when we mess up in work, how often do we think 'wow, I usually get things right, and this is unusual and no one will hold it against me' as opposed to 'I am such a complete idiot and will never get anything right again'. Dr Russ Harris writes:

> Thus, evolution has shaped our brains so that we are hardwired to suffer psychologically – to compare, evaluate, and criticise ourselves, to focus on what we're lacking, to rapidly become dissatisfied with what we have, and to imagine all sorts of frightening scenarios, most of which will never happen.[7]

Our minds are drama queens, even into respectable middle age. The minds of children are indisputably even more dramatic. Learning to understand and control our responses to negative thoughts is something worth teaching to everyone.

Cognitive behavioural therapy

The NHS describes cognitive behavioural therapy (CBT) in the following way:

> CBT aims to stop negative cycles such as these by breaking down things that make you feel bad, anxious or scared. By making your problems more manageable, CBT can help you change your negative thought patterns and improve the way you feel … You and your therapist will analyse your thoughts, feelings and behaviours to work out if they're unrealistic or unhelpful and to determine the effect they have on each other and on you. Your therapist will be able to help you work out how to change unhelpful thoughts and behaviours.
>
> After working out what you can change, your therapist will ask you to practise these changes in your daily life. This may involve: questioning upsetting thoughts and replacing them with more helpful ones; recognising when you're going to do something that will make you feel worse and instead doing something more helpful.[8]

The essence of CBT is to start changing the direction of your thoughts, and the way we experience thought. Underlying this is an assumption is that we can and should take charge of our thoughts: 'We can control and direct our thoughts, but it often feels like our thoughts have minds of their own, controlling us and how we feel.'[9] Furthermore, we reinforce our negative thoughts when we don't challenge them, instead accepting thoughts as they come as reality; as our identity. For therapists like Avy Joseph, we must challenge our natural proclivities and take charge of our minds: 'This is the principle of emotional responsibility: you are largely responsible for the way you feel and act.'[10]

The increasingly popular practice of mindfulness aims to challenge a blind acceptance of our thoughts. With mindfulness, practitioners stay still with their thoughts for ten or more minutes at first, observing thoughts as they come or go, but refusing to engage with them. Those who have taken up the practice will almost all say it is incredibly hard, and extremely frustrating – at first. After a while, though, the ability to separate yourself from your thoughts lends tremendous calm: instead of, 'Wow, she didn't even notice me – I bet she hates me and is going to fire me – if she fires me I wonder how I'm going to pay my rent – I bet all my friends think I'm a loser too', we might be able to stop at the first paranoia and think instead, 'oh, that's a thought I'm having. How interesting.'

The leadership expert Brene Brown has a helpful phrase for this: 'the story I'm telling myself is'. When met with something upsetting on the surface, instead of immediately assuming what the issue is, she instead says: 'the story I'm telling myself is'.[11] By framing our negative thoughts in this way, we can make it clear to ourselves that this is not the objective reality, but our subjective version of reality.

CBT also forces us to analyse and engage with anxieties, rather than seeing them as facts of life or that 'I am an anxious person'. It classifies worries – practical worries ('I have a headache') and hypothetical worries ('what if my train is late and I'm late to work?'). Sarah Knight has a great way of dealing with these kinds of anxieties: first, ask can I do something about it? If yes, do something. If no, stop worrying about it. It sounds logical and simple, but is surprisingly tough to train ourselves to think this way.[12]

CBT is much more complex than this, and the subject of many an entire Masters-level study, but these are the general principles most pertinent to educational settings. So, how should we use it?

Preventative work in schools

We can use CBT principles in schools to help the children in our care cope with the inevitable negativity they will feel at some point in their education towards school or peers, and we can use these same principles to set our children up to lead calm and balanced lives into the future.

In my opinion, the most helpful precepts of CBT we can teach children are:

■ You can control your thoughts.

■ Thoughts are not reality – they are your perception, and can and should be challenged.

■ Don't worry about what you can't control.

■ Observing thoughts and feelings can help to manage our responses to thoughts and feelings.

Tutor time or PSHE

The most obvious place to incorporate these teachings is in tutor time or in PSHE. Children are more likely to respond and engage on such a personal level with an adult they trust a lot, or one who is specifically trained to deliver PSHE content. (Where possible, tutors are best; for a few years I had the lucky job of being wheeled in to teach PSHE – a subject I have no expertise or real interest in – to a number of groups I did not know. The results were not impressive, and I came to dread those periods more than any other classes I taught.)

I would suggest beginning with the concept of mindfulness, and then instituting a weekly practice as a class. Practice only needs to be five minutes long. The app Headspace has some superb and short videos freely available on YouTube to illustrate key concepts of mindfulness.[13] Once students understand the concept, you can use a five-minute guided meditation from the app which talks you through it – at the time of writing, Headspace is free to all teachers. Ask the students how it was at the end, and what they struggled with.

This is a good introduction to CBT, because if a child can meditate and observe their thoughts, it is a small step to recognising they can begin to take control of their thoughts. Move on to this notion – that our thoughts create our feelings, and if we are feeling unhappy we can change the way we *think* about it as our first step, rather than feeling we have to change everything (or many things) in our lives.

The next two concepts can be tackled in either order. If you have children who are fractious and often argue with one another, move next to: 'the story I'm telling myself is'. This will start to help young people to acknowledge multiple versions of the truth, and to begin to be more honest with one another, while acknowledging that much of what they feel is projection rather than reality.

For less fractious teens, but those who are still experiencing anxiety – which in my experience is a shockingly large proportion – move onto worry and how to start understanding what they can and cannot control. This should help with a plethora of issues, from time management (worried about not doing your maths homework in time? How about … Doing your maths homework?) to reality checks (worried about failing all your GCSEs? What can you *do* to make that not happen? OK, now do that), to dismissing outlandish worries (worried everyone will suddenly hate you? Is that likely? What do your friends say about you? Do you know any adults with zero friends?).

Having the tools is one thing; using them is quite another. Revisit this using anonymised examples of negative thoughts, and ask the students to give their verdict on how to think more healthily.

Individuals

Teachers are not counsellors. I certainly wouldn't advocate turning tutor time into a group therapy session, nor would I advise getting children to anonymously suggest their own negative thoughts for group discussion. (I once got my PSHE class to anonymously submit their questions about sex while we covered this topic, and I don't know if I will ever get over the terribleness of that idea.)

Nonetheless, well-trained teachers can use the skills of CBT to support individual tutees who are struggling. While serious disclosures should always go to the school's safeguarding lead, when students come to us with fallings out or upset over feeling unaccepted by a group of friends, we can use the skills of CBT to help them think through this. Just by asking questions: 'why do you think this? What would you say to someone if they told you this? Is this the truth, or is this your version of this story?' we can begin to help children to think more positively and realistically.

Normalising negativity

It is easy for children to think they are alone. As an English teacher, I am duty bound to say that great literature dispels this myth. I began this chapter with *Catcher in the Rye*: for me, this was the first recognition. 'Oh – other people feel this way.' Rather than the depressing 'I'm not special', I thought: 'I might actually be normal.'

The more we read, the more we encounter those flashes of recognition in fiction that reassure us we are not alone. Reading R. J. Palacio's *Wonder* can help children to open up and talk about bullying and discrimination of those who look physically different. Reading Harper Lee's *To Kill a Mockingbird* opens up the conversation about racial discrimination. Reading widely is a great comfort and a balm to children, and should be encouraged and drawn on as frequently as possible. (The first PE teacher I hired clinched her position when she mentioned: 'I love to read. I can't stop reading' in her interview.)

Let's help children to talk about the normality of negativity healthily.

Take-aways

■ Negativity is normal; we can teach children how to cope with it.

■ Teach children coping mechanisms in curriculum time.

Notes

1 J. D. Salinger, *The Catcher in the Rye* (Penguin, 2010), p. 1.

2 'New research led by Sarah Coyne, a professor of family life at Brigham Young University, found that the amount of time spent on social media is not directly increasing anxiety or depression in teenagers. "We spent eight years trying to really understand the relationship between time spent on social media and depression for developing teenagers", Coyne said about her study published in *Computers in Human Behavior*. "If they increased their social media time, would it make them more depressed? Also, if

they decreased their social media time, were they less depressed? The answer is no. We found that time spent on social media was not what was impacting anxiety or depression."' Retrieved from www.sciencedaily.com/releases/2019/10/191022174406.htm (accessed 3 August 2020).

3 Hans Rosling, in *Factfulness* (Sceptre, 2019), argues: 'the vast majority of the world's population lives somewhere in the middle of the income scale … Their girls go to school, their children get vaccinated, they live in two-child families and they want to go abroad on holidays, not as refugees. Step-by-step, year-by-year, the world is improving' (p. 13); 'the misconception that the world is getting worse is very difficult to maintain when we put the present in its historical context' (p. 55); 'your own country has been improving like crazy. I can say this with confidence even though I don't know where you live, because every country in the world has improved its life expectancy over the last 200 years. In fact almost every country has improved by almost every measure' (pp. 62–63).

4 Retrieved from www.magonlinelibrary.com/doi/full/10.12968/pnur.2019.30.5.218 (accessed 3 August 2020).

5 'There is ample empirical evidence for an asymmetry in the way that adults use positive versus negative information to make sense of their world; specifically, across an array of psychological situations and tasks, adults display a negativity bias, or the propensity to attend to, learn from, and use negative information far more than positive information. This bias is argued to serve critical evolutionarily adaptive functions' (retrieved from www.ncbi.nlm.nih.gov/pmc/articles/PMC3652533, accessed 3 August 2020).

6 Johann Hari, *Lost Connections* (Bloomsbury, 2018).

7 Paraphrased in S. J. Scott and Barrie Davenport, *Declutter Your Mind: How to Stop Worrying, Relieve Anxiety, and Eliminate Negative Thinking* (Old Town Publishing, 2016), p. 35.

8 Retrieved from www.nhs.uk/conditions/cognitive-behavioural-therapy-cbt/how-it-works (accessed 25 May 2020).

9 Scott and Davenport, *Declutter Your Mind*, p. 9.

10 Avy Joseph, *Cognitive Behaviour Therapy* (Capstone, 2016), loc. 352.

11 Retrieved from https://brenebrown.com/wp-content/uploads/2019/08/Integration-Ideas_Rising-Strong.pdf (accessed 3 August 2020).

12 Sarah Knight, *Calm the F**k Down* (Quercus, 2018), p. 46: 'Anxious and overthinking? FOCUS: Which of these worries takes priority? Which can you actually control? Zero in on those and set the others aside.'

13 Retrieved from www.youtube.com/watch?v=pDm_na_Blq8 (accessed 25 May 2020).

 # How can we teach our children to be polite?

Politeness is a social good: everyone is happier when people are polite. The English, as they say, love a queue, and hate nothing more than those who cut in front of them. Indeed, I don't think I have ever felt a deeper shame than bouncing up to a colleague by a coffee urn, greeting him enthusiastically and then helping myself to a cup … Before realising I had, in my enthusiasm to greet him, inadvertently cut to the top of a very long queue, and had around fifteen other colleagues scowling and muttering at my rudeness. It was at a work event, and I immediately called a friend to panic I thought I might be about to be sacked on the spot for this kind of inexcusable error, or that I would need to resign from shame.

Politeness matters. We might not notice it, but when we behave politely good things happen to us. When we lose our tempers and rage against the world, people don't tend to want to help us out. But politeness makes people want to help us and want to fight for us.

An assembly I often trot out is the story of how I once lost my temper. I like to think of myself as a very calm individual, and rarely have I ever lost my temper (I am sure my family and friends would have their own version of this, but I have chosen to not survey them to fact-check this part of the book). One Christmas Eve, when I was at the very start of my teaching career and earning that unqualified teacher's salary and living in London and paying rent that was more than half of that salary, I had pre-booked my train ticket home several months in advance.

On trying to collect this ticket, it became clear that I had booked it on a credit card which had since expired, and which I had dutifully cut up and thrown away many, many weeks previously.

Luckily, I always get to the train station hours before I need to travel, and so I queued up (I managed to queue this time) and after many minutes, met with a harried and stressed ticket seller. I explained my predicament.

'I'm sorry, we can't release the ticket without the original payment card.'

I explained what had happened, and she repeated her phrase. This is where I lost my temper. I pushed every card I owned up at the clear screen, saying 'This is me! How else can I prove to you that it is me!'

DOI: 10.4324/9781003097075-9

'I'm sorry, but you will have to buy a new ticket.'

The new ticket, for a return journey on Christmas eve, was over a hundred pounds. I rattled and raged and cried. Then I called my mum.

'Don't worry sweetie,' said my mum. 'Worst case, I can just drive to the end of the tube line and collect you.'

So I felt pretty stupid when I went back to the same ticket lady.

'I'm so sorry,' I said. 'I'm so sorry I shouted at you.' I had worked for eight years in customer service of some kind before I became a teacher – as a waitress, a shop assistant, as a ticket seller in a theatre, and I was *very* familiar with customers doing exactly what I had just done. I was so ashamed, and I think I tell this story in so many assemblies, and indeed here as well, to try and rid myself of some of this shame.

Sadly, I did not redeem myself with my petty apology at this point. I was dead to the ticket seller. Luckily, my partner at that time was (and probably still is) a much better person than me.

'I'm really sorry to bother you,' he said. 'We're just really anxious to get home, and we're worried we might not make it in time for Christmas if we can't get the tickets. I'm so sorry to ask you, but is there any possibility at all of you making an exception this one time? Again – I completely understand if there isn't, and thank you so much for being so understanding about all this.'

His politeness was the key that unlocked those tickets. She smiled, said 'I really, really shouldn't.' And then she did.

I tell this story to illustrate the real-world value of politeness. When we rant and rage and get angry, people shut down. They don't want to help us, and they don't have to help us.

When we are polite, though, and respectful, and see others as humans, and speak softly, and ask nicely – people bend over backwards to help us.

We see this lesson being acted out with our students time and time again. If students are kind, and polite, and thank us for our lessons, when they come by after school and ask for extra help, we want to help them. We probably want to help all the students who come by after school, but laying the groundwork of politeness undoubtedly makes people more disposed to help you. A lesson we want children to learn at least part of in life is that most rules can be bent for the right attitude.

Politeness makes us happy. Think how we feel when someone, particularly a student, opens a door for us. When someone takes time to thank us. When someone greets us happily and asks how we are. I hope I'm not alone in feeling inordinately pleased when an American waiter gives me completely standard service – and if you haven't experienced the American service industry, I would absolutely recommend it. These are people trained to make your day better by smiling and saying nice things. I strongly believe the world would be a better place if we all channelled the American service industry.

Moreover, politeness makes every situation a happier one. Even when you make a mistake and upset someone, being kind and polite about it makes a bad situation better.

But politeness is not innate in any of us. No human on earth was born saying 'please' and 'thank you'. We should not expect politeness, even at secondary school. We should expect to explicitly teach politeness and remind children of it.

Explicit teaching

We have established that explicit teaching of core knowledge is the best way to ensure all pupils learn to a high standard.[1] The same is true when teaching pupils to be polite. From my colleagues Joe Kirby and Barry Smith, I learned a simple but helpful acronym to ensure all pupils behave politely: STEPS.[2]

STEPS stands for:

- Sir and miss.

- Thank you.

- Excuse me.

- Please.

- Smile.

In explicitly teaching each of these terms, we talk about when they are used. 'Always address your teacher saying "Sir" or "Miss"!' 'We always ask using please and thank you to show our appreciation for what others do or might do for us.' 'Don't forget to smile! A smile brightens everyone's day.'

Teach STEPS to year 7s when they first join the school; teach it to every year group at the start of the year. Teaching is easy. The challenge is keeping it up.

Forming the habit

Children will only become polite by habit if they continually practise, and this means being held to account by their teachers. Teachers must also believe in the value of politeness, because the second they are reminding a pupil to say 'please' is the second they are not teaching subject content – which every teacher agrees is of critical importance.

Make use of the moments between lessons to get pupils to practise politeness – talk to students in corridors on the way to lessons (while not slowing them down of course!) and on the playground at break time. Remind them of how they address their teachers as they are answering questions in class.

To secure the habit, reward it. That doesn't mean shower prizes on people, because one of the most valuable rewards we have in our arsenal as teachers is our approval. 'Thank you for saying "Miss" at the end of your sentence – so polite!' 'I love the way you are holding the door for your peers', 'Great smile! Brightens up everyone's day around here.' Positive reinforcement is key to ensuring that politeness isn't just taught as a one-off, but genuinely ingrained as a habit in all members of the school community.

It's always a trade-off, in any school, between the amount of time we spend practising habits and the amount we spend teaching subjects. I'm not sure any of us know definitively what the right balance is. I've visited superb schools where every teacher shakes the hand of every child coming into the room (though recent pandemics may curtail this practice) – for me, this takes too long. There is a time to teach the handshake, and a value in practising it, but to do this six times a day seems overkill to me. Nonetheless, I respect the colleagues who do this and I'm sure their children will go on to have firmer interview grips than those in the schools I work in. It's a risk I'm willing to take.

Behaviour

It would be remiss to write about school culture without mentioning student behaviour. Student behaviour is one of the strongest indicators of a school's culture. When behaviour is poor, learning suffers; when learning suffers, children do not achieve what they could achieve. It is inevitable in such a situation that children are likely to mistrust their school, dislike school, and not buy into what school is about.

Conversely, in an environment where everyone follows the rules, where there are clear sanctions when rules are broken which are seen to be applied fairly and justly, where there is clarity on what one should and should not do, there is a calm environment well-placed to ensure learning. When children are learning, they are more motivated to succeed.

There are those who believe that good teaching causes good behaviour. There is an argument which is often made, that if teachers planned their lessons more effectively the children would behave better. This argument is not without a grain of truth: if a lesson is pitched too wildly high or low, children will check out of it and turn to off-task behaviour.

Nonetheless, I would still argue that good behaviour is the necessary foundation for good teaching. My reasoning comes from my experience in schools. As a brand-new teacher in a school with no discernible behaviour system, I planned terrible lessons and endured a chaotic classroom of my own making. Conversely, my more experienced colleagues planned great lessons and enjoyed calm, purposeful classrooms. So it would be easy to determine that their planning created their classes.

Yet even in my most impressive colleagues' practice, they had classes they were more impressive with than others. Even the best teachers in the school had classes they struggled to control. The variable did not seem to be them or their planning, but the particular group of children.

It is true that as I grew more experienced, my students improved their behaviour. But again, my sense is that this was less about my planning than about the relationships I had built up with my classes. I know this, because I had three classes in my third year of teaching who I taught only once a week. The quality of my planning was the same as the lesson I delivered from the group I saw four times a week, but the reception was markedly worse.

A school that does not value teachers building positive relationships with children will never reach a school culture of excellence. It is imperative that teachers like the children they teach, and display this in an appropriate and clear way. We need to be even more explicit than we ever think – I think of myself as an especially effusive teacher who constantly tells my classes how great they are, and yet I am struck by the number of times a child has thought I 'hated' them after I've issued them a single detention. If we don't genuinely like children, we are, frankly, in the wrong profession.

But a school that relies on relationship-building alone to forge a behaviour policy is in trouble. This is fine in schools where teachers are all experienced and never leave. Sadly, the nature of our profession means that schools with 100% teacher retention are vanishingly few, and the pipeline to replace those who leave is not exactly heaving with brilliantly trained, experienced teachers. Our schools, particularly those serving challenging communities, which I have spent my career working in, are always going to be an unavoidable mix of the brilliant, experienced, high-flyers, and the new, out of subject, training and struggling. Our behaviour system must be strong enough to support *everyone* to teach effectively.

Explicit teaching of routines

It is not enough to say to young people: these are the rules. Very few young people – indeed, very few adults – are likely to say straight away: 'I fully understand those rules and will follow these in any and all circumstances.'

Moreover, one person's definition of 'perfect behaviour' will not be the same as another person's. Time needs to be invested to ensure that every member of staff has the same view of what great behaviour looks like: we need our mental models of this to align so we are all applying sanctions in a consistent and fair way.

First, we must teach the teachers: it is worth revisiting the behaviour system each year, and using examples to find consistency together. What happens if a child is late, or forgets their pen, or is wearing trainers? There are a hundred such questions, and if you can get consistency on all of them you are in an incredibly strong position as a team.

Then we must teach the children, and explicitly teach them, every rule and routine, along with why this is important. Explaining the 'why' behind rules is extremely important in securing student buy-in. Particularly at secondary, having rules we follow 'just because' does not inspire children to follow them. While most of the children we encounter will be happy to do what we tell them, the few who won't may very well undermine the culture for everyone.

As well as explicitly teaching routines, we must practise these routines. It is not enough to say: come into the room silently. They need to practise it, so the teacher can be explicit: that is (or is not) silent. The more precise we can be, the better: 'quietly,' for example, is one of those ambiguous terms for which everyone has their own definition – adults as well as children. 'Silence' is far easier to interpret and encourage for its lack of ambiguity.

Deliberate practice of routines

Practice is one of those triumphs of will over awkwardness, as any teacher who has been made to practise with other adults will attest to. With children, over-communicate how much time is saved through having tight routines, and then make it a mission to save as much time as possible, using timers or stop watches and competing to beat the time, perhaps with incremental improvements of that class, perhaps with the times of other form groups in the same year.

In setting aside plenty of time for explicit practice, you ensure you can get it right. For schools most in need of instituting new routines, set aside a whole day or half a day to ensure the practice is perfect. If you're rushing, you might have to accept less than 100%. I visited a school with incredibly challenging classroom behaviour, but was stunned to watch all one thousand students line up in complete and total silence on the playground after the lunchtime whistle was blown. The disparity was stunning.

'How did you do this?' I asked the kind deputy head who was showing me around.

'We spent about two hours out here at the start of term', they replied, 'until they got it right.'

It is a massive investment of time, but it only needs to happen once if you maintain it, and probably no more than twice a year if you need a reset. Had the school invested two hours in explicitly getting those classroom routines right, I could imagine what a delight the school would become to work in.

Collective practice in a large school is equally helpful, as it ensures everyone calibrates with one another. It is hard to accept students talking in your line when everyone around you has theirs silent and facing forwards. We accept what we see as the norm, and it is a brave teacher who steps away from that norm to enforce additional regulations of their own. That is why SLT must ensure behaviour is right, from the beginning. The first week of term is the most crucial time, where SLT need to be everywhere: in every classroom, on every corridor during every transition. They need to call out poor behaviour when they see it: 'this isn't how we behave,' or 'you know the rules – we expect you to face the front in silence. When I come back at the end of this lesson, your teacher better have good news for me.' If you invest time up front explaining why we have the rules we have, and teach those rules explicitly, there is no excuse for students not following them.

Behaviour reset

So your school has an Ofsted 'Good' for its behaviour. Great! Well done. The work continues. Getting it right at one point in time is no one's aim here. Schools need to get it right all the time.

I taught at one school that had moved from being the worst in the area to being among the best, and where behaviour was better than that of any other school I had worked in. What struck me was that the principal of that school never stopped thinking about behaviour. Despite impeccable behaviour in classrooms, she was determined to improve corridors. Despite improvements on corridors, she then became concerned that the isolation room wasn't running very well. She sought out reports on behaviour from members of staff at all levels, teaching and non-teaching, and shared those concerns with SLT: 'what are we going to do then?' Behaviour never left the agenda, because she knew that it was the crux of a good school. Behaviour would never be perfect, but it could always get better.

When we returned to school after a long holiday, tutor time and period one were given over to a revisit of our routines, with an added focus on anything we had noticed at the tail end of the previous term. The two weeks before holidays were spent fact finding, chiefly with the school's pastoral leaders and form tutors. If answering back was the key issue, that was the one we spent most time re-teaching. After a short holiday, we would spend tutor time on the routines, and possibly a period if we felt behaviour required more investment that term. And after the long summer holiday, it was between two and four periods depending on the year groups.

Different schools will need different approaches, and this needs to be managed carefully. If you give over a day to teaching routines, it has to be managed tightly with a lot of active student practice to break the day up. Putting children in a classroom at a challenging school to look at slides is likely to have the opposite effect to the one you are hoping for.

I would argue for two to four days of induction for year 7s, but higher up the school this is unnecessary, unless you have completely changed the behaviour code – and even then, you should be able to communicate and practise this in two to four periods. The chief thing with a school in a very difficult position is flexibility on whole-school set pieces. Give yourself a period for a thirty-minute assembly, so you can ensure you only speak when you have every single child listening. Ensure form tutors are aware and have a task to fill thirty minutes should the children settle more rapidly. Have a period to practise line-up outside, but tell the teachers of the next period to meet the class on the playground because this will be going on until the children get it right.

To be clear, if you have a routine, the children need to have some practice doing it. I would avoid saying 'from now on, we're going to come into the classroom silently' and expect them to just do it. Practise it until you get it right.

A whole-school behaviour reset requires careful logistical planning and total buy-in from staff. Don't reset student behaviour until teachers are fully trained in managing behaviour. Use staff practice to ensure everyone knows what the bar is, and ensure heavy SLT presence in the behaviour reset sessions to ensure consistency. You need to walk through the lesson from start to finish and be ready to know exactly how a teacher should respond to the most likely challenges.

One task for the member of SLT with responsibility for whole-school behaviour might do is to list twenty common things a child might do to contravene the rules, and to make these as small and everyday as possible – indeed, when a child throws a chair, even in the least structured schools there is generally no question as to what needs to happen next. What happens when a child forgets a pen is often less clear.

I have often said that the policy itself doesn't matter – what matters is that everybody follows it. We all have our favoured terms – demerit, detention, check, sanction, catch-up, and a dizzying array of acronyms to describe the kind of detention you are sitting. There are isolation rooms and exclusion rooms and inclusion rooms that serve the identical same purpose. Ultimately, it doesn't matter what you call it. What matters is you all call it the same thing, and when a situation arises you call it in the same way.

Relationships

I mentioned above that to rely on relationships alone to manage behaviour is inadvisable. I would not, however, say it is impossible: I have spent my career working in schools in inner London and outer Kent, serving communities which are often economically deprived and culturally diverse, combined with teaching staff who don't tend to spend twenty-five years in the same school – such teachers are the glorious minority, sadly, often due to a combination of house prices, workload and poor student behaviour depending on the school.

The longer you teach in a school, the easier managing behaviour tends to be. This is because the first five hundred times you issue a detention, children don't always think you will follow through (and if you are a new teacher, there is a non-zero chance you *won't* follow through – due to changing your mind under the child's pleas, or simply due to having a thousand more pressing things to do). If you repeatedly maintain strict behaviour in your class, it is only a matter of years before the majority of children comply. Your reputation spreads through the school, and if you are strict but loving this is normally a very good thing. (Being seen as strict and uncaring will be similarly good for behaviour, but bad for your soul.) One of my colleagues moved schools within the same local authority, and found the children in the new school surprisingly responsive to her – before finding out that her reputation for being an excellent teacher who had very high standards of behaviour had found its way to that school.

Ultimately, who wouldn't want to teach somewhere where we didn't need any sanctions? Who wouldn't want to quell an argumentative child with a raised eyebrow? Who wouldn't want to only walk down a corridor to find only respect and happy greetings? We all aspire to such actions, but such respect is earned in today's culture.

There are those who argue that this is a terrible tragedy – that children should respect their teachers (as 'in my day' we respected ours, and so on) no matter what, and that society has gone to hell in a handcart and that this needing to earn respect is one of the signs of our impending apocalypse. I have sympathy for this view, and also long for such days I'm not quite sure I have ever experienced, even as a student.

There are rules children need to follow in schools because schools are large, complex places filled with too many people to let everyone do their own thing. You wouldn't have a rule in your own home about which side of the stairs to walk up, because it's unlikely two hundred people are ever trying to get to the other floors of your house at the same time. Schools are different. In a classroom of one, we can be completely led by the child's needs – we could teach faster or slower, break if they felt distracted, start later or finish later because they worked better at different times of the day. But in a school of a thousand, such individualism does not work. Children need systems and rules for moving, turn-taking, and bathroom visiting, because otherwise chaos happens. I've yet to find a school where children move freely at their will or speak when they want to speak where 100% of children can learn.

So, children have to follow the school rules, but not because we, the adults, say them. There is nothing, in my personal opinion, naturally superior about an older person than a younger person. The rules aren't because we say so, the rules are because we *all* need to learn. The rules protect the pack.

With this in mind, I almost put rules to one side. They're there, they're set in stone, they're nothing personal. A child keeps talking, they get a sanction. It's not personal, it's a rule. It doesn't mean you like the child less, it means you like the learning of the class more.

We have to build relationships with our classes not because we need them to follow the rules – the rules are irrelevant to this conversation. The rules must be followed, relationship or no. A child I don't teach needs to follow a rule I remind them of when I see them doing something wrong on the playground or in the corridor. That's the rules part, that that part is really, really important. But when we teach our classes, we need to build relationships with those children so they learn more.

The power of relationships is clear in my experience of how children learn. The number of times I've watched a 'less good' teacher leave, and seen a star teacher take on a class the following year. That new teacher can have been the best in the department. It doesn't matter. The class still dips. They dip because they knew their previous teacher. Because no matter how weak the teacher was, they had a relationship with them. Indeed, the only time I don't see this dip is when the class disliked the teacher. When the class disliked their last teacher, often another teacher swoops in and the children are immediately more successful. I don't have data for this, it's just something I have seen time and time again.

I can't count the number of times someone told me when I started teaching: 'they don't need to like you, they need to respect you.' And they do need to respect you, but I'm afraid they do also need to like you. This is just my experience, and yours may contradict mine. Children who like their teachers work harder for them. They want to impress them. They want to do well for them.

As a side note, occasionally it works the other way, actually – children want to 'show that teacher' who didn't believe in them. I had a Latin teacher in school – one of the greatest teachers I was privileged to have – who repeatedly told me I was on course to fail my A level. She told me I was intellectually lazy – true – and didn't understand grammar – also true. She ripped into me once in class so viciously I argued back – the sole time I have ever argued with a teacher – and told her with typical teenage arrogance: 'I'm going to get an A. You wait and see.' To her credit, she didn't put me in detention, as she should have done. Instead she paused, looked me dead in the eye and said: 'I admire your tenacity.' I studied so hard to prove her wrong, and on results day when I said: 'I got an A!' her response was a genuinely mystified: '*Really*? How?' I loved Miss Coote, then and now. She knew exactly how to get me that A. (Though when I went back to school after university to see her and told her I was considering teaching Latin as well as English she did say to me: 'I don't think your Latin is strong enough for that.' And actually, I decided to let that one go. Miss Coote was many things, but she was never wrong.)

In both extremes, of course, the teacher–student relationship is key. We have to like the children – of that I am sure. Going further, I often say you have to *love* the children, but I'm aware this concept is not without its arguments. Some of the best teachers I have known disagree with me on the love front, so I've come to think that love is a very personal thing. I also know that love is one of my own core values – it is deeply important to me that I feel love for every child in the school, and every member of staff as well. But in the absence of love, I will insist on liking. We have to like the children.

Including the difficult ones. It is often said that the children who are hardest to love are the ones who most need it, and I absolutely agree with this. In my career, some children have certainly been harder to love than others. But love changes everything.

Working in a Church of England school probably helped with my love ethos. We talked about love a lot in that school, which worked well for me and for the children. Once, I shared a safeguarding admission from a student with a Head of Year and the child in question made my life extremely difficult. I'll never forget the ensuing meeting when the child had stormed out of my room and behaved appallingly. In the meeting, they explained how betrayed they felt that I had passed on their concern.

'Ms Facer had to tell me,' the head of year said to the child. 'Because Ms Facer loves you and wants you to be safe.'

'Miss loves me?' The child looked to me. I was in my first year of teaching, and this was the first time I'd heard an adult say that word so directly to a child. I nodded. 'I do.' The child nodded and looked the other way. But from that day forward, she was nothing but a complete joy to teach, and remains one of my favourite children I have ever taught. (You don't have favourites. You must not have favourites. But there are children you think about ten years after you last saw them, and hope they have every success they deserve in their lives. This child's thank you card to me one year read: 'Your card is twice as big as the other teachers'. Laugh at those peasants.')

As my career went on, I found myself often teaching the 'challenging' class, and almost without exception those children are easy to love. They bounce towards you with their energy and sometimes their insults, but they tend to have hearts of gold and are full of remorse when they do something wrong. But every so often, there's a hard shell on a child.

I have yet to meet a hard-shelled child who has had a delightful upbringing, though I'm sure they exist. Without exception, the hard-shelled hard-to-love children I have worked to love have experienced more hardship in their little lives than I have been lucky enough to have in my much longer one. These are the children who most need our love.

With complete honesty, I say here that I have never taught a single child who I did not love. That is not to say I loved them all immediately. But those who I found harder I worked harder with – I asked them more questions, I called home more often to say more nice things, I took an interest in something they took an interest in and chatted to them about it at lunch time. There's an awful lot you can do in the minute before a lesson begins and the minute after it finishes to show you care about a child's progress and them as an individual. Even these hardest of children have the potential for joy in them.

One of the toughest children at a previous school was the subject of a number of exclusions – he was abusive to members of staff on a regular basis, and had earned his most recent exclusion by breaking a plastic lunch tray in half with sheer force and threatening to hit a member of staff with it, before being restrained by another member of staff. Not only was he hard to love, he was pretty scary when he lost his temper. But watching him effortlessly pick up his baby brother in the parent meeting that followed the exclusion and soothe him with complete assurance and expertise; watching his big hands care so tenderly for the tiny baby while his wonderful mother worked tirelessly with the school was a turning point for my perception of him. Children are so much more than their mistakes. It doesn't excuse their mistakes, but it helps them if we can see far beyond them into their future possibilities. We have to find some redeeming feature to ensure all our children are human to us.

That is not to say we have to excuse their flaws because they have something brilliant about them. Too many times I have been told by SLT to 'let it go – he's having a tough time', or 'just keep her in the classroom, no matter what – she's got a very difficult background'. I actually had a vice principal walk a child out of my detention when they had ten more minutes to sit because 'she's had a bad day. She can sit the rest on Monday.' (She didn't.)

Stuart Lock shares one poignant outcome of such well-intentioned care for children in a blogpost simply called 'Kevin', about his brother. Lock describes how Kevin felt he did not belong in school:

> Kevin didn't think he belonged at school. He was in the bottom set for almost everything. He didn't really have much in common with his peers, and he certainly didn't like sitting in classrooms. He had failed, at that stage, to master the basics. He didn't really like football, and he still tries to get into it to this day. In fact, sport was no passion of his.
>
> The only time Kevin felt he belonged was when he was disruptive. He avoided work. He wouldn't listen. It is fair to say that he was not good for others' education. It's also fair to say that many other pupils would laugh and play along with him. There would be dozens of people paying him attention. And Kevin would be congratulated by them. He doesn't really remember the trouble... By the time he reached year 11, Kevin was almost impossible to teach. School was a battleground. And he was 'stressed out' by school. In an effort to help him cope, his mum would give him one 'stress' day a week and not insist he went in.
>
> For the last couple of years that Kevin was at school, whenever Kevin was in trouble, he would have a meeting. Senior staff or the Headteacher of the school would meet with Kevin, and his mother, and outline what he had to do to improve his behaviour. They would say to him that he should 'probably' be excluded, but would give him one more chance. They would, for very good reasons, say that they are working together.[3]

This rings true to me. There are, in my experience, no schools that take a 100% consistent approach with every single child. There are always mitigating circumstances, and no one situation is identical to any other. The difference comes where different schools draw that line. Are the exceptions genuine exceptions, or is the exception the new rule?

Too often, schools spare children the sanction they deserve because they want to protect them, which is exactly what it sounds like happened in the case Lock writes about. But we pay a heavy price if we protect children from the reality of life. For Kevin, an experience of exceptions and excuses made had catastrophic results, as Lock writes about what happened two years later:

> Kevin was out with a friend in a pub in Weston-super-Mare. As is the case in seaside towns, the pub was crowded on a hot day. Kevin had a pint of beer, and was knocked by an older man. As Kevin had had a few drinks that day, he challenged the man, saying 'Watch it!' or equivalent.

The well-built stranger turned, and provocatively blew Kevin a kiss, and laughed at him.

Kevin was somewhat enraged, and suggested they leave the pub.

In a nearby carpark, with his friend watching, Kevin and the stranger had a fight. Despite the stranger's size, Kevin won easily, and his friend and he returned to their night out.

At 3.30 a.m., Kevin was arrested. His friend was also arrested. They were charged with GBH with intent. His friend had struck no blows, but had been charged with the same charge because it was a joint venture.

With Kevin and his friend standing in court, his mother, father and family watched the CCTV images of Kevin kicking a body on the tarmac.

They wailed, his mum sobbing and his brother saying 'No', as he was sentenced to 2.5 years in prison. He ended up serving half of this, largely in HMP Parc in Bridgend. His friend also got 15 months.[4]

We have to like our students – that, for me, is a non-negotiable. But we have to like their futures more than we like their present. If we remain too attached to the children's present, we are more likely to forgive them things we should not. We can like them, *and* ensure they experience appropriate discipline.

Good parents know this dilemma well. All parents want their children to be happy, but all parents know that they cannot make their children happy at the expense of their developing characters. If a parent gives a child what they want and ignores their poor behaviour, they will make a monster. Ice cream might make them happy, but it will also make them sick. As children grow older, the stakes grow higher.

I often tell students that giving a detention is hard. Teachers actually don't like doing it. If I ignore your poor behaviour, my life is easier – first, because I don't have to log your detention (or in many schools, stay after school to supervise your detention, and call your parents before or after), but more importantly, because in the moment I ignore your behaviour, you probably like me more. 'Miss is alright', the children say on the playground. 'She never makes us work', or 'she lets us talk'. It's nice to be that person.

'Miss is so strict', the children will instead say when I give the detention. 'It's so unfair. No one else would have picked up on it. Why did she?' Even in the most consistent of schools, children will tie themselves in knots to persuade themselves that this single teacher is the problem. We all try to evade blame, even as adults who should know better.

'Tactical ignoring' is a method I was encouraged to use in the early days of teaching. Tactical ignoring means you see something happen, but you pretend you haven't. It sounds like a good idea, because you can continue to teach the class. And perhaps tactical ignoring works if you are genuinely the only person who saw something bad happen, and absolutely no one else did *and* the child thinks you haven't seen them either. I would argue that such a circumstance is so rare as to be a fantasy.

The problem with tactically ignoring something is that everyone thinks you're stupid, and they assume they can get away with similar levels of poor behaviour. In my experience, tactical ignoring is swiftly followed by deteriorating behaviour over time.

Instead of tactically ignoring, address issues calmly and without rancour. If your school system is strong, you don't have to be a force of personality when enacting it. You can assert your belief in the child's potential and how much you like them as a person *at the same time* you sanction the poor behaviour. A child is not their behaviour.

So relationships *are* key – they are the glue that holds a school together. We have to love, or at least like, our charges. But liking the children means making difficult decisions for the sake of their futures.

Group norms

Of course, schools are not only places where adults and children interact. They are also places where children interact with other children. As we will all know from our own personal experience of school, our peer group is an incredibly powerful force. The human connections we make with our peers are, and remain, the most important connections in our lives. We might look up to a role model (who might be a teacher), but if their message goes against our group's, we are not likely to diverge away from the herd.[5]

In areas where gang culture pervades, or where the majority of families are without work, it can be very challenging for schools to ensure the message of hard work, academic success, and professional employment is delivered. Children are shaped by the culture around them.

I noticed this in a big way when I moved from an inner-city London school to one in Kent. In London, children are surrounded by images of success – walk down any street in any area and you see mansions next to social housing, individuals wearing designer suits walking past the homeless on the way to their glass towers of work. For context, I once worked at a school placed on what was known as the most expensive street in north London. Over 70% of the children attending the school received free school meals. Every morning when I did the gate, I would watch a child come out of the mansion opposite, dragging her cello, get into a range rover with her mother, and drive who knows where to attend another school. The windows of the first-floor classrooms had an excellent view into that mansion's upper floors, and I'm not going to lie – it was a lovely way to dream. If I could see their bookcase lined, marble floored library, so could the children I served.

Where households are geographically disparate, it is hard for them to see that success. I grew up in country villages, where the people I knew lived in homes exactly like mine. I remember being in complete awe of the first 'rich person''s house I went to, and feeling that hunger for a different life from the second I walked through their enormous door. My enduring memories there were of family meals on a weeknight so long they stretched on for what seemed like hours around a table so large someone had to get up to pass the salt.

We are unavoidably influenced by our peers. We do what they are doing. In the school I went to, every single person in our tiny year group applied to university – it would have been unusual not to. So I applied. I remember hearing from old friends at the state school I would have attended had I not won a government assisted place in 1997 – friends who were far smarter than me, who had done far better than I had in their GCSEs and A levels – about how they weren't sure they were going to go to university. They were thinking about it, as if it were a choice.

David Didau asserts that we must 'shape the peer culture in schools so that children come to believe it's cool to be clever.'[6] He lists three core methods to do this, which are helpful: 'defining group norms', 'defining the boundaries of the group' and 'defining the image children have of themselves'.[7]

Defining group norms is more complex and challenging than it sounds, and is perhaps everything about the culture of a school. It starts with behaviour – in this school, we behave in this way. Behaviour norms have to be the first step, because to begin to control the narrative you need to have everyone's attention. It feeds into teaching, because if children are experiencing an excellent curriculum, with high-quality lessons, they are learning something. A knowledge-rich curriculum lends itself well to this aim, because it is very clear to children that they know more today than they knew yesterday; more this term than last. They experience their schemas strengthening and broadening.[8]

Building behaviour norms

But you can't get children succeeding academically without securing behaviour norms. Behaviour is the foundation for everything else in a school. You need behaviour first, because the children need to be able to hear and act on all the many other messages you give them.

I've written in depth about behaviour in *Simplicity Rules*, so I'm not going to repeat that level of detail on behaviour systems and implementation. I'm simply going to say that you must have a system, it must be clear and simple enough that everyone can use it consistently, and you must check that it is working.

There is a school of thought that there are no bad systems, only bad implementation. This is true to a certain extent, but with behaviour we have to also consider the amount of effort it might take to implement our systems. If the system only works when everyone puts Herculean effort in, it's probably not the right system.

Once you have the system, you need to teach the children each part of that system – and that does not mean just telling them. You need to show them, and then practise until the reality matches the ideal. That does mean a lot of entering classrooms, walking down corridors, lining up outside and handing out books you then immediately take back in. Behaviour induction looks odd, because it is odd, because the rules that govern schools are odd.

We must over-narrate the 'why' in behaviour. Our rules are strange, and while some will follow them unquestioningly, the proportion who will do this varies by school. No one is harmed by you explaining why a rule is the case, and others are helped by it. It builds buy-in with all children if they feel our rules are purposeful.

We need to harness as many points of the school day as possible to narrate the why and celebrate our students. Many schools now do a line-up before morning lessons; some have added this after break or lunchtime. It takes minutes (when you've practised it), and gives you an opportunity to reinforce key messages and to celebrate students or whole classes or year groups doing well.

On key messages: choose three to six and hammer them home, for five to seven years. Schools often fall into the trap of variety – I've seen so many assembly rotas packed full of hundreds of different ideas and stories. It isn't necessary. Tell the children those same messages, and tell them over and over again.

At Ark John Keats, at the start of the year I chose two messages I wanted to tell the children and I worked every assembly (with one or two exceptions for timely new stories and the like) around those messages. For me, everything that first year would be focused around kindness and effort. All I wanted was for the children to be nice to each other and to work very, very hard.

By teaching and encouraging politeness, teaching and rewarding following the rules, teaching children how to cope with the inevitable challenges life throws at them, we will make our schools happier places to be.

Take-aways

- Politeness is a social good.

- Explicitly teach children the steps to politeness (like STEPS).

- Forming the habit of politeness will serve children for the rest of their lives.

- Explicitly teach children how to behave in the classroom, and practise these routines more than you think you need to.

- Relationships are also important in classroom behaviour, but probably less than routines.

- Group norms matter, to take care to shape the peer culture in schools.

Notes

1 Well, this is clear to me at least. For a more detailed argument, if you'd like to have it, do read Jo Facer, *Simplicity Rules* (Routledge, 2019), ch. 1, or, even better, the entirety of Daisy Christodoulou, *Seven Myths about Education* (Routledge, 2014).

2 If this acronym originated before these two individuals, my sincere apologies. I try very hard to credit those who have shared ideas with me, but ultimately in teaching we are

always only borrowing from others better than ourselves. At this point in human history, I suppose it is inevitable that we are not likely to find originality.

3 Retrieved from https://mrlock.wordpress.com/2018/07/14/kevin (accessed 23 March 2020).
4 Ibid.
5 For a great explanation of the sociology behind why we do this, have a look at David Didau, *Making Kids Cleverer* (Crown House, 2019), ch. 4.
6 Ibid., p. 111.
7 Ibid., p. 107.
8 I've written about a knowledge-rich curriculum in *Simplicity Rules*, ch. 3.

8 How can we help our children value education?

The question of what education is for is debated by teachers, school leaders, politicians and the general public alike. It is not one on which I anticipate agreement in my lifetime, but it is crucial to unpick, because when we ask how we can get pupils to value education, we also must bear in mind that if we are not clear on what education is for, we might understand why they are not clear on what they are valuing.

The simplest view of education is as a stepping stone to something else, but this is also arguably its most reductive. How can you value a stepping stone that happens to last thirteen years? If education is a stop-gap, it is an unusually drawn-out one.

We might consider education as the thing that prepares us for work, more specifically. Yet we then run up against all manner of outrages: quadratic equations, enzymes and historical figures have yet to feature in most people's jobs. It is clear that we learn more in school than we ever need to actively draw upon.

Perhaps we believe it is the skills we learn along the way that matter – how to research, how to study, how to debate, how to put together a firm hypothesis, how to work as a team – and that the subjects themselves are immaterial. In which case, students may well ask why they can't learn these things through their preferred medium – whether that be dance or football or video games.

The purists, who I am afraid I have a great deal of sympathy with, being myself a teacher, believe in the inherent beauty of their subjects. I once worked with a group of middle leaders in developing their curriculums, and asked them in one to one meetings what their subject was *for*. Almost everyone told me some variation of: 'Maths/geography/science/history is all around us! Our whole world revolves around [my subject]! It is the universal language! It unlocks all of life!'

I empathise. I feel the same way about English – I have learned about people, relationships, and emotions from books. I have also learned about society, what has come before us, inner lives – from books. Conversely, for example, science opens no world for me. I understood very little of it in school, I crammed for an exam I managed to pass respectably, I promptly forgot everything, and I now make

DOI: 10.4324/9781003097075-10

embarrassingly obvious mistakes when I have to cover a colleague's year 7 science lesson. ('This stuff is *hard!*' I exhale to the eleven-year-olds who look at me like they've just realised Santa doesn't exist, and adults don't have all of the answers after all.)

For me, education is the language that unlocks other worlds. All of our worlds – no matter our backgrounds, rich or poor – are narrow ones. We are confined within the limits of our own experiences. A child who is the offspring of two doctors may well have untold advantages in life, but it is likely they will grow up knowing more about science than music or art, more about the middle classes than any other classes, and run the risk of therefore placing value on one over the other.

I don't know much about science, and that is not a good thing. That is another world, closed to me. I could remedy this, but, being human, my brain is inherently lazy, so I do not. I don't want the children in my school to grow up like me, ignorant of all science's glories. For one thing, of course, that will close some pretty lucrative doors (as anyone with an arts degree probably has found out by now). But more importantly, I want the children in my school to have a deep and thorough understanding of this wide and complex world. I want them to bring their knowledge to bear on everything they read and write and say; to enrich the lives of others with their understanding and intelligence. To make good choices in all areas of their lives, because they knew the range of things they could do, and had the wisdom to choose the right one.

Parents' aspirations

Much has been made of the role of 'aspirational' parents in changing the trajectories of their children's futures. Amy Chua publicised the idea of the pushy parent who ensures her child's success in her 2011 book *Battle Hymn of the Tiger Mother*. There are two key messages in this book. The first: hard work pays off. The second: strict discipline is the best way to ensure your child succeeds.

Chua notes:

> In one study of 50 Western American mothers and 48 Chinese immigrant mothers, almost 70% of the Western mothers said either that 'stressing academic success is not good for children' or that 'parents need to foster the idea that learning is fun'. By contrast, roughly 0% of the Chinese mothers felt that way.[1]

Of course, this is not purely a question of belief – it is also one of method. Chua writes that: 'While the other kids were learning to count from 1 to 10 the creative American way – with rods, beads and cones – I taught Sophia addition, subtraction, multiplication, division, fractions, and decimals the rote Chinese way.'[2] Underpinning this book is the core belief that children can learn anything, as long as they work hard enough and their parents make them do it.

While the book was hugely contentious for some Western audiences, in the same year of its publication the *Guardian* reported:

> The domestic statistics show that, at GCSE, children of Chinese ethnicity – classed simply as 'Chinese' in the data – who are eligible for free school meals (FSM) perform better than the national average for all pupils, rich and poor. Not only that, but FSM Chinese pupils do better than those of most other ethnic backgrounds, even when compared with children from better-off homes (those not eligible for free school meals).[3]

It seems clear that not all Chinese parents have the skills to teach their children the way Chua, a university professor, describes herself doing in her book. And yet, the statistics, year on year, show Chinese students of all backgrounds outperforming their peers. This is not a question of academic tutoring, but one of a powerful culture.

Of course, all parents want the best for their children. But we are all also human, and we fear disappointment – for ourselves, and our offspring. Our own experiences in schools will throw up memories of parents who ask us: 'is he happy?' or 'is she behaving?' and appear to care more about that than whether the child is succeeding. The parents of children who receive top marks across the board rarely ask such questions. Some secondary school teachers, therefore, might reach the conclusion that their parents are 'unsupportive' and have 'low aspirations' for their children, this may be a misdiagnosis. Is it that excellent performance leads to increased parental interest, or that strong parental support is the driver of excellent performance?

The Sutton Trust's 2014 report, *What Makes Great Teaching?*, memorably says 'the poor motivation of low attainers is a logical response to repeated failure. Start getting them to succeed and their motivation and confidence should increase.'[4] Perhaps the same is true for parents. Perhaps low expectations, low aspirations, are simply a logical response to their child doing poorly in school for the majority of their time? Perhaps low aspirations are a necessary psychological buffer to disappointment?

I don't think it's fair to say that some parents don't value education. I think it is fair to say that some parents don't believe their child will be academically successful, based on a plethora of evidence, and that schools need to change the narrative, urgently.

It is a surprisingly short journey from wanting your child to exceed expectations to wanting them to be happy. 'I just want him to be happy' is something I've heard more parents say than I can count. 'Happy' is possibly even more elusive than 'successful', but more easily accomplished in a superficial way. Children can seem happy when they are getting their own way – I know, I've taught enough naughty classes as a training teacher to remember seeing the glee in their faces of winning control of the class.

For children to really learn and really succeed, especially if they are academically behind, is tough, because we need them to work really hard. To get long-term happiness, they need to endure some short-term pain. The roots of education are bitter, but the fruits are sweet.

Aspiration

But achievement is not enough. Children also need to aspire. This is where it gets more complex. I once taught a wonderful student, who I'll call Sally. I taught Sally for three years – from year 9. She spent most of year 9 doing not very much. She was, in the kindest terms, a joker – I found her very funny, but she didn't learn very much. This was combined with the fact that I was in my first year of teaching, and part of her joking around and not learning was certainly down to me.

In year 10, Sally changed. Suddenly, she was putting her hand up in class and saying intelligent things. One lesson, during independent writing, she wrote an entire page. I remember her looking at me, cheeks puffed out, in frank amazement. 'I don't know how I did it', she said, as I read it with glee. Something had clicked. Sally was suddenly very, very good at English.

It might have been about this time that she discovered drama, but perhaps she had always been an actress. I don't know. But I do know that I went to see her in the school play, and I foolishly sat in the front row, and her monologue brought me to tears which I tried and failed to hide. She just *was* another person. When I told her how good she had been, I was not alone – Sally was crowded with friends and relatives and teachers at the end. Her drama teacher, who had been a professional actor before becoming a teacher, was in agreement: something very special was happening here. Sally could really do something with her talent.

So, midway through year 11, a massive alarm bell rang for me when Sally told me she was applying to college to be a hairdresser. 'But you're on track for As,' I said, 'in English and drama at least. I thought you wanted to be an actor?'

'I did,' said Sally. 'But it's a really hard profession and I'd probably never make it.'

'Well, there are lots of things you could do to do with drama. You could study it at university. You can make a career out of what you love. Like Mrs Robinson has!'

'Really?' she asked.

'Absolutely! Do some A levels! Do a degree! Have a go at the career of your dreams! If it doesn't work out, hairdressing will always be there!'

And I convinced myself Sally was going to think about it. The next thing to do was alert her mum, who would surely be horrified to find out what Sally's plans were.

'So, Sally tells me she's going to go to college next year to do hairdressing?' I said.

'Yes.'

'I was just talking to her – I mean, her work is very good. If she keeps this up she's guaranteed two Bs in English and I wouldn't be surprised if she got As. And her drama, as you know, is spectacular. She's got a real talent.'

'She wants to do hairdressing.'

'Yes. I mean, I know that's what she thinks she wants *now* –'

'I'm a hairdresser. Something wrong with hairdressing?'

'No! No. Absolutely not. I … I just mean … I suppose what I'm saying is …'

'You know, some kids aren't academic. That's OK. I was never good at school. I always struggled. Found it really tough. Some kids are academic and they're smart and they get a lot of qualifications and they do all of the university stuff. And some kids aren't. I wasn't good at school.'

'But Sally *is* good at school! Her grades are really strong! She's incredibly bright – she would be well suited to university –'

'Look, some kids just aren't academic. You have to accept that.'

To date, that remains the strangest conversation I've had with a parent. Of course, I have to unpick my own biases here and be honest: I really did think it would be better for Sally to not be a hairdresser. Not because I don't think hairdressers are important – I've had three in my lifetime and I got to know and love each of them dearly. But because Sally had a gift and a talent and a *love* for something, and it wasn't hairdressing. Because she had the potential to do the thing she wanted, and it wasn't hairdressing. And because that career is one you can take up at 16 or 18 or 23 or 30, but if you wanted to go to university first it wouldn't make that much difference (I suppose all careers are like that if you think about it).

I bothered Sally a lot after that about sixth form. I talked to her about the options she could do. I talked to her about drama courses at universities. I told her many, many times that she could still be a hairdresser even if she followed her dreams for a few years first. To her credit, Sally seemed to like me despite my badgering.

In my mind, it was a case of belief. Sally didn't believe in herself, or her talent, enough. On GCSE results day, I scanned the year group eagerly for my class. I still have their results, and I looked at them to check Sally's before I wrote this chapter – to see whether my memory matched the reality. I'm still so proud of that class. They were set two, but almost every grade is an A for both English language and English literature. They worked so hard.

And there, proving my memory, are Sally's grades: an A for English language and an A for English literature.

When the students came in, I sought mine out to celebrate with them. Results day really is my favourite day of the year. There were a few who had especially proved themselves, and Sally – with her prediction of two B's – was one of them.

It seemed strange then that I hadn't seen her – a student who did genuinely seem to like me. I finally caught her trying to sneak out, and physically stepped in front of her, grin on my face.

'Well done!' I shrieked.

Sally beamed. 'Thank you miss! I'm so happy.'

'Where are you going?' I asked.

'I've got to get to college to sign up for my course.'

'But your grades! You can stay in sixth form here, Sally.'

'Miss,' she said, 'I told you. I'm doing hairdressing.'

'But you got such good grades.'

'I know. I'm really happy,' said Sally, and off she went.

Sally's story felt deeply personal to me. Her rejection of the grand plans I had laid out felt like a kick in the teeth for educational equality, and stood in stark contrast to the majority of aspiration issues I had encountered up to that point. Taking on bottom sets in my Teach First placement school, I had spent most of my initial parents' evenings talking to parents of Year 10 students who were barely literate about how an A* was probably not the most likely expected grade, especially as their child had done no homework and little classwork in my experience of teaching them. 'But my child should be getting A*', I had heard, or 'but if I'm going to be a doctor, I need all As.'

But Sally was the opposite. She was brilliant, and bright; she came from a part of the world that was full of challenge, and, it sounded, from a family who had no idea of her potential – or knew, but encouraged her away from the risky arts she loved and towards the safety of a career they knew well.

Sally worries me because she defied the peer effect of school. In the rest of that set two English class, I don't think anyone else went on to college to do a practical course – everyone else was doing A levels somewhere. In terms of a culture of aspiration, the school had cultivated that brilliantly – and yet it hadn't brought Sally along.

As you can probably tell, I haven't made peace with Sally's path yet. Family ties are often the strongest ones in our children's lives, and it takes an overwhelming school culture to go up against these – and of course we might want to ask whether we even want to. Do we want children to diverge from the path their families want to put them on? It is also a question of value – do we value some jobs and some qualifications more than others?

I think we can make our peace with that. I've talked before about my own experience of being the first in my family to go to university, and the difficulty of feeling disconnected being overwhelmed by the later support and unconditional love I hope that most families give their young people.[5] I think the recent coronavirus pandemic gave us all a newfound appreciation for the under-appreciated in society: all of a sudden, we were saluting supermarket workers and leaving gifts for the bin men and acknowledging that while nurses do an extraordinary job (the fact of which no one has argued with), it is the bus drivers and transport workers who get large numbers of them there, and the cleaners and porters who keep a hospital moving and safe.

It is possible to value jobs and to still push children to aspire to other jobs. Is it 'higher' to aspire to a university degree than to an entry-level train driver? If you spend your whole childhood obsessed with trains and dream of the latter, then no. For children with a calling and deep love for a profession, let them go there.

For some children, a school's peer culture will never raise their aspirations. All we can do is to build a place where success is valued: Sally worked hard and achieved good grades. I console myself in thinking that firstly I hope she is profoundly happy in her career of choice. I hope she goes to work every day excited to cut hair. I hope she gains enormous satisfaction from the happiness she undoubtedly gives her clients.

And if Sally doesn't feel any of that, she's got some amazing GCSEs she can spin into anything she might choose in the future.

Building the norm of success

Making it normal or desirable to be successful is a challenge with some communities. This is especially the case when working in schools which have been historically unsuccessful – we make many of our judgements about school from our own experiences of school. If parents have been ill-served by education, it is little wonder they might view the school with suspicion and all its promises of aspiration.

To build success as a group norm is simple but difficult. The first aspect is ensuring all children can be successful. We've spoken before about motivation, and that success motivates children (and all of us, actually). A curriculum and teaching style that starts where the children are and which moves them rapidly along, having them finding success at every point, will encourage them to continue to put in effort. Pitch your curriculum too high and ask them to grapple with the tough stuff straight away and you risk early defeat.

Once you have set up success, you have to recognise and reward it. Don't say things like 'but this is really easy' – narrate how challenging what they are doing is (authentically, of course – there's an easy and difficult way to approach Blake's 'The Tyger', but if you start talking about religious symbolism with year 7 that's a genuinely challenging concept and poem they should feel proud of studying; don't try to tell secondary school pupils that the *Mr Men* books are challenging). I'm always surprised by schools that make merits hard to come by – to my mind, most children who put in a lot of effort in a lesson should get recognition. A merit is a quick way to stop you drowning them in words. For the younger year groups, merits are especially important while they develop their habits and their intrinsic motivation.

Even more important than merits though is a culture of excellence. That means holding the children to high standards, which includes how they present their work. It should be a privilege to have your book held up as an example for all, and if you get the narration right you will find it will be. They will want to get the merits or the praise, even in the most challenging contexts – in my early days of teaching, back when I marked books all the time, I'd frequently see the children writing things like: 'why didn't I get a merit this time?' beside my lengthy 'what went wells' and 'even better ifs'. It struck me that many were too shy to ask me this in class, and I took to narrating each time what children needed to do next time to get a merit – the messages stopped coming after that.

Marshmallows

The infamous 'marshmallow test' – a 1972 Stanford University study in the impact of delayed gratification at an early age – has been largely discredited.[6] In the original experiments, four-year-olds were told that if they did not eat one marshmallow, they would be later rewarded with two marshmallows. As suspected, some children waited for their later reward, while others ate the single marshmallow. The experimenters later found a correlation between those who waited for the marshmallow and their academic success in later life, which makes intuitive sense – those who impatiently seize the immediate joys are not best suited to the grind of studying. In the years since, this correlation has been discredited as it does not hold when controlling for family background, home environment and early cognitive ability.

Though the science may not hold up to scrutiny, the nugget of the idea remains: in order for children to reap the fruits of education, they must endure the bitter roots. Studying is difficult for all of us, but even more so if you are behind.

Families can do much to close this gap: there are children from all backgrounds who close the gap due to a combination of their own dogged determination and the families behind them telling them to work hard and respect their teachers. A simple reward and sanction system, combined with consistent messaging about the importance of school along with the belief and support their children need to succeed, can propel children a very long way.

For other children, building in the drive and stamina to work hard requires a many-pronged approach by schools.

Working with parents

The first step is to work with parents, which sounds obvious, but is not always done. When I started working in education, there was a feeling about parents from certain schools which was essentially: they just need to get out of our way and let us do the right things. Such schools saw parents as either useless or openly obstructive, and I worked in some schools that subscribed to this view.

Conversely, some Charter Schools in the US were finding quite the opposite: parental support was actually key to their children exceeding expectations. The most highly publicised of these are the Success Academies in New York City. Spending a year in a succession of these schools, the education author Robert Pondiscio lifted the lid on practices that had helped to propel Success schools to top of the league tables on every single measure. And those results are astonishing: at the time of writing, on state standardised tests, the network averaged 95% proficiency in maths and 84% in English, far above even the state's most selective schools, while at the same time serving incredibly deprived communities, as evidenced by the high proportion of children receiving free or reduced lunches. This is in part due to curriculum and teaching, but in large part also due to the way the schools work with parents.

Pondiscio notes the divergence of Success Academies to the standard working practices of other US Charter networks:

> Among education reform advocates, there is a regrettable tendency to view urban communities through a lens of dysfunction ... 'Schools should not expect much from parents at all,' the founder of one national charter school network told me ... Success Academy's relationship with its parents suggests precisely the opposite view. The network makes significant demands of parents, assumes significant leverage, and makes no discernible negative assumptions about parents' ability to contribute materially to their children's education. Very little in the network's expectations, for good or for ill, suggests a view of low-income parents as any less capable and competent than affluent ones.[7]

The book is a lesson in how to involve parents in their child's education. Throughout, we learn of the almost constant contact with parents and the logistics of how this works. Teachers call, text and email frequently, and daily during important testing preparation periods, about children's progress, behaviour, or test scores. We are treated to a blow-by-blow account of a parent meeting, where the teacher explains the minutiae of the school day to ensure parents understand why she is asking for what she is asking for, along with offering to support them in any way they need: 'You need more stickers? Just ask! You need more cubes, tiles, index cards? Just ask, ask, ask. We're happy to give you anything you need to support your child at home.'

This latter point is an important one. For too long, schools have essentially said to parents (though never in so many words): just stop interfering. Let us get on with teaching, and we'll let you know once a year what the issues are. In other quarters, there is a reluctance to give resource to parents – one school leader I worked with refused to provide uniform or equipment for children who came without it, using instead the isolation room and detentions where this was absent, because they believed that to provide things for children that parents should provide would erode the personal responsibility of families. I have a lot of sympathy for this view: the argument is that parents value what they put into financially, and I have also seen this. It is a shame that whenever as a school we have given children free theatre tickets, for example, we have had only 75% of those who sign up actually *turn up* to the show. When we tweaked this and charged a nominal amount, 100% would come. It's a sad reality that we value more what we have to sacrifice something else to choose to do this for.

At the same time, the Success teachers aren't talking about providing uniforms or equipment for the students. They maintain a minimum bar for parents. What they are recognising though is that for full support, parents may need even more additional equipment. This seems to me the right approach, but does not resolve the question of how parents who are struggling might afford expensive uniform and extensive equipment lists.

Where teachers at Success Academies have 'deliverables' – measurable markers of success, such as the percentage of students focusing in lessons, so do parents, who are advised to aim for: '97% of students present, 96% on time, 97% in uniform, 97% of homework completed.'[8] Pondiscio even describes a 'parent report card', which was received without argument. (I brought this concept up in a parent meeting as a joke once, and while some parents nodded enthusiastically, others looked extremely uncomfortable at the idea of having firm markers around key aspects of school life. I've not yet managed to work out a way to make this palatable to the parent communities I serve.)

Conversely, home-school agreements have become commonplace. When seeking advice from a colleague at another school on dealing with a particularly challenging parent, I was told:

> You need a home-school agreement. Put things like that they must come to meetings when the schools requests them to in it, and get them to sign it in year 7. Then when they argue like this, you can say: 'look, here's the home-school agreement you signed'.

Buoyed with this idea, and raced to my Headteacher ... Who told me we already had a home-school agreement.

A home-school agreement is as much of a big deal as you want it to be, but I'd suggest it seems to be an under-utilised resource. First, review the agreement to make sure it is a genuinely helpful one. Then, use it. Use it in your year 6 parent meetings, or in your first parents' evenings with tutors. Go through it. Talk about it. If it reflects what you care about, it is well worth investing the time in it. Have the argument with the parent when it is still in the theory stage, rather than something very personal and current. It is unlikely their child will have managed to be naughty between the door and the desk on their first day of year 7, or before, so make use of this to set the ground rules together. Too often, transition meetings are overwhelmed with admin and logistics – in one school I worked in, they managed to be forty-five minutes long and contained travel advice without once mentioning the home-school agreement.

Many schools in my network conduct home visits prior to children starting in year 7. I am in two minds about these. Those who have conducted them swear by their utility, though I often wonder if I had sunk over two hundred hours of time into something I might also be inclined to attest to its usefulness.

In a home visit, a senior member of staff visits the family in their home. This visit is scheduled and planned. They go over the key rules, expectations, and home-school agreement in the family home. It is, I am told, a powerful way to show the school the lengths we are prepared to go to to ensure your child starts strong. Having been in the family home is a hugely powerful thing.

For me, two hundred hours is too much staff time. It makes sense to do this if you are a brand-new free school and you need to get that first cohort of children fully on board. It might also make sense if you are in a notably challenging area, where parents mistrust school (although some parents may well feel uncomfortable having teachers inside the home).

The main reason I am reluctant to say home visits are a great investment of time, though, is the message they deliver. For me, the message is perilously close to: I care so much about your child succeeding, I will come to your house to make sure you agree with me on this. I have come to your house once, so you better believe I will come again if I ever need to.

For me, this flies too close to the 'whatever it takes' motto adopted by some early charter schools. Some charter schools believed it was their duty to do 'whatever it takes' to ensure their children achieved academic success. This was rapidly translated into long school hours, weekend school and summer school. The children did well, undeniably, but such systems do not scale. There are currently over 500,000 teachers in the UK, and we cannot expect even half of those people to want to work seven days a week, fifty-two weeks a year. Undoubtedly, some will want to – at least at first. But relying on the excess efforts of some is both unfair to the children whose teachers do not or cannot for whatever reason commit such Herculean efforts, and unfair to the teachers themselves who might find themselves one day unable to commit such hours – for example, when they choose to start a family of their own – and cannot square lower hours with their current profession.

Success Academies are built on just such a model. In Pondiscio's book, he writes of the culture of expecting only a short number of years from their teachers before they will inevitably leave. They do so leaving an incredible legacy of learning for their children, and I hope to not undermine the efforts of the superhuman educators who do commit a few years of their lives – and their whole lives – to educating the children who most need it.[9]

I'm just not sure this is the best way to run a school for the long run, and perhaps that is because I also work in a school, and I'm a bit selfish. I'm possibly selfish because I personally do not want to work seven days a week – partly because I am much better at my job when I take two whole days off a week, but partly because there are other things I want to do at least as much as I want to work in a school. I want to walk the dog and see my friends and visit things and people and places on the weekends. I don't want to always run revision sessions and mark books and plan lessons.

The other reason it's probably selfish is because I do want to work in schools for the very long term, and a high turnover of staff is therefore unpalatable for me. Working in a school is, of course, about working with children, otherwise you'd work in an office (have you ever worked in an office? I have. They are where hope and joy go to die, in my very subjective opinion). Schools are also about working with teachers, and teachers are humans, and humans work on interactions and trust. The longer we work together, the easier and more enjoyable that relationship is. The number of teachers I've seen describe someone as 'my work wife' or say 'we've worked together for fifteen years' is surprising, and the work people do when they really trust one another is extraordinary.

I'm veering dangerously away from the topic though. There are many, many things we can do to build better relationships between home and school – we must just remain mindful of workload and staff time with whatever we choose to do.

Responsibility

The final point, and this is one of values which many will disagree with, is that I strongly value personal responsibility. I think it is one of the most important qualities children develop, and if they do not develop it, it narrows their choices and options for later life. I believe this because it is my opinion that personal responsibility empowers people. There are, of course, limits. A four-year-old should not be taking responsibility for feeding and clothing themselves, but some must, and this is evidently wrong and worth providing interventions for. But by the time children reach their teenage years, we must ensure they are responsible for themselves, and their parents are responsible for them.

A small and tangible example is in equipment. In 2010, I visited a school where the children were not expected to bring in any equipment. The school served a deprived community, and I felt this was exactly right: how wonderful that the school valued equity, and that every child had pens and pencils and rulers aplenty on their tables!

But what the school won with equity it lost in terms of responsibility. How, I found myself wondering, were these children completing their homework, if the pens were all at school? And isn't there a value in having your own materials which you look after and replace when they are broken or when they run out? While there are always edge-case families who simply cannot do the bare minimum, this is not the reality for most children: being on free school meals does not mean you cannot have a working pen, and to assume the two are inextricably linked is to limit your expectations of what it means to be a young child growing up in disadvantage.

The non-negotiables

The clearer we can be about our school's non-negotiables, and the more transparent about these we can be with parents, the better.

I'm a big fan of a parent handbook which is succinct (less than ten pages) and lays out clearly for parents what they can expect from the school. The focus needs to be on what the parents' responsibilities are. Parents must play their role so schools can play theirs, but we will get further in these if we know what our responsibilities are.

Parents need to know the times of the school day and the approach to lateness. They need to know the school calendar and the days school is and is not open. They need to know the uniform in all its specificity, ideally with images to support guidelines (while 'long sleeved white shirt' is fairly unambiguous – though necklines can vary – 'smart hairstyle' can mean very different things to different people). Parents need to know what equipment their child needs to bring with them each day. They need to know the behaviour policy – what are the expectations their child needs to follow, and what will happen if they don't. They need to know who the key people are involved in their child's education, and how to contact them if they need to.

But all of these are only supporting parents to help children meet minimum expectations. Perhaps the most important thing for parents to have clarity on is homework. After all, most secondary children only spend 25 to 27.5 hours a week in school, thirty-nine weeks a year.[10] At just 5.5 hours of learning a day, and allowing for nine hours of sleep, that still leaves nine and a half hours of the day spent away and not in school. Of those hours, how many are spent on homework? Judging from the variable submissions I've encountered in my years in the classroom, not many.

I take responsibility for the poor homework of my students – I set it, and if children weren't doing it it's because I wasn't following it up adequately. To be entirely truthful, I don't think I've ever managed to get 100% homework completion 100% of the time from any of the classes I have taught with the exception of my sixth formers. Indeed, the only time I reached towards 100% was when the school I worked in had a centralised homework policy, where form tutors checked daily homework in a specific thirty minute 'prep' slot at the end of the school day.

In this environment of minimal compliance, parents have a huge role they might play if we could only harness them. If we had hours in the day to call every parent of every child who had not completed their homework, I imagine the response would be exceptional. Sadly, we do not have this kind of time. There are a few things we can do.

The first is to be clear about the purpose of homework. I know from my teacher colleague parents how frustrated they feel when their children are set 'pointless' homework tasks, like building an instrument from cereal packets or baking a cake. While busy work is better than no work for some parents who long for some peace in the evenings, work that essentially requires a parent to do it is certainly not welcome.

We need to communicate the purpose of homework, whatever that may be: extended reading, writing, or knowledge recall. We need to be clear about the format homework will take, the days it is expected to be completed by, and the support parents can provide – even if that is just to ensure their children have somewhere relatively quiet to work for two hours each evening.

We then need to uphold our end of the bargain and set the homework. It is pointless tee-ing up parents to be ready to support us if we don't actually set it. Upholding our end also means sanctioning homework when it isn't complete, and at some point contacting parents. A good centralised detention system will send parents a notification of a detention being issued; a great system can tag this for parents as 'no homework', and the best will enable tutors or Heads of Year to track students who struggle to complete homework and dig a little further into why this might be, and ways the school can support them.

Contacting parents

Although contacting parents is time-consuming, if we are going to invest time in it I'd do it straight out of the gate in September. I'd invest a lot of time in the first two weeks making pre-emptive positive calls. Target children who haven't always had the best behaviour or who haven't yet found success in secondary school – so often, children come back in September resolving to do better. Notice their efforts and let their parents know.

At the same time, now is the moment to secure your expectations and talk about learning. The first time you take in students' books (and I hope you're giving them feedback rather than having to mark them), anyone who does not meet your high standards of presentation or amount of work – let parents know. In an age of universal email, you might even take a photo and send it along so they can see what you mean (though I always caution use of email as I think it can spiral rapidly out of control).

One of the most powerful things schools can do is to invite parents in during the normal school day. A lot of schools shy away from this, but there really is no better way to reassure them that you're doing a great job at educating their child than to send the invite. Having worked at a school which did this, I can relate that very few parents will ever take this offer up. The ones who do will be grateful (the behaviour of a boy in my class was transformed when his mother, standing at the back, enjoying the last ten minutes of year 7 English, *clapped* when I finished the class and thanked me profusely as the children filed out. I still can't work out if it was the vote of parental confidence that made him start to behave or the humiliation of having his mother approve his teacher publicly), and the ones who don't will appreciate that the offer is there should they ever choose to take it up. A word of caution on this is that your day to day school has to be where you want it to be – you lose your advantage if parents see things aren't going well, and you lose your staff if teachers have to 'be on their best game because Sammy's Mum is in tomorrow.' This only works if teachers just continue to do what they do, and parents just happen to be there to enjoy it.

With parents who are suspicious of school, who do not buy in, we have to be ready to meet them where they are. Being flexible over meeting times is an important, though annoying, part of senior leadership: while I would never expect a head of year to stay late into the evening to meet a shift-working parent, as a VP I frequently found myself being shooed out by the site manager who locked the door behind both myself and the parent as we left in the last moments of the site being physically open. I hope the chapter on workload has emphasised how deeply I care about reducing this, so I'm not setting a blanket expectation that your SLT meet parents late – I simply mean in the rare cases where parents explain why they cannot get to the school before a certain time, try as much as you can to accommodate this, while ensuring you maintain regular meeting times for 99% of meetings.

In the even rarer occasion that parents cannot get to the school *at all*, and again this will be less than 1% of your intake, it can build a huge amount of trust to be willing to visit them at home if that is easier for them. This is, of course, a much larger investment of staff time, particularly if your parents live far from the school and public transport is unreliable. But again it is not a blanket offering, but an occasional willingness to go beyond the grounds to meet parents where they are.

In parent meetings, particularly where school and home are not yet aligned on the best thing for the child, it helps to allow the parent to speak first. This allows the teacher not just to model good listening, but to *genuinely* listen. We go into meetings – often busy, and as SLT rarely in possession of the full story, particularly if we are picking up a major incident and protecting the staff member who might not want to be in the meeting – with preconceptions and our own ideas about what the issues will be. It always pays to listen first.

At the same time, you will find parents who enjoy being granted the floor, and who subsequently try to talk over you repeatedly. If you have genuinely given them the opportunity to speak and they aren't listening to you, just say calmly: 'I've listened to you. If you could just listen to me for one more minute then you will have a chance to come back after that.' Staying calm is not always easy: in difficult meetings, when parents become argumentative, the temptation to argue is immense. Never rise to it. When a parent argues back, take a breath, pause, go slowly. You have the power and opportunity to slow the meeting down and to defuse its tension.

The thing I always keep in my mind in meetings is: this person loves their child more than I ever can or will. When you disagree with a parent, it is tempting to think that you want the best for the child and the parent doesn't. But that simply cannot be the case: whether the parent is right or wrong, they absolutely want the best for their child.

The more you can assert that you are on the same side and want the same things, the better. But there will be times when you fundamentally disagree. I had a challenging meeting with a parent over a child who was going to be referred to alternative provision after not one but three fights in one week with three different individuals. The parent's argument was: 'If someone hits my son, he hits back. That's what I've taught him.' Nothing I could say would dissuade the parent of this ethos, and I left the meeting deflated and still worry about how that lovely smart warm boy who fought when provoked is doing now.

Writing reports

I have been blessed in that I have managed to never work in a school which provides written reports to parents. In all the schools I have worked in, reporting to parents has been a case of scraping data off the system and presenting that on a sheet of paper.

When I clean out my own cupboards at home, I often uncover a chunk of school reports I can't bring myself to throw away, and which move from place to place with every spring clean. They are a tick box exercise – literally – with my teachers ticking one of four boxes (normally 'poor' to 'excellent') with subject-specific skills on one side ('accuracy', 'use of complex vocabulary' and so on). Below, the teacher has painstakingly written (with a *pen*) a comment about my performance in their lessons. I cannot begin to imagine the time it must have taken, and as the years go on I grow new respect for the two teachers whose comments are typed, and which consist of a generic paragraph which could apply to anyone in my class, with my name slotted in in a clear case of an early-adoption of mail-merge.

Some schools still make teachers write to parents. While I can begin to understand this in primary schools where a teacher has thirty children – where such a task, though painful, might conceivably be completed in a couple of evenings – this makes far less sense for the average secondary teacher who is likely to have well over a hundred charges.

Furthermore, many school reports are all but impenetrable to parents. Many parents are confused – having failed to get their heads around levels, schools are now reporting all kinds of grades and numbers. Is the number what they *would* get if they sat their exam *now*, or does it represent a flight path? Is 72% on an exam good or bad? Some schools give a percentage and then the average percentage of the class – this is good to put the child's grade in context, but risks complacency in those who have outperformed the average. All the contingent issues with data outlined in previous chapters apply to data-driven reports.

Parental contact is more important than the time we tend to invest in it. But annual reports do not tell you what you need to know – they are reassuring to parents because they are written to be reassuring. A teacher raising major issues through a report meets with a barrage of additional work in follow-up calls and meetings. The worst issues will have been raised earlier. For some of the worst performing children, the report won't reach their parents anyway.

We must always consider the effort to impact ratio. A past colleague of mine, Joe Kirby, used to talk about 'hornets' and 'butterflies'. A 'hornet' is something that takes a huge amount of teachers' time but has limited impact – writing reports falls into this category. A 'butterfly', in contrast, is something which takes little work but has a large impact – whole class feedback might fall into this category.[11]

Instead of impenetrable reports full of numbers and instead of reports full of the tired teacher's scribbles, we should be speaking to parents more and helping them to understand how they can support their child to improve their performance. Surely this is all that matters?

To satisfy parents' wishes to hear something about their child twice a year – not an unreasonable expectation, after all – and to avoid sending a lot of meaningless numbers, at Ark Soane we had planned to trial 'formative' reports once a year, and to send the impenetrable data only at the end of the year. In the formative report, we would tell parents their child's attendance, punctuality and number of homework detentions they have accrued – all within the parent's control to improve. We would tell parents the number of merits and demerits their child has received, and hope they know that more merits than demerits is the goal.

Teachers would then choose from a drop-down menu of pre-prepared comments curated by the Head of Department to be subject specific. There would be no more than five comments so that this exercise does not take too long. In the first column, the comment would relate to an aspect of the curriculum the student needed more practice or support in. The second column would indicate what the parent could do to support their child.

This second column is the most important one, in my view. For too long, schools have had an attitude of shutting parents out, assuming they cannot help in the way we want them to help. I too shared this misconception, and saw schools as a way to incubate children away from homes. Yet in Robert Pondiscio's *How the Other Half Learns*, a clear lesson can be drawn from the Success Academies Charter School chain in New York City.

Throughout his book, we learn of the almost constant contact with parents and the logistics of how this works. Teachers call, text and email frequently, and daily during important testing preparation periods, about children's progress, behaviour, or test scores. We are treated to a blow-by-blow account of a parent meeting, where the teacher explains the minutiae of the school day to ensure parents understand why she is asking for what she is asking for, along with offering to support them in any way they need to ensure their children can learn effectively at home. Parents, according to Pondiscio, are a hugely under-used resource and can transform the educational outcomes of the children in our care.

Contacting parents

So while lengthy written reports are a 'hornet' – hugely time consuming and without clear evidence of transforming student attainment – parents are not, as a result, to be ignored. If anything, the opposite.

I have yet to meet a parent who does not want the best for their child. Though there are some who insist their child would be 'just as happy' with no formal qualifications, it is rare to find parents of high-achievers, no matter what their background, who do not have high expectations of their child. Our job as educators, then, may be less about convincing parents of the benefits of academic qualifications and university, which almost all of them will know, than convincing parents their child can get there – or helping them to get their child there.

When I speak to parents, I am clear that for some there will be a choice to make. Some children arrive at secondary school painfully far behind. No matter how far behind, though, they can catch up – but only if they are willing to put in the work.

We make the commitment to be honest with parents about what extra help their child will need to succeed in higher education, but then let the parent decide. We don't seek to control the child's life beyond the school gates – we respect what happens with their family, and that many people hold values different to our own. All we can do is explain carefully to the parent what they as a parent need to do, and give them all the resources to do it. If you are given the task of two additional hours of online maths homework every night to catch up, you have to make that choice as a family.

There is a school of thought that says we should be ready to impose extreme actions that will lead to student achievement on families, such as the founding KIPP[12] principal who would go to families' homes (and even removed a television from one to help a student better focus on their homework).[13] I admire leaders who have this level of commitment, but for me there has to be a division between school and home. We agree with parents when they begin that they should never undermine the school in front of their child, but we encourage them to speak to the adults at school directly about any issues, including disagreeing where necessary, adult to adult.

I am always mindful of a peer who was smarter than me throughout school, read constantly, and continues to be smarter than me now. They left school at age 16. Having worked for their whole career in a legal firm, the firm offered to pay to send them to college to begin to be qualified as a solicitor. They turned the offer down – they loved their job in legal support. When I heard this, I couldn't believe it. I was outraged. Couldn't they see what they could be?

And of course there is a strong argument to be made for moving children's aspirations. I've already mentioned the response of my favourite teacher when I told him I wanted to be a hairdresser. I never mentioned my 'dream' again, and his dismissive comment set me on a different path – one I am hugely grateful to have been put on. Yet if that teacher had come into my home and told me to stop watching television and reading trashy magazines, I wonder if I might have reacted in quite a different way.

There should be boundaries between home and school. We must do all we can within our ability to encourage children to aim high, but nothing moves a child's aspirations more than academic success.

The very vast majority of parents will want to do more to help their child succeed. Our job as professionals is to harness this power and to deliver honesty. As someone without children myself, I often prompt myself to think: what would I want to hear if this were my child?

If I had a school-age child, I would want to know how far behind they were, and what I as a parent could do to help them catch up. One of the most heartbreaking conversations I have had was with a year 6 parent who knew her child was behind ('he can't do maths'), and who had asked the school for extra work … Only to be told the school didn't believe in homework, and her son would be fine. Such parents are gold dust: rather than wanting the school to solve all her son's learning needs, she was more than willing to put in hours with him at home; she just did not know what to do.

Your messages

The best headteachers I have worked with emphasised repeating core messages over variety. A strong assembly rota to me is not one with all different ideas and people and voices and ideas, but one with the same three to five ideas, repeated over and over, perhaps by different people and using different stories, but ultimately the same messages.

What are your core messages? These might be linked to a school mission statement, or your school values – but I'd simply advise taking a bit of time to think: if I could brainwash children to think five things by the end of their time here, what would those five things be?

Brainwashing sounds negative. I don't mean it that way. Clearly you won't be brainwashing children to harm others or themselves. And all of us, to a certain extent, feel the power of the influence of those around us. Our children will come to us with deeply ingrained ideas, and we need to decide on what ideas we would ingrain in them if we are able to over five or seven years.

For me, the key messages are:

1 Work hard – the harder you work, the better the things that will happen in your life.

2 Be nice – to be successful is not enough; you must be a nice person and do good in life.

3 Team beats individual – stolen shamelessly from the US Charter schools, the idea that we are a team – as a school, as a class, as a year group – no matter what the group, we do better when we work together.

4 You have limitless potential – you can do absolutely anything, and here, by the way, are a few of the million options of careers and pathways you might want to think about in life.

5 Responsibility – you must take responsibility for your actions and your choices. Only you can drive your destiny, and you won't get there by blaming others and making excuses. Closely linked to your responsibility for your future is your responsibility for representing our school – you leave these gates wearing our blazer, and other people will judge our school based on your actions.

Of course these messages are hugely simplified – that is what propaganda is. The complexity inherent in these core messages is what the assemblies, guest speakers, tutor time sessions and all other holistic work will complement over the time the students are in school.

And of course, many of you will read these messages and think: no, I don't agree. If I could only give five messages over the course of a year, it wouldn't be those five. While I would hope nobody reads these messages and thinks: 'well, that's a wrong and stupid thing to say to young people', you will have your own powerful messages and your own way of phrasing them. These messages will stem from what you value, which is why it is so important we as leaders take time to consider our values and the actions that stem from our values, and why it is so important to take time with teachers over exploring our school values together.

How to arrive at these values? I would anticipate the headteacher having a strong steer, but equally a member of the leadership team responsible for the pastoral care of young people could lead this. I would encourage taking feedback while resisting deciding the core messages based on a collective. After all, so the saying goes, a camel is a horse designed by committee.

Once your messages are decided, organise your culture moments of the school based around these. If, for example, a core part of your messaging is around the possible future students might enjoy if they work hard, you will want to make that future tangible for them, and a series of assemblies on the realities of university will help students to see this as something real that they can aspire to. Many universities, particularly those local to your school, are keen to welcome younger students. In my view, the earlier and the more frequently students visit university the better. Experience, and knowledge, is power. I will never forget sitting with my mum, age seventeen, looking at a university's fledgling website on our dial up computer, trying to work out if we wanted to order the undergraduate or postgraduate prospectus. Although I now think this seems almost ludicrous in its obviousness, it wasn't obvious to me then or to Mum. The less you know about university, the easier it is to reject it.

Assemblies

It's hard to get children to change the way they see their future, so ensuring the assemblies about university reflect a diversity of experience is important. I watched a colleague's assembly, all about the parties she had gone to and the clubs she had joined, with unbridled jealousy. My experience of university was skipping lectures to pick up extra shifts at work when money was tight, and working shifts in a bar meant I never got to go out at the same time as the people who might have been my friends did.

Perhaps my favourite assembly I've seen about university was that of a colleague who got pregnant just before first year, and managed to have not one but eventually two babies while at university. It certainly put my minor and common financial struggles into perspective. Watching this woman describe how hard she had fought to stay and succeed at university was inspirational: she told the story that the easy route would have been to raise her child and not try to both have children, study and earn her living. She took the tough route. For the children listening, it seemed to me that anything was compatible with further study: whatever they saw their imminent future as, there was really no reason it could not also take place at a university.

Line-up

A number of schools I have worked in and visited do line-ups. This is a prime opportunity to inject an ethos message to the students, because you have the whole year group there with members of SLT and heads of year, who tend to have experience in addressing large groups effectively. Although the primary purpose of a line-up is to ensure the children enter the school calmly and silently, it is, in my view, too good an opportunity to pass up for talking to them and amping them up with our ethos messages. It only needs to be twenty seconds, but the constant drip feeding of messages makes a difference.

Lunch

A significant number of schools also use family lunch to develop the ethos of their schools. I am in two minds about family lunch. I have seen this done gloriously well, where pupils are genuinely serving one another food over tables small enough to enable genuine conversation, and where they give their thanks to their peers publicly in a way that is supportive and developmental of their speaking skills.

But I have also visited schools where family lunch had no discernible difference to a canteen dinner, the only difference being the food was brought to the table rather than the children moving to the servery. Family lunch is an enormous investment of staff time, and carries with it significant catering costs. Although I think having teachers eat with pupils is hugely important, I am not yet convinced it must be family style.

There are some small tweaks you can make to your dining policy to allow children to develop the ethos of the school. At one school I worked in, we operated using five long rows of dining tables, and each year group had to file into the next available seat on their year group's row. This meant that no child was ever sitting alone, or anxious about where to sit. At another school, teachers were given a free lunch if they chose to eat it with the children, and again seats were filled in order to ensure full tables conducive to conversation.

Tutor time

In the best schools I have visited, a programme of structured activities during tutor time has contributed to building the culture of the school. The most important consideration in tutor time is the form tutor themselves. As a middle and senior leader, I have recently had a lot of experience in covering form time once a week for my part time or absent colleagues. It is difficult to build a relationship with a group of people you see for fifteen or twenty minutes a week, to the extent that for me a hard rule is that only full time members of staff should be form tutors, unless you can cover the final day or days with the group's head of year, who already has a rapport with those young people, or another solution such as their form tutor from a previous year who knows the children. In the scenario when you have someone covering form time on a long-term basis, even more structured form time activities need to be enforced: if one tutor checks planners and the other doesn't bother, for example, the system stops working.

Giving form tutors structured information to share about their group is a good way of shaping the conversations that occur there. For example, if tutors are given the number of merits their form as accrued as well as the number of detentions, they are better able to narrate the form's story. One of the most powerful uses of form time I have seen was at a school which had form time at the beginning and end of every day, meaning a tutor could set the form up for the day with a target, and review it at the end of the day.

Extending form time, even to thirty minutes or so, once a week means you can cover the PSHE curriculum with form tutors. In my opinion, this is the only way to make PSHE meaningful. The curriculum depends on the group being able to share their thoughts and ideas, and often their fears and uncertainties, and the group must feel safe enough to do this. For the most crucial topics, it is important to have subject experts deliver these. If you have that expertise on staff, amazing; most schools do not find this expertise in all their tutors, however. In this situation, it can be helpful to use a drop-down day to have your most knowledgeable members of staff deliver parts of the curriculum, or to even use external providers for this.

Everything we do in the school day builds our culture, and while every good choice we make can make children value education, every badly conceived assembly or pointless tutor session has the potential to undermine children's buy-in. We tend to be very good at checking that lessons are of good quality – we should apply this same level of scrutiny to all aspects of school life.

Take-aways

- Almost all parents want great things for their children, though many are afraid to believe in the possibility of this happening and take refuge in prioritising their children's happiness.

- Build the norm of success by recognising and celebrating it.

- Harness parent power to propel kids further.

- Expect pupils to take responsibility.

- Decide on your key messages and over-communicate them.

Notes

1 Amy Chua, *Battle Hymn of the Tiger Mother* (Bloomsbury, 2011), p. 5.

2 Ibid., p. 7.

3 Retrieved from www.theguardian.com/education/2011/feb/07/chinese-children-school-do-well (accessed 4 April 2020).

4 Robert Coe, Cesare Aloisi, Steve Higgins and Lee Elliot Major, *What Makes Great Teaching?*, retrieved from www.suttontrust.com/wp-content/uploads/2014/10/What-Makes-Great-Teaching-REPORT.pdf, accessed 20 March 2020), p. 27.

5 I found university incredibly challenging, and wrote a series of blog posts in 2017 in an attempt to make my peace with those years: see https://readingallthebooks.com/2017/01/07/first-year-or-why-i-didnt-drop-out-in-the-end (accessed 11 August 2020).

6 In 2018, the *Guardian* reported that the link between delaying gratification in youth and academic success in later life was limited (retrieved from www.theguardian.com/education/2018/jun/01/famed-impulse-control-marshmallow-test-fails-in-new-research, accessed 11 August 2020).

7 Robert Pondiscio, *How the Other Half Learns* (Avery, 2019), p. 97.

8 Ibid., p. 36.

9 Ibid., p. 294.

10 Robert Long, *The School Day and Year (England)*, House of Commons Briefing Paper, 19 July 2019, retrieved from https://researchbriefings.files.parliament.uk/documents/SN07148/SN07148.pdf (accessed 28 July 2021), p. 7.

11 Retrieved from https://pragmaticreform.wordpress.com/2015/06/06/hornets-and-butterflies-how-to-reduce-workload (accessed 31 July 2020).

12 KIPP is a chain of American Charter schools.

13 Jay Matthews, *Work Hard Be Nice* (Algonquin Books, 2009), p. 189.

Part III
Culture change

A culture, once set, will not endure immortally for the following hundred years. While there may be examples of schools for whom this occurs – the more famous private schools come to mind – this seems all but impossible in the modern school. We live in a changeable culture – each year brings new developments. For the private schools established before the turn of the nineteenth century, their benefit in culture has meant evading the shifting sands of multiple governments who changed schools. Where grammar schools became comprehensives, middle schools became secondary schools, and external qualifications were reformed over and over again, established private schools were affected by only the latter change.

Modern state schools, without the hundred-year heritage of 'this is what we have always done', have been open to changes, which many would argue is a good thing. I disagree. I am a traditionalist. I like stability, I loathe change. Part of the reason I went into teaching in the first place was because I liked the rhythm of the school week and school year. Not everyone feels the same, which is absolutely fine if we're talking about a personal emotional response to tradition. Yet even the public school bastions of tradition will change over time, if more slowly.

School culture changes over time because people change over time. Largely, this happens when the leadership of the school changes. With new leaders come new priorities, and new ways of working. Inevitably, staff leave when a new leader comes. They may dislike the new leader or disagree with their values or priorities. That isn't, of course, the only reason people leave. They may have intended to leave earlier, but had a relationship with the previous leader who convinced them to stay. They may have had their sights on a promotion internally which suddenly seems less likely now the person deciding roles hasn't had the benefit of an insight into their last five years of stellar work, and will instead sit them next to a large panel of external applicants for the post. And the knock-on impact of all of these relationships – if a deputy head leaves, your head of department might go with

DOI: 10.4324/9781003097075-11

them, and you might have been staying for the head of department – often means large staff changes in a very short time.

Suddenly, the local school can go from beacon to sink school in a year – or the reverse. This section touches on the reasons schools change, and hopes to illuminate some ways new leaders might safeguard against a cultural decline.

Why can school cultures decline?

Whose fault is it when a school declines, and how do we know? The second question is clearer cut than the first: the first sign of a school's decline is behaviour. It is evident to the people who work in the school that there is trouble by the sounds coming from classrooms and corridors, and frequently this disturbance is transmitted to the outside world by the conduit of an identifying school uniform. Children in the best schools in the country do awful things in uniform out of school hours, but there tends to be an increased prevalence of this when a school is in decline, and it is particularly evident at points where children congregate before and after the school day.

The second clue to a school's decline is its results, but this is a lagging indicator. Children who have attended an excellent school for four years do not usually collectively fail their GCSEs in the fifth. Excellent schools' results will go up and down by a few percentage points each year very naturally due to the changing nature of the humans who make up exam cohorts. A sudden drop in results normally reveals a decline in school culture which has started many years before.

So, who is to blame? This question is needlessly punitive, but what we want to know is why school culture declines, to allow us to prevent it. I have been lucky enough in my career to work in a series of wonderful schools, yet each role was challenging. Schools are hard places to work. Poor culture makes them so hard to work in, you don't want to work there anymore. How can we prevent this extremity?

Leadership

Ultimately, the success or failure of a school's culture begins and ends with the leadership of the school. I have yet to encounter a badly run school where excellent teachers manage to enable a great school culture – that is, one where children learn lots, achieve in exams, and behave well.

The job of leadership is simple, but hard: to do the right thing in the right way. This becomes harder when doing the 'right' thing changes with the successive

DOI: 10.4324/9781003097075-12

changes of government policy. Once upon a time, schools were successful when they pulled more children over the C grade boundary in at least five qualifications including English and maths. Schools built entire strategies around this fact, deploying their strongest teachers to year 11, and to that crucial group of children we called 'borderline.' Around this time, the right thing to do was to invest heavily in what we could control: coursework. This combination of exam preparation and endless tweaking of a single set of essays was at the expense of the wider curriculum, but nobody really minded if the children left with amazing results. The kids were happy, their parents were happy, the teachers (praised heavily for their role in all of this) were happy.

Of course, goalposts do move. Leadership teams have had to marshal their staff through changing priorities to match up to new markers of success. All of a sudden, the best teachers need to be redeployed to the top end, because that's where we don't hit the progress measures yet – in some schools at least. The curriculum needs to be rewritten from the ground up, because we can't get children through these more challenging qualifications without a five-year run of good stuff. The absence of coursework means we need to find different ways of preparing children for that all-important exam, and suddenly everyone cares about memory and how children learn. Middle leaders suddenly become the most important people in the building, as Ofsted decides it doesn't need to talk to an SLT anymore, it barely needs to talk to the headteacher, but instead focuses on heads of department showcasing their curriculum in the neat boxes of intent, implementation and impact of their curriculums.[1]

And then, more change, more upheaval, when for a (I hope) brief moment in time schools' success is judged on how few children manage to attract a deadly virus that might harm their families and lock down their communities.

The personal stuff

External factors have an impact on school culture, and I certainly remember feeling a dip in the school I worked in when the new reformed GCSEs came in, for example, as teachers who were used to teaching the same thing they'd taught for many years struggled with the demands of doing their day job well and planning for the future texts they would be teaching the following year.

But external changes will never have the impact of leadership changing. New leaders inevitably bring change. The largest change is felt with a new headteacher, but a new deputy or a vocal assistant head can make similar waves. Ultimately, you feel the most change with the person you have most contact with – your head of department, if you are a teacher – but everyone feels the ripple down effect of the top boss.

Headteachers set the tone of the school. The way they manage others, their priorities, the things they praise and censure – it all filters down. Schools are incredibly hierarchical, and full of people who seek to please (otherwise known as 'humans').

Schools that have gone through tough times or uncertain times tend to welcome leadership, even when it might make them do things they wouldn't necessarily choose to do. I remember working in a difficult school as SLT and being surprised when a series of big ideas were accepted and enacted by a group of middle leaders I was working with, with no discernible outrage. 'They just want to be led', the executive head told me. 'They haven't had any leadership for years. They just want a direction.'

But for schools where the leadership has been greatly loved, succession is challenging. Internal candidates have the advantage of being known, but this only plays well if they are known for something good. But headship is not the same as being a deputy: I remember a colleague telling me about the star deputy stepping up to headship and disappointing everyone (what a crushing review). While they had seemed completely self-assured in their remit, they became unable to make clear decisions in headship.

Change is inevitable when new leadership takes over. Old alliances shift, and working practices change. There are a thousand reasons people leave, but these seem to coalesce at a point of leaders leaving. When the headteacher of one school I worked in announced they were leaving, suddenly people began reprioritising – some moved to schools closer to home, others moved to the private sector, more still overseas. Pipelines stall – conversations about progression had over the course of the year suddenly seem one for 'the next person', and many choose to look elsewhere for certainty.

I don't think some degree of turnover is terrible, but we must acknowledge that it is destabilising. Even the most gifted leaders must work hard to prevent instability leading to a culture decline. And no matter how similar two leaders might be, they will never be identical – investing teachers in the 'new vision' sounds fluffy, but is important: if everyone's still rallying around the last guy, inconsistencies can arise.

Finally, leaders have different ways of working. One of the best (of many great) pieces of advice in Jill Berry's excellent *Making the Leap* – a book about deputies becoming headteachers – is for the new principal to find out how people worked with the previous headteacher. This means asking what worked and what didn't, but also being aware of working practices: if your VP has been used to having what is grandly termed in the *West Wing* as 'walk-in rights' to the head's office, they will feel disoriented to suddenly have to book a slot to meet in.[2]

In the next short chapter, we will explore what leads might do to prevent a cultural decline in their schools.

Take-aways

- The job of leadership is simple but hard: do the right things in the right way.

- Changing external goalposts (DfE, exams, Ofsted) mean schools are often in flux even when leadership remains the same.

- The headteacher sets the tone.

Notes

1 I fully anticipate a new Ofsted framework obliterating everyone's memory of what this is, so if you are reading this in the framework of the future, it is exactly as odd as it sounds.
2 Jill Berry, *Making the Leap* (Crown House, 2016).

How can schools improve their culture?

In this short chapter I hope to give some general pointers on how we can improve school culture by focusing on some of the levers of improvement which can enact some of the ideas suggested in the bulk of this book without alienating or overloading teachers.

From the previous chapter I tried to illustrate that the central issue affecting school culture was change and its inevitability. Here, I will explore some key ideas around change management.

When I trained to teach, I was inexplicably introduced to theories of change. I think it was assumed that I would be a 'change agent' in the classroom, or some other cringe-worthy moniker, and that it was therefore critical that I understand how to get others to go along with what would inevitably be hugely influential ideas that would rock the school.

Rest assured, like any unqualified and then newly qualified teacher, I struggled to rock my own classroom and retain my sanity.

Since those days, I have been told to reference 'change theorists' for certain professional qualifications that were once thought essential to predate headship, and so I have reluctantly read these and found them of limited use.

For example, what kind of leader are you? I'd like to describe myself as a leaderly leader, who leads the be-leds towards a leadership vision of leading. This is how these books read to me. I was once interviewed for a vice principal role and was asked what kind of leader I was. In the feedback, I was told: 'you gave a lot of examples of times you had led people and what you had done … But what we really wanted to hear was: "coercive leader". Or, "conciliatory leader".' Assuming this was some sort of joke (because this was before I had to read those books on change management) I asked with genuine curiosity: 'What is a "conciliatory leader?"' and the individual replied: 'Well, it's sort of what you said you did.'

So you might call me a little biased against leadership theory.

There may well be gems in leadership theory, but sadly my own biases prevent me from finding them. No matter, dear reader, because there is absolutely no shortage of books on leadership theory for you to peruse at your leisure.[1] Instead

DOI: 10.4324/9781003097075-13

of a drawn-out thesis, I'm going to share a few short nuggets of experience and my thoughts on leading change, and luckily this chapter is extremely short, so if you want to skip it and instead read one of those very erudite tomes in the footnote, be my guest.

Align around the change

Whether a new leader's vision succeeds or fails relies on one thing and one thing alone: whether everyone else wants it to happen or not. If you blaze into a school with your ideas and your dreams and these are roundly rejected by your colleagues, even if these are the best ideas in education since chalk first met slate, they will not happen. One person cannot change a massive organisation through force of personality and a willingness to forego sleep for several years.

Similarly, because successful change is predicated on alignment, different people in the school may have very different views about what the new leadership is doing. I visited one turnaround school that had made significant gains under a new principal, but heard the full gamut from 'I'm really excited about the direction we're going in' to 'it was so much better three years ago'. The culture and way of working in a school is key, and one size will not suit every member of staff.

To align people around changes, you need to do a sell job and it needs to start with the senior leadership team. There are two ways this can work: you can tell everyone what's going to happen and be very clear about who, how and when. This approach is well suited to schools in serious distress, with the full sheet of poor behaviour and poor results. In these kinds of schools, people seek clarity and systems, so give them both. It is important to be clear on *how* as well as *what* – just telling people the end goal ('get great results!') is unlikely to lead to change if it hasn't so far. People must be marshalled around the plan and know how to execute it.

The other route is to get buy-in for your changes. Start at the leadership team and have a lot of respectful arguments. Begin your one to ones with leaders by asking about how they have worked with the previous headteacher. Ask them what worked and what didn't, and what their expectations are for this relationship. Then tell them yours.

I like to encourage dissent and enjoy argument for a few reasons. The first is, admittedly, because I am argumentative: by nature, I enjoy arguing. The second is because I read *Radical Candour* and it suggested that arguing with your people was a good way to ensure nobody ever sat quietly by and let you do something stupid.[2] And the third is because I think people are much more likely to commit to an idea they don't like if they have had a chance to say their full piece on it.

To return to point two momentarily: this is a real risk. When you don't know people, and they 'outrank' you, it is very hard to tell them they're wrong. I myself have spent whole swathes of my career nodding when I'm with my bosses and complaining afterwards about how idiotic their ideas were because I didn't have the guts to tell them to their faces (or, in some cases, because I tried once and it didn't work out that well for me). You have no idea what people's past experiences of their bosses will be, and it is very natural in humans to want to please, so in my experience you really do have to encourage the dissent. Unless someone is actively grinning, nodding and saying 'yes, that's exactly right, and here's another reason I think that's right', I try to probe them to tell me I'm wrong. Some good phrases I've probably stolen from the books of smarter people are: 'tell me why I'm wrong', 'how do you disagree?' 'would that work here?' 'I'm not sure this is right', 'this is only my experience – how does yours differ?'

On this approach, which I believe management consultants call 'disagree and commit', there is something clear in the psychology of it. You are much more likely to support an eventual direction if you have had an opportunity to say your piece about why it's the wrong direction.

How you get people to disagree is something to be mindful of. I found out in my first year of middle leadership that putting across a new idea to a large group of people would most usually lead to it being shot down – people were quick to critique, everyone piled on, and more often than not, they killed it. Momentum is not your friend in large meetings.

After this, I tended to try and share new ideas one to one. This meant I could take feedback from key individuals, and so when I presented the idea (a) the idea was better than it would have been without the initial feedback and so less likely to be rejected, and (b) I had some invested parties who had created parts of the new idea who would speak positively about it in the meeting.

For principals, this usually means investing an SLT before bringing a new idea to teachers. If you have enough people who have critiqued something enough they are much more likely to advocate for it.

And in terms of seeking feedback, I'd continue to do everything outlined in Chapter 2 around genuinely welcoming the views of others, and calling out with credit when people make an idea better through their candour.

Change around the people

As an incoming headteacher or leader, you must listen to a range of views. Different people tell different stories about the school, or the department, or the team, and in time you will come to work out which are true and which are less likely. There are normally common threads in what people say which will help you get to the truth – the extremes of positive and negative are rarely the reliable stories.

I'd advocate hearing a wide range of views of existing staff, and being willing to bend plans to build buy-in. If everyone in your team hates your idea, you probably should not press ahead regardless. Build in compromises or tweaks, or abandon it entirely and revisit it when you have built more trust with people.

Ultimately, the changes you enact as a leader should be informed by the people you lead in the first instance. I firmly believe that every single member of staff has something to add to improve the school. If harnessed, listening to others can radically improve the changes we enact and ensure strong staff buy-in so that those changes have their desired impact.

Accountability

A final often little noted element of school culture is around accountability. It is all very well to have great ideas, but doing them is another matter.

I've often reflected on whether accountability is necessary in schools. When I started teaching, I was much more inclined to argue that leaders should trust teachers to get on with it and teach their classes. I still largely think this: for a main scale classroom teacher, we need to expect them to teach great lessons. This involves planning, teaching, giving feedback and building strong relationships with students and colleagues.

But for anyone who is a post-holder, accountability is nothing to be feared – indeed, it is a necessary lever to ensure the school improves.

I have two favourite line managers who had vastly different styles, and who I try to channel when I work with others. The first was someone who made line management not feel like line management. Going to his office was something I looked forward to and genuinely enjoyed. We would sit on his little table, and we would right the wrongs of the school. We would come up with what felt like brilliant ideas, and he would say things like: 'great – if you do that, I'll do this'. It felt like a partnership, not a superior talking to his inferior. I felt energised and stretched by the work.

But largely, this person totally trusted me to get on with things. While this was great for my peace of mind and my ego, I wonder a couple of things. I wonder whether I actually got the things done I needed to get done. What slipped off my radar in that job? What did I pay too little attention to? The second thing I wondered was what mistakes I made, either in my job or my 'leadership'. How could I have grown more as a leader?

Only recently have I begun to realise that feedback is both intensely uncomfortable *and* hugely helpful. Previously, I've tried to convince myself 'feedback is a gift!' But receiving feedback in this overly positive way did not feel authentic. I'm going to get to that place genuinely one day, but right now I have to confess to being in the 'I hate what you're saying, but you're right' phase.

For my last job interview, for example, I had to create a presentation during half term. I was very pleased with my efforts. I practised it over and over, and then a friend let me practice it with them. 'It's in a very odd order,' he said. 'It doesn't really make sense.'

'It does,' I asserted. 'You just don't understand education.'

But the second they left, I went back to the presentation. They had suggested an alternative thread through, which meant changing every aspect of the presentation. I poured another few hours of work in, and then had to make a phone call – the best, worst phone call you can make – to say: I'm sorry, you were right.

Being told you're wrong by someone who wants the best for you and who is very skilled at their job is a good thing. That's not to say you accept all feedback unthinkingly, but if someone is good at what they do and likes you, they probably have the best intentions.

More mundane but perhaps even more important than candid feedback is holding people to account for the things they say they will do. My other favourite line manager was the boss of this. Each meeting she took short notes, and flagged all the actions. Then, at the start of the next meeting, she would go down the list of previous actions and say: 'Have you done that yet?'

I know, it shouldn't be revolutionary. But from what I've heard in many schools, this is extremely rare. I have worked in five schools, and she was the only person to ask me about actions. I found this useful for a couple of reasons. The first was that, as someone who enjoys ideas and theories and proposals, it made me focus on action and what I was *doing*. Secondly, the job of a leader in a school is one of extraordinary pace and it is inevitable that things get lost. With this method of line management, things didn't get lost. In fact, I would often talk with my SLT colleagues about how we all hung our heads in shame in our individual line management meetings as the head would say: 'and have you done this yet?' if we had not. Her system was impeccable: by week two she would say: 'second time for this one – is it done yet?'

As a young middle leader, I vividly remember an interview where I struggled with the question: 'how do you hold others to account?' In the feedback, the principal said I simply had no examples and seemingly no experience. At the time, I agreed with her: in my mind 'holding to account' was synonymous with 'telling people off'. I didn't tell people off, because I worked with people who did the things I asked them to do, either when I asked them or when I chased them.

I wish I had known then what I know now: holding to account is a systematic way of saying: 'have you done this yet?' And it makes schools better.

Leadership actions to improve culture

To ensure a school culture improves rather than declines, leaders need to communicate clearly, align around the key ideas, robustly challenge privately and defend publicly, and then do what they say they're going to do.

Take-aways

- One person cannot change a massive organisation – you need others to rally around your changes.

- Encourage disagreement and debate robustly and genuinely.

- Holding people to account usually just means asking if they've done the things they said they'd do.

Notes

1 I've read quite a lot of them, and would recommend the following leadership books: Kim Scott, *Radical Candour* (Macmillan, 2017); Brene Brown, *Dare to Lead* (Ebury Digital, 2018); Paul Bambrick Santoyo, *Leverage Leadership* (Jossey-Bass, 2012); Susan Scott, *Fierce Conversations* (Piatkus, 2017); Patrick Lencioni, *The Advantage* (Jossey-Bass, 2012); Matthew Evans, *Leaders with Substance* (John Catt Educational, 2019); Daniel Coyle, *The Culture Code* (Random House Business, 2019).

2 Kim Scott (*Radical Candour*, p. 80) shares a wonderful story of Steve Jobs winning an argument, his idea failing, and him being furious with his subordinate. When the subordinate points out it was Steve Jobs's idea, Jobs replies: 'Yes, and it was your job to convince me I was wrong.'

Part IV
Case studies

Introduction

I have been lucky enough to visit around 30 schools in the course of my career, and have seen aspects of real greatness in every single one. I particularly rate the very many Ark Schools I have visited and worked in, but am wary of this chapter becoming an advertisement for my employer (who I must say are excellent; I would highly recommend working for them). I have, however, included Ark Elvin for three reasons: because it stands out to me as such an impressive turn-around, because I spent a significant amount of time in it during a second school placement, and because I have come to know its principal, Becky Curtis, extremely well as she is my executive principal at Ark John Keats. The other schools I have chosen because, while excellent in any number of ways, each had a culture that felt special, and even unusual.

Reach Academy Feltham

Reach Academy Feltham was founded in 2012 by Ed Vainker, who remains at the helm of the organisation 9 years on. Feltham is an area of not just high deprivation, but high educational deprivation: whereas 62% of pupils of similar deprivation go onto higher education in neighbouring Osterley, in Feltham that figure is just 19%. The school takes as part of its inspiration Geoffrey Canada's Harlem Children's Zone, with the firm belief that school does not begin and end at the gates. The school prides itself on its community outreach and wrap-around care, and forges close relationships with families to support them through accessing social workers, legal support and mental health counselling, as well as providing a number of these services themselves for families.

Walking around the academy on an average day is breath-taking. The school is quiet and calm, but never eerily so. It's the kind of school – and I'm glad to say I have visited or worked in a lot of these – when you often raise your voice too loud

DOI: 10.4324/9781003097075-14

under the impression no lessons are going on down a particular corridor, only to see scores of children silently focused on their work.

This calm continues into family lunch, where the children chatter excitedly – particularly in the primary setting – while simultaneously never bubbling into excess. Adults smile benignly and speak patiently and lovingly to the children in their care; no adult I saw looked stressed or pressed for time. There was a wonderful flow to the day. Everyone knew what they were doing and seemed to have plenty of time to do it in.

Walking around the primary school, I saw a class of year 5s eagerly listening to their teacher explain Maths to them.

'All maths lessons are centrally planned,' my teacher guide told me, 'which means the TA can deliver them.'

'That's a teaching assistant?'

It was. The teacher was not far away – just outside the room in a break-out space with six children.

'These are the children most struggling with maths, so the teacher is going through the content with them while the TA teaches the rest of the class.'

It is with such thought that children can make great progress, but none of this learning is possible without the strong systems to ensure great student behaviour which allow this teaching to occur.

Children at Reach Academy Feltham buy into the culture of the school: they have spoken of Lemov's 'warm/strict'[1] since their foundation, pride themselves on the warmth of their interactions with pupils. Pupils call teachers by their first names, which – combined with the rigour and clarity of teachers' high expectations – makes for an unusually familial atmosphere. The work Reach does with parents supports this – indeed, the small tweak of pupils calling teachers by first names extends naturally to the parent/teacher relationship and forges closer and more personable bonds between school and families. The school invests heavily in securing these relationships from day one: every family who is new to Reach can expect a home visit, and in the primary school when the class teacher changes they will visit every member of the class. Strong centralised planning and a no-marking expectation frees teachers up after school to make these visits outside lesson time without having a harmful impact on teacher wellbeing. Prior to the start of term, new pupils are inducted thoroughly during summer school, which ends with a picnic to which families are also invited.

An important aspect of the school is it is an 'all-through': children can come to the school in reception and leave after sixth form. Despite Reach's year 6s scoring the highest of feeder schools on the local grammar school entrance tests, they lose remarkably few pupils to other schools: 90% of Reach's primary cohort go on to attend secondary, and 80% of their year 11s stay on for sixth form. A further innovation is the smallness of the year groups: the school accepts only 60 children into each year group, which means that all teachers can genuinely know every child in the school. This leads to an enormous sense of warmth, love and community.

With such a small number of pupils admitted each year, and with glowing reports and results, the team at Reach soon recognised their catchment area would shrink and begin to favour those who lived close to the school. This is a common event in the UK school system, where great schools drive house prices up, creating schools only those who can afford such houses can attend. To guard against this, Reach Academy changed its admissions policy to ringfence 30% of places for children in receipt of the pupil premium, a correlating measure for disadvantage in the UK, to ensure that they are always a beacon of opportunity for pupils of all backgrounds.

Ark Elvin Academy

When you take the National Professional Qualification for headship, you have to spend nine days at a contrasting school. I chose Ark Elvin Academy partly for their phenomenal turn-around, and partly because one of the most inspirational educators I know, Sarah Donachy, worked as a vice principal there.

I worked with Sarah a few years ago, and found her to be one of the most relentless and intelligent professionals I have ever met. While I could not foresee what I might glean from a second placement, I knew that time spent with her would be developmental – it was a sure thing. She had moved to Elvin, a school I only knew by its reputation some four years previous as being pretty difficult – if not as the most difficult school in the borough. The high level of exclusions and reported poor behaviour of pupils both in and out of school was legend in the area. Sarah assured me it was very different now.

I could tell from day one she was right. When I arrived, children were waiting calmly outside the gates, speaking in low voices with small groups of friends. When the receptionist opened the gate for me, a flood of children also came in, walking purposely to their courtyard.

What I saw, in every aspect of school life, was hugely impressive. Any child whose opinion I asked about school could only say positive things. On the first day, I watched over 900 students fall into year group lines in total silence and then, when dismissed, walk to their lessons in around three minutes. I turned to Sarah and grinned. She grimaced: 'Needs to be quicker.'

And that attitude summed up every interaction I had with teachers: everyone was constantly asking 'how can we improve'? When I asked the principal, Becky Curtis, for her thoughts on the school's transformative journey, she started by noting: 'we approach everything in the spirit of constant improvement. We know we've still got a long way to go. Our children are not getting the grades they need to transform their lives.'

When Curtis took over in January 2017, she was the year 11s' fifth headteacher. In her first six months as Head, she took a narrow and laser-focus to the actions she felt would have the highest leverage in improving the school: making line-up (before school, after break and after lunch the students line up silently to transition quickly to their next lesson) more efficient and a more positive experience for students; ensuring a purposeful start to each lesson; and behaviour management. For the third action, again she broke this down into just a few clear focuses: teachers should use 'three step instructions' (1, tell them the task; 2, tell them how long they have; 3, clarify the voice level expected) and then positively narrate what they saw. Only once this training had been embedded did Curtis review the sanctions system, centralising detentions in an early move to ensure staff were supported.

Similarly, as the school goes from strength to strength, the SLT retain this laser-like focus on only a small number of priorities. This is especially evident in teaching and learning, where the school will focus on only three core ideas until they are embedded, usually for the whole academic year.

For Curtis, a great school is one that can be sustainable over time. She has much to build on: staff satisfaction is high. Curtis attributes this to making Elvin a team effort: teachers know they are cared for and that their opinions count. Curtis talks about ensuring people have both the training and time to do their jobs well. Such pragmatism is typical: Curtis says that 'at the heart of school improvement is an organised school.' She means this on every level: clear systems, strong training, and a sensible calendar with deadlines planned in advance so nothing comes as a surprise and people can plan their workloads.

In fact, one of my favourite take-aways from Elvin was the time spent thinking about when people will do the work. During meetings, Curtis includes 'togetherness' time so everyone can plan in any new projects. They also work out what might need to be dropped in order to fit in a new priority.

Another learning point was Becky Curtis herself. She is stunningly clear on what she wants in Elvin and how she will rally the team to get there. She and others continually say: 'what does great look like?' For all the staff, the first step is to be clear on what ideal practice is. In my nine weeks at Elvin, I too started to internalise three core principles I heard Curtis say again and again:

▪ Evolution not revolution.

▪ Less is more.

▪ If something is worth doing, it is worth doing it right.

So, where next for Elvin? Curtis is still focused on dramatically improving outcomes, and the school will also reopen its sixth form in 2020. For 2019–2020, Curtis wants to make sure all teachers and children can articulate the purpose of why they are doing what they are doing. She also says 'structure should liberate': the school is a well-oiled machine. Now what? With the safety of these strong structures in place, Curtis wants to untap creativity within the school, so staff and students take ownership. Finally, she wants to build what she calls 'a genuinely developmental culture of constant improvement.' Curtis's aim is to sustain excellence over time, a concept I saw scrawled large on the whiteboard in her office that the leadership team had used for planning their next academic year: 'excellence isn't a prize you win once; it is continuously earned.'

Bedford Free School

We believe that, given the right circumstances, all children are capable of extraordinary things.

So reads the wall in the reception of Bedford Free School. The school was established in 2012, and has been working out exactly what those 'right circumstances' are. In 2016, for example, under a previous Principal, Mark Lehain, the school introduced silent corridors. It is hard to imagine the peaceful halls of the school otherwise, but the children have taken to them well, and are grateful for the calm atmosphere. One year 10 who showed me around the school when I visited in 2017 said: 'it's great, because we get fifty minutes of learning in every fifty-minute lesson with the silent entry'.

Across the school, and including in cover lessons, behaviour is exemplary. On the day I visited, one class's teacher employed Doug Lemov's 'do it again' technique to line up her class anew outside when there was 'some silliness' on the stairs (standing in the stairwell, I heard nothing). Standards are very high here. Executive Principal Stuart Lock tours the school, asking of teachers his trademark: 'is everything to your satisfaction, sir/miss?' to provide a supportive climate for teachers.

Bedford's context is unusual: a commuter town to London in part, it is said that a larger than average number of children attend long-established private schools. The intake of state schools in Bedford, therefore, doesn't always reflect the full demographics of the area.

Apart from behaviour, I was struck by the focus on knowledge at the school. All children carry '100% books', which contain knowledge maps collating the core knowledge of most subjects. These are referred to, used, and tested in lessons. In history, pupils began their lesson by filling in a partially blanked-out knowledge map, allowing the teacher to assess their recall. In art, pupils completed a knowledge-based end of unit exam, where they were asked to identify paintings and techniques, among other aspects. In science, I saw a teacher going over a recent exam practice paper, re-teaching questions the class had struggled with.

The school is increasingly using booklets like these in English to ensure pupils' focus is on the text and linked questions, and this has led to remarkable consistency across classrooms. The writing in these booklets is supplemented by work in their books.

Bedford Free School have a generous approach to guests, offering for me to take away any booklets I saw. ('All we ask is that you send them back to us if you make any improvements so we can all improve!')

Every pupil reads for 30 minutes a day in what the school calls 'DEAR (drop everything and read) time', but which is improved immeasurably by having the whole class read a text together with a teacher, thus ensuring all pupils are held accountable to be reading during this time, and no child can just stare into space. This also ensures the pupils are constantly being exposed to high quality texts, improving both their literacy and their cultural literacy.

In addition to academics, the school day is structured to include 'electives' built into the timetable, so every child enjoys extra-curricular activities. Incredibly, last year 96% of pupils at the school participated competitively in a school sports team, despite the fact that the school cannot host matches due to its lack of facilities.

As with all the best schools I have visited, the focus is on relentless improvement, and there is no complacency. Principal Tim Blake and his team are working hard each day to tweak the conditions to ensure every pupil at Bedford Free School can achieve their full potential.

Dixons Trinity Academy

Founded in 2012 by Luke Sparks, Dixons Trinity Academy towers over the north, a pillar of exceptionalism in education, based in Bradford. At DTA, visitors are struck with the clarity of the school's vision and an unparalleled approach to school culture. But all of this visionary work is embedded in their championing of their community. The demographic and deprivation data of the school speaks for itself and yet this is rejected as oftentimes unhelpful rhetoric by the leadership. To say they love their community and love their children would do little justice to their commitment. As Jenny says, they do what they do in service to their community, never in spite of it.

At Dixons Trinity, intentional, considered design permeates – for the leadership, a maximally effective culture is the origin of, and amplifier for, all else. Perhaps most importantly is that Dixons Trinity delivers – not just in their delightful, articulate and purposeful children who will certainly be future game-changers – but outcomes. In the cold, hard data of education, Dixons Trinity is exceptional delivering P8 scores between +1.21 and +1.55 every year (with disadvantaged students often outperforming their peers and students with SEND often making the highest rates of progress).

The school day begins not with tutor time, but with charismatic members of the SLT and some heads of year leading whole year groups in large spaces in the school through targeted intervention, assembly messages or quizzing. As culture is so strong, these large groups are supported with skeleton staffing freeing up the rest of the team to participate in morning practice – a team activity where staff work together on the school's micro-scripted routines framed through role-play. As Luke and Jenny recently wrote in *The ResearchEd Guide to Leadership*:

> this is a designed to build consistency, but it is so much more than that: it facilitates cohesion through trust, through vulnerability and, critically,

through humour. We can strip away everything else and call it what it is: fun. It is a great way to become better but also to develop the relationships that are a foundational prerequisite to constructive conflict ... If we can laugh together as a team, we can challenge each other because everyone has played the fool at some point (happily without a child in sight).[2]

Dixons Trinity was among the very first schools in the UK to introduce family dining, and they maintain this today, with form tutors eating lunch with their tutees each day. Over the course of an academic year, every student will give a 'shout out' to the rest of their year group, both practising their public speaking and building a culture of kindness towards one another.

Sparkes and the team who have succeeded his leadership were highly influenced by Dan Pink's *Drive*.[3] In *Drive*, Pink argues that people are motivated by three things: *mastery*, *autonomy* and *purpose*. These three drivers underpin every decision the leaders have made in the school and the students' commitment is so much more than compliance – it is tangible self-determination.

Conclusion

As I said in the opening of this section, I am not intending to cover off cultural excellence in all schools: hundreds or perhaps thousands of schools exist which can also boast similarly impressive cultures. I share these specific examples partly to showcase their tremendous work, and partly to put down in words my deep thanks to every single leader in these schools who opened their doors and welcomed me so warmly; who gave (and continue to give) very generously of their time when I ask questions or favours; and who are, to me, the very best that education has to offer in terms of practice but also genuine kindness.

Notes

1 Doug Lemov, *Teach Like a Champion 2.0* (Jossey-Bass, 2015), p. 438.
2 Stuart Lock (ed.), *ResearchED Guide to Leadership* (John Catt, 2020).
3 Daniel H. Pink, *Drive* (Canongate, 2011).

Bibliography

Rebecca Allen and Sam Sims, *The Teacher Gap* (Routledge, 2018)

Paul Bambrick Santoyo, *Leverage Leadership* (Jossey-Bass, 2012)

Phil Beadle, *How to Teach* (Crown House, 2010)

Jill Berry, *Making the Leap* (Crown House, 2016)

Roy Blatchford (ed.), *The Secondary Curriculum Leader's Handbook* (John Catt, 2019)

Brene Brown, *Dare to Lead* (Ebury Digital, 2018)

Peter C. Brown, Henry L. Roediger III and Mark A. McDaniel, *Make it Stick* (Harvard University Press, 2014)

Daisy Christodoulou, *Making Good Progress* (Oxford University Press, 2017)

Daisy Christodoulou, *Seven Myths about Education* (Routledge, 2014)

Amy Chua, *Battle Hymn of the Tiger Mother* (Bloomsbury, 2011)

Jim Collins, *Good to Great Good to Great: Why Some Companies Make the Leap ... and Others Don't* (Random House, 2001)

Stephen Covey, *The Seven Habits of Highly Effective People* (Simon & Schuster, 1989)

Daniel Coyle, *The Culture Code* (Random House Business, 2019)

Caroline Criado Perez, *Invisible Women: Exposing Data Bias in a World Designed for Men* (Vintage, 2020)

David Didau, *Making Kids Cleverer* (Crown House, 2018)

Rolf Dobelli, *The Art of Thinking Clearly* (Sceptre, 2013)

Emily Esfahani Smith, *The Power of Meaning* (Ebury Digital, 2017)

Matthew Evans, *Leaders with Substance* (John Catt Educational, 2019)

Jo Facer, *Simplicity Rules* (Routledge, 2019)

Deborah Frances-White, *The Guilty Feminist* (Virago, 2019)

Michael Fullan, *Change Focus: The Sequel* (Falmer Press, 1999)

Johann Hari, *Lost Connections* (Bloomsbury, 2018)

Maia Heyck-Merlin, *The Together Leader* (Jossey-Bass, 2016)

Avy Joseph, *Cognitive Behaviour Therapy* (Capstone, 2016)

Sarah Knight, *Calm the F**k Down* (Quercus, 2018)

Doug Lemov, *Teach Like a Champion 2.0* (Jossey-Bass, 2015)

Patrick Lencioni, *The Advantage* (Jossey-Bass, 2012)

Stuart Lock (ed.), *ResearchED Guide to Leadership* (John Catt, 2020)

Jay Matthews, *Work Hard Be Nice* (Algonquin Books of Chapel Hill, 2009)

Eva Moscowitz, *The Education of Eva Moskowitz: A Memoir* (Harper, 2017)

Eva Moscowitz, *Mission Possible* (Jossey-Bass, 2012)

Michelle Obama, *Becoming* (Penguin, 2018)

Daniel H. Pink, *Drive* (Canongate, 2011)

Robert Pondiscio, *How the Other Half Learns* (Avery, 2019)

Kiley Reid, *Such a Fun Age* (Putnam, 2019)

Hans Rosling, *Factfulness* (Sceptre, 2019)

Sheryl Sandberg, *Lean In* (W. H. Allen, 2015)

Sheryl Sandberg, *Option B* (Alfred A. Knopf, 2017)

Kim Scott, *Radical Candour* (Macmillan, 2017)

S. J. Scott and Barrie Davenport, *Declutter Your Mind: How to Stop Worrying, Relieve Anxiety, and Eliminate Negative Thinking* (Old Town Publishing, 2016)

Susan Scott, *Fierce Conversations* (Piatkus, 2017)

Dylan Wiliam, *Embedded Formative Assessment* (Solution Tree Press, 2011)

Index

Printed in Great Britain
by Amazon

85508657R10113